MONEY
LAND

ALSO BY OLIVER BULLOUGH

The Last Man in Russia
Let Our Fame Be Great

MONEY LAND

THE INSIDE STORY OF THE CROOKS AND KLEPTOCRATS WHO RULE THE WORLD

OLIVER BULLOUGH

ST. MARTIN'S PRESS ▨ NEW YORK

MONEYLAND. Copyright © 2019 by Oliver Bullough. All rights reserved.
Printed in the United States of America. For information, address St.
Martin's Press, 175 Fifth Avenue, New York, NY 10010.

www.stmartins.com

Library of Congress Cataloging-in-Publication Data is available upon request.

ISBN 978-1-250-20870-5 (hardcover)

ISBN 978-1-250-20871-2 (ebook)

Our books may be purchased in bulk for promotional, educational, or business use. Please
contact your local bookseller or the Macmillan Corporate and Premium Sales Department at
1-800- 221-7945, extension 5442, or by e-mail at MacmillanSpecialMarkets@macmillan.com.

First published in Great Britain by Profile Books Ltd.
First St. Martin's Press edition: May 2019

10   9   8   7   6   5   4   3   2   1

CONTENTS

1   Aladdin's Cave   1
2   Pirates   28
3   Queen of the Caribbees   49
4   Sex, Lies and Offshore Vehicles   64
5   Mystery on Harley Street   72
6   Shell Games   83
7   Cancer   101
8   Nasty as a Rattlesnake   115
9   The Man Who Sells Passports   131
10 "Diplomatic Immunity!"   153
11 Un-write-about-able   161
12 Dark Matter   176
13 "Nuclear Death Is Knocking Your Door"   191
14 Say Yes to the Money   204
15 High-End Property   211
16 Plutos Like to Hang Out Together   225
17 Breaking Switzerland   233
18 Tax Haven USA   244
19 Standing Up to Moneyland   258

Acknowledgements   273
Notes on Sources   275
Index   287

MONEY LAND

1

ALADDIN'S CAVE

London wears many different faces, depending on whom it's talking to. There is the pageantry and ceremony of the Changing of the Guards: all red-jacketed soldiers, glossy horses and cheering crowds. That's for the tourists. There is the steel and glass of the City, London's financial district, garrisoned by an army of bankers and clerks who teem across the bridges in the early morning. That's for the business folk. There are the suburbs, with their semi-detached houses, hedges, no-through-roads and parks. That's for the locals.

And then there are places like Finchley, in northwest London, and the short street called Woodberry Grove, where the cars were new a decade ago, and the nearest stores sell Polish beer and tabloid newspapers. It isn't a street you'd visit, or even notice, unless you had a good reason to, which is perhaps why Paul Manafort situated one of his companies—Pompolo Ltd—at house number 2.

According to the indictment prepared by the Office of Special Counsel Robert Mueller, Manafort, Donald Trump's former campaign chairman, moved some $75 million through various offshore bank accounts, much of which he used to buy high-end properties and luxury goods. He earned this money working in Ukraine, primarily for thuggish ex-president Viktor Yanukovich, and was found guilty of hiding it from the Internal Revenue Service, as well as assorted other crimes. The meticulous indictment listed the companies through which he owned the bank accounts that channeled this money, which is how we know about Pompolo Ltd. Pompolo controlled a bank account that paid $175,575 to a Florida home entertainment company and $13,325 to a landscape gardener in the Hamptons on the same day—July 15, 2013.

That may well be all that Pompolo ever did. It had been created just three months earlier and was dissolved by the UK's Companies House a year later, something that happens automatically if companies do not file the necessary paperwork. I had come to 2 Woodberry Grove to look at the street address that was Pompolo Ltd's supposed base of operations.

It was an uninspiring destination, a two-story office building of russet bricks, some of them overlaid with beige stucco. Its roof tiles appeared to be held together by clumps of moss, and the window frames were stained so dark they were barely recognizable as wood. A row of doorbells ran down the side of the door. I pressed one of them and was greeted by a middle-aged man with a South African accent and a faded T-shirt advertising the English heavy metal band Iron Maiden. He ushered me inside.

I wasn't quite sure what to expect from a place that had been a junction in the financial plumbing that Manafort used to suck money out of Ukraine and pour it into luxury goods in New York and Virginia, but I'd imagined something more exciting than a tidy, dull office with an institutional gray carpet and a poster advising workers on how to sit at their computers to avoid damage to their backs. While I waited for the Iron Maiden fan's boss, I listened to two women gossiping about their weekend plans, and tried to peek into their cubicles. Sadly, the boss wasn't available, and I left with nothing more than an email address (his reply, when it came, included a denial of any wrongdoing and a strong tone of exasperation: "I cannot speak with any authority as to what motivations 'people like Manafort' may have, so I am afraid that you will have to draw your own conclusions") as a reward for the fifteen-minute walk to Woodberry Grove from the Tube station.

There are two places to go next with this story. The first would be to give up on Pompolo as a dead end and instead focus on Manafort, on his sordid client base, his amoral maneuvering and his remarkable appetite for luxury goods. The second would be to look back at 2 Woodberry Grove and to ask why Pompolo—a company with access to significant amounts of cash—would base itself in an unglamorous part of an unfashionable corner of London.

It's understandable that most journalists would prefer the first approach. It makes a more compelling story to write about ostrich-skin jackets and luxury condominiums, about the way Manafort laundered the reputations of dozens of unlovely politicians and oligarchs, than it does to describe ugly British institutional architecture. But the second approach is the more rewarding, because if we can understand what links Manafort to Woodberry Grove, we gain a glimpse behind the personalities, into the hidden workings of the financial system, into the secret country that I call Moneyland.

The indictment against Manafort, and against associate Rick Gates (in whose name Pompolo was registered), revealed the existence not just of Pompolo Ltd, but also of companies in the Caribbean states of St. Vincent and the Grenadines, and on the Mediterranean island of Cyprus, as well as in Virginia, Florida, Delaware and New York. And these companies had multiple bank accounts, supposedly independent of each other, but in reality connected by their shared—and hidden—owners. They moved money back and forth between each other in a ceaseless and bewildering dance, the patterns of which are far too complicated for even many experts to understand. Trying to draw the complexity of the financial arrangements among all of these entities is a job for a whole team of law enforcement professionals; it's all but impossible for a layman.

Manafort and Gates exploited this system for a decade or more, but they didn't create it. Nor did they seek out 2 Woodberry Grove and decide to make it their base of operations. That was done for them by an entire industry of people who enable the crimes of people like them, people with money to hide. The real tenant of the office building in Finchley is A1 Company Services, which creates companies for its customers and gives them a postal address. A1 Company Services is emblematic of something far greater than a political scandal, even one as big as this. It represents a system that is beggaring the world by hiding the secrets of the rich and powerful.

Manafort's secrets were so well defended that had Robert Mueller not started investigating the former Trump campaign chairman, he would almost certainly have gotten away with his crimes. And this is a worrying thought, because there are many other people still using the exact same system. House number 2 on Woodberry Grove is or has been home to *thousands* of other companies—16,551, according to one database—as have the addresses Manafort used in the Grenadines, and in Cyprus, not to mention those in the United States.

Most people view Paul Manafort as important only insomuch as he revealed corruption surrounding the election of Donald Trump. But in fact, his link to Trump inadvertently gives us a window into something much bigger, a shadowy system of which few of us are aware. It's a system that is quietly but effectively impoverishing millions, undermining democracy, helping dictators as they loot their countries. And we can learn more about this world by looking at one of the biggest clients for Manafort's services: Viktor Yanukovich, ex-president of Ukraine.

***

Yanukovich ruled Ukraine for four years, from 2010 till 2014, during which time he enriched himself and bankrupted his country. Finally, Ukrainians got fed up, and thousands protested throughout the cold winter of 2013–14, until he fled. The riches he left behind revealed him to have had tastes so baroque as to make even Manafort look restrained. The spreading grounds of his palace at Mezhyhyria included water gardens, a golf course, a nouveau-Greek temple, a marble horse painted with a Tuscan landscape, an ostrich collection, and an enclosure for shooting wild boars, as well as the five-story log cabin where he indulged his tastes for the overblown and the vulgar. It was a temple of tastelessness, a cathedral of kitsch, the epitome of excess.

Everyone had known that Yanukovich was a criminal, but they had never seen the extent of his haul. At a time when ordinary Ukrainians' wealth had been stagnant for years, he had accumulated a fortune worth hundreds of millions of dollars, as had his closest friends. He had more money than he could ever have needed, as well as more treasures than rooms to store them.

All heads of state have palaces, but normally those palaces belong to the government, not to the individual. In the rare cases—Donald Trump, say—where the palaces are private property, they tend to have been acquired before the politician entered office. Yanukovich, however, had built his while living off a state salary, and that is why the protesters flocked to see his vast log cabin. They marveled at the edifice of the main building, the fountains, the waterfalls, the statues, the exotic pheasants. Enterprising locals rented bikes to visitors. The site was so large that there was no other way to see the whole place without exhaustion, and it took the revolutionaries days to explore all of its corners. The garages were an Aladdin's cave of golden goods, some of them perhaps priceless. The revolutionaries called the curators of Kiev's National Art Museum to take everything away before it got damaged, to preserve it for the nation, to put it on display.

There were piles of gold-painted candlesticks, walls full of portraits of the president. There were statues of Greek gods, and ivory carved into intricate oriental pagodas. There were dozens of icons, antique rifles and swords, and axes. There was a certificate declaring Yanukovich "Hunter of the Year," and documents announcing that a star had been named in his honor, and another for his wife. Some of the objects were displayed alongside the business cards of the officials who had presented them to the president. They had been tribute to a ruler: down payments to ensure that the givers remained in Yanukovich's favor and thus could continue to run the scams that had made them rich.

There was an ancient tome, displayed in a vitrine, with a sign declaring it to have been a present from the tax ministry. It was a copy of the *Apostol*, the first book ever printed in Ukraine, of which perhaps only a hundred copies still exist. Why had the tax ministry decided that this was an appropriate gift for the president? How could the ministry afford it? Why was the tax ministry giving presents like this to the president anyway? Who paid for it? No one knew. In among a pile of trashy ceramics was an exquisite Picasso vase, provenance unknown. A cabinet housed a steel hammer and sickle, which had once been a present to Joseph Stalin from the Ukrainian Communist Party. How did it get into Yanukovich's garage? Perhaps the president had had nowhere else to put it.

Soon the queue at the gate stretched all the way down the road. The people waiting looked jolly, edging slowly forward to vanish behind the museum's pebble-dashed pediment. When they emerged again, they looked ashen. By the final door was a book for comments. Someone had summed it up nicely:

"How much can one man need? Horror. I feel nauseous."

And this was only the start. Those post-revolutionary days were lawless in the best way, in that no one in uniform stopped you from indulging your curiosity, and I exploited the situation by invading as many of the old elite's hidden haunts as I could. One trip took me into the heart of a forest outside Kiev. Anton, a revolutionary I'd befriended, stopped the car at a gate, stepped off the road into the undergrowth, rustled around and held up what he'd found. "The key to paradise," he said, with a lopsided smile. He unlocked the gate, got back behind the wheel and drove through.

To the right was the glittering surface of the Kiev Reservoir, where the dammed waters of the Dnieper River swell into an inland sea dotted with reed beds. Then came a narrow causeway over a pond by a small boat-house with a dock. Ducks fussed around wooden houses on little floating islands. Finally, Anton pulled up at a turning circle in front of a two-story log mansion. This discreet residence, which went by the name of Sukho-luchya, was where Yanukovich came with old friends and new girlfriends when he wanted to relax.

Anton first came here with his daughter in the few hours after the president fled his capital in February 2014. He drove down that immaculate road to the first gate, where he told the policemen he was from the revolution. They gave him the key, let him pass. Now Anton opened the door and led the way in. He had changed nothing: the long dining table with its eighteen over-stuffed chairs were as he had found them, as was the heated marble massage table. The walls were dotted with low-grade sub-impressionist nudes—the kind of thing Pierre-Auguste Renoir might have painted if he'd moved toward soft porn. The floor was of polished boards, tropical hardwood; the walls were squared softwood logs, deliberately left unfinished, yellow as sesame seeds. There were no books.

Strange though it sounds, it was the bathrooms that really got to me. The house held nine televisions, and two of them were positioned opposite the toilets, at sitting-down height. It was a personal touch of the most intimate kind: President Yanukovich had been someone who liked to watch television, and someone who needed to spend extended periods on the toilet. The positioning of the televisions had clearly been intended to prevent the necessity from getting in the way of the hobby. While Ukraine's citizens died early, and worked hard for subsistence wages, while its roads rotted and its officials stole, the president had been preoccupied with ensuring that his constipation didn't impede his enjoyment of his favorite television programs. Those two televisions became a little symbol for me of everything that had gone wrong, not just in Ukraine, but in all the ex-Soviet countries I'd worked in.

The Soviet Union fell when I was thirteen years old, and I was highly jealous of anyone old enough to be experiencing the moment for themselves. In the summer of 1991, when hard-liners in Moscow tried and failed to re-impose the old Soviet ways on their country, I was on a family holiday in a remote part of the Scottish Highlands, and spent days trying to coax the radio into cutting through the mountains and telling me what was going on. By the time our holiday was over, the coup had failed, and a new world was dawning. The usually sober historian Francis Fukuyama declared it to be The End of History. The whole world was going to be free. The Good Guys Had Won.

I longed to see what was happening in Eastern Europe, and I read hundreds of books by those who had been there before me. When at university, I spent every long summer wandering through the previously forbidden countries of the old Warsaw Pact, reveling in Europe's reunification. At graduation, most of my fellow students had lined up jobs, but not me. Instead, I moved to St. Petersburg, Russia's second city, in September 1999, overcome with excitement, drunk on the possibilities of democratic transformation, of the flowering of a new society.

I was so full of the moment that I didn't realize I had already missed it, if indeed it ever existed in the first place. Three weeks before my plane touched down at Pulkovo Airport, an obscure ex-spy called Vladimir Putin had become prime minister. Instead of writing about freedom and friendship over the next decade or so I found myself reporting on wars and abuses, experiencing paranoia and harassment. History had not ended; if anything, it had accelerated.

By 2014, when I found myself contemplating presidential toilets, I had already written two books about the former USSR. The first grew out of the misery I'd seen in and around Chechnya, and described the peoples of the Caucasus and their repeated failures to secure the freedoms they desired. The second addressed the ethnic Russians themselves, and how alcoholism and despair were undermining their continued existence as a nation. Beneath both books, though unaddressed (I now realize) by either of them, was a question: What went wrong? Why had the dreams of 1991 failed to become reality? And that question was forcefully presented to me by the en suite bathroom at the hunting lodge of Ukraine's exiled head of state: Why had all these nations gained not liberty and prosperity, but politicians who cared more about their own defecatory comfort than the well-being of the nations they ruled?

Because this wasn't an isolated example. A Bentley showroom within half a mile of the Kremlin sold cars that cost hundreds of thousands of dollars, and the Russian media boasted that it was the busiest outlet for the luxury brand anywhere on Earth. Just a few hours' travel away—and this was well into the age of the iPhone—I once met a man who offered to swap his entire farm for my Nokia. In Azerbaijan, President Ilham Aliyev commissioned Zaha Hadid, perhaps the most glamorous architect in the world at the time, to build a spectacular, swooping, sinuous museum in honor of his late father (and predecessor as president) on a prime location in the center of Baku. Thousands of his subjects lived in makeshift refugee centers and had done so for the two decades since losing their homes in a war with neighboring Armenia. In Kyrgyzstan, the president created a three-story yurt (yurts are a kind of tent, and like all tents they usually have just one story) in which he could pose as a nomadic horse lord of old, while residents of his own capital still went to communal pumps for their water.

In Ukraine, Yanukovich and his ruling clique ran a shadow state operation, which operated alongside the official government apparatus. Instead of ruling, they stole. Where taxes were to be paid, they took bribes to help people avoid them. Where permits were being given, they awarded them to their friends. Where businesses were flourishing, they sent policemen to demand protection money. State officials moonlighted for the shadow state, neglecting their real duties for their more lucrative side careers. Ukraine had 18,500 prosecutors, who operated like foot soldiers for a mafia don. If they decided to take you to court, the judge did what they asked. With the entire legal system on their side, the insiders' opportunities to make money were limited only by their imagination. (Manafort's job was to present Yanukovich to the West as a statesman, as if none of this was going on.)

Take medicine, for example: the government bought drugs on the open market for a health system that had a constitutional duty to provide free care to everyone who needed it. Any company that met the relevant standards was technically allowed to participate. In reality, officials found endless ways to exclude anyone who wasn't prepared to pay them off. They would disqualify entries for being written in the wrong font, if the signature at the foot of the document was too large or too small or for anything else they could come up with.

Excluded companies could appeal, of course, but that required them going to a court that was another part of the corrupt system, enmeshing them further in the scams, so they tended not to bother taking action in the first place. After all, if they made a fuss, they would be hassled in perpetuity by one of the several dozen state agencies empowered to conduct on-the-spot inspections: for compliance with fire regulations; for compliance with hygiene regulations; and so on and so on. That meant the medicine market was dominated by the bureaucrats' friends: shady intermediaries, registered abroad, who colluded with each other and with insiders to jack up prices. The trade abided by the letter of the Ukrainian law, and still made big profits for the businessmen and officials who dominated it.

The health ministry ended up paying more than double what it needed to for anti-retrovirals, the drug needed to control HIV and prevent it from developing into full-blown AIDS, despite Ukraine's having Europe's fastest-growing epidemic. When international agencies took over procurement after the revolution, they managed to reduce the cost of medicine by almost 40 percent, without compromising on the quality of the drugs. Previously, all of that money had gone into officials' pockets.

And that was just the beginning. The government bought everything it used from someone, and every single purchase was an opportunity for an insider to get rich. Fraud of the state procurement system may have cost the government as much as $15 billion a year. In 2015, two Ukrainian children caught polio and were paralyzed, despite its being a disease that had supposedly been eradicated from Europe. A faulty vaccination program, undermined by corrupt and cynical politicians, was to blame. What went wrong?

It may seem like this question is specific to Ukraine and its former Soviet neighbors, but it has a far wider significance. The kind of industrial-scale corruption that enriched Yanukovich and undermined his country has driven anger and unrest in a great arc stretching from the Philippines in the east to Peru in the west, and most places in between. In Tunisia, official greed became so bad a street vendor set himself on fire, launching what became the Arab Spring. In Malaysia, a group of young, well-connected investors looted a sovereign wealth fund and spent the proceeds on drugs, parties and Hollywood stars. In Equatorial Guinea, the president's son had an official salary of $4,000 a month, yet bought himself a $35 million mansion in Malibu. All over the world, insiders have stolen public money, stashed it abroad, and used it to fund lifestyles of amazing luxury, while their home countries have collapsed around them.

***

As I walked out of the hunting lodge, still mulling over the toilets, the televisions and the unwelcome visions they conjured up, I asked Anton how the Ukrainians had let their ruler get away with this. How could they not have known what was going on? "We didn't know the details; of course we didn't," he replied, with a hint of frustration. "This land we're standing on—it's not even in Ukraine, it's in England. Look it up."

He was right. If you wanted to know who owned this 76,000-acre former nature reserve, perhaps because you wondered how it had come to be privatized in the first place, you could look in the registry of land ownership. And in the registry, you would find that the official owner was a Ukrainian company called Dom Lesnika. To find out who owned Dom Lesnika, you needed to look in another registry, where you would find the name of a British company, which yet another registry would tell you was owned by an anonymous foundation in Liechtenstein.

To an outside observer, this looked like an innocent piece of foreign investment, the kind of thing all governments are keen to encourage. If you had been particularly persistent, and had tried to reach Yanukovich's private hunting lodge in Sukholuchya to check it out for yourself, the police officers guarding the road through the forest would have stopped you. That might have made you suspicious, but there would still have been no proof that anything wrong was going on. The theft was well hidden.

Thankfully for investigators, Yanukovich kept records of what he was up to. His palace sat on a wooded hill, which sloped down to the Dnieper. The shoreline below his palace was adorned with a yacht harbor and a bar shaped like a galleon. In their haste to leave, the president's aides dumped 200 folders' worth of financial records into the harbor, hoping they'd sink, which they didn't. Protesters fished the papers out and dried them in a sauna. They provided a fascinating glimpse into the heart of the financial engineering that had allowed Yanukovich to fleece the country.

It wasn't just Yanukovich's shooting lodge that was owned overseas—the palace was, too. So were his coal-mining companies in the Donbas and his palaces in Crimea. And he wasn't the only outsider to use these offshore schemes: the medicine racket was run out of Cyprus; the illegal arms trade traced back to Scotland; the biggest market selling knockoff designer goods was legally owned in the Seychelles. All of this meant that any investigator trying to unknot this densely woven cloth of official corruption had to deal with lawyers and officials in multiple tax havens, as well as with police forces in dozens of foreign countries.

"These high-ranking officials are all registered abroad, in Monaco, or Cyprus, or Belize, or the British Virgin Islands," one Ukrainian prosecutor tasked with trying to recover these stolen assets told me. "We write requests to them, we wait for three or four years, or there's no response at all. As a rule, the BVI don't reply; we don't have an agreement with them. And that's that, and it all falls apart. We wait, and it has been re-registered five times just while we're waiting for an answer to come. It's all been re-registered, and that's our main problem, checking and receiving these documents."

This makes me dizzy, like a math problem that's too complicated to understand, or a deep hole that sucks at my feet. These assets are attached to Ukraine, yet legally they are elsewhere, somewhere we cannot follow them to. It's no wonder crooked politicians have found these vertiginous structures so useful: they defy comprehension. And Ukraine is just the start of it.

Officials in Nigeria, Russia, Malaysia, Kenya, Equatorial Guinea, Brazil, Indonesia, the Philippines, China, Afghanistan, Libya, Egypt and dozens of other countries have likewise stashed their wealth beyond the reach and oversight of their fellow citizens. Estimates for the total amount stolen each year from the developing world range from a massive $20 billion to an almost unimaginable trillion dollars. And this money makes its way, via the offshore

secrecy jurisdictions, into a handful of Western cities: Miami, New York, Los
Angeles, London, Monaco, Geneva.

***

Once upon a time, if an official stole money in his home country, there wasn't
much he could do with it. He could buy himself a new car, or build himself
a nice house, or give it to his friends and relatives, but that was more or less
it. His appetites were limited by the fact that the local market could not ab-
sorb endless sums of money. If he kept stealing after that, the money would
just build up in his house until he had no rooms left to put it in, or it was
eaten by mice.

Offshore finance changes that. Some people think of shell companies as
getaway cars for dodgy money, but—when combined with the modern financial system—they're more like magic teleportation boxes. If you steal
money, you no longer have to hide it in a safe, where the mice can get at it.
Instead, you stash it in your magic box, which spirits it away at the touch of
a button, out of the country, to any destination you choose. It's the financial
equivalent of never feeling full, no matter how much you eat.

It's no wonder officials become such gluttons, since there is now no limit
on how much money they can steal, and therefore no limit on how much they
can spend. If they want a yacht, they can send the money to Miami and choose
one at the annual boat show. If they want a house, they can send the money
to London or New York, find an estate agent who doesn't ask too many questions. If they want fine art, they can send the money to an auction house.
Offshore means never having to say "when."

And the magic does not stop there. Once ownership of an asset (be it a
house, or a jet, or a yacht, or a company) is obscured behind multiple corporate vehicles, hidden in multiple jurisdictions, it is almost impossible to discover. Even if the corrupt regime from which the insider profited collapses, as
it did in Ukraine, it is difficult if not impossible to find his money, confiscate
it and return it to the nation it was stolen from. You may have read how
millions of dollars have been sent back to Nigeria, Indonesia, Angola or
Kazakhstan, and indeed they have. But they represent less than one cent of
every dollar that was originally stolen. The corrupt rulers have got so good at

hiding their wealth that, essentially, once it's stolen it's gone forever, and they get to keep their luxury properties in west London, their superyachts in the Caribbean and their villas in the South of France, even if they lose their job.

The damage this does to the countries that lose the money is clear. Nigeria has lost control of its northern regions, and millions of people are refugees. Libya is barely recognizable as a state, with multiple warring factions battling for control, leaving a free path for people traffickers. Afghanistan's corrupt rulers have stopped battling opium growers, meaning cheap heroin continues to flow wherever smugglers wish to send it. Russia, which consumes much of the heroin, has more than a million HIV-positive inhabitants, while its health service remains underfunded and its government pursues cheap propaganda wins rather than helping its citizens.

Ukraine, meanwhile, is a mess. The roads running between its cities are poorly maintained, while those in the villages are scarcely maintained at all. Traveling around the country is an ordeal, made worse by the constant threat of being stopped and shaken down by traffic cops looking for infringements of the dozens of traffic regulations, or inventing them if necessary.

At independence in 1991, pretty much everyone in the country had the same amount of stuff, thanks to the way the Soviet Union mismanaged everything. In two decades, that changed utterly. By 2013, on the eve of the revolution, just forty-five individuals owned assets equal to half the country's economy. And this again is a feature of many developing countries that have been wrecked by corruption. The daughter of Angola's longest-serving president became Africa's richest woman, and sashays around the West like an A-list celebrity, while the rest of her nation struggles by in what is essentially a failed state. The daughter of Azerbaijan's president produces films and publishes glossy magazines, while the sons of two of his ministers have run lobbying operations from London and Washington DC. It is all but impossible to imagine countries with such skewed economies building healthy democracies, or honest political systems, or even being able to defend themselves.

The consequences had been obvious in Crimea, right after Ukraine's revolution. Crimea was technically part of Ukraine, and had been since the 1950s. Yet, when Russian troops—in unmarked uniforms, but driving vehicles with Russian military number plates—fanned out into the peninsula's cities and blockaded its military bases, the authorities were so demoralized that no one tried to stop them. An admiral turned over not just himself, but the ships of the Ukrainian navy, to Russia, despite the oath of loyalty he had given to Ukraine. The border guards in the airport stamped my passport with the Ukrainian trident while the country they were serving evaporated around them. Later, in eastern Ukraine, the same pattern repeated. No one wanted to defend Ukraine against armed and well-trained Russian-backed insurgents. Corruption had so hollowed out the state that it had all but ceased to exist, except as a means of illegal enrichment. Why, after all, would anyone defend something that spent its time making their lives miserable? Corruption robbed the whole country of legitimacy.

This kind of anger undermined Ukraine, and it undermines other countries too. It helps motivate people to join terrorist groups in Afghanistan, Nigeria and the Middle East. "The great challenge to Afghanistan's future isn't the Taliban, or the Pakistani safe havens, or even an incipiently hostile Pakistan. The existential threat to the long-term viability of modern Afghanistan is corruption," said US Marine Corps general John Allen, formerly head of international forces in Afghanistan, in 2014. "The ideological insurgency, the criminal patronage networks and the drug enterprise have formed an unholy alliance, which relies for its success on the criminal capture of your government functions at all levels. For too long, we've focused our attention on the Taliban as the existential threat to Afghanistan. They are an annoyance compared to the scope and magnitude of corruption with which you must contend."

And I keep wanting to ask everyone—just like I asked Anton—how can they not know what's going on? It's so obvious, isn't it? Well, no, Anton's right. It isn't. It's only easy to find this money when you already know where it is. Likewise, this problem is only obvious if you already know it exists.

***

On the morning after Halloween 2017, a carved pumpkin appeared on the doorstep of 377 Union Street, a handsome brownstone in the extensive grid of streets south of Brooklyn Heights. The pumpkin, when examined closely, bore a good likeness of Robert Mueller, the special counsel for probing whether

Russia illegally interfered in the election of Donald Trump. The pumpkin was the work of a local photographer named Amy Finkel, and it sat beneath a makeshift "designated landmark" sign declaring the property to be "The House That Brought Down a President." Locals, who voted overwhelmingly for Hillary Clinton in the 2016 presidential election, were having some fun with 377 Union Street.

The indictment charging Paul Manafort with money laundering had been unsealed just two days earlier, and it stated that he bought the property in 2012 with $3 million from a Cypriot bank account owned by a Cypriot company called Actinet, then mortgaged it for $5 million and used that money to buy other properties and to pay off loans in a complicated tax-dodging scam.

When he worked for Yanukovich, Manafort perfected the campaign style he would later use for Trump. Under Manafort's skilled guidance, Yanukovich styled himself as a plain-talking, no-nonsense guy who would stand up for the forgotten and the left behind. Mueller's charges against him relate to this Ukraine work, and what he did with the money he earned from it. "They lobbied multiple Members of Congress and their staffs about Ukraine sanctions, the validity of Ukraine elections, the propriety of Yanukovych's imprisoning his presidential rival," the indictment states.

He used the money he earned to spend almost as lavishly as his patrons did. According to the indictment's exhaustive breakdown of his expenses, Manafort spent $934,350 on antique rugs; $849,215 on clothing; $112,825 on audio and video equipment (perhaps he too had televisions at sitting-down height in the toilets). But it was the property that was the biggest expense. A condo in New York cost him $1.5 million, and a house in Virginia another $1.9 million (like Yanukovich and indeed Trump, Manafort appreciated the votes of people left behind by economic change, but did not like living near them), all of it money that came from the government of Ukraine.

And here the questions are uncomfortable. It is amusing that Manafort's Brooklyn neighbors trolled him with pumpkins and homemade signs, but it is also worrying that they didn't know who owned the house in their neighborhood, any more than Ukrainians knew the true owner of Sukholuchya. And it is worrying too that there is no way that they could have found out. If they had looked up the name of the company that owned the brownstone—MC

Brooklyn Holdings LLC—on the New York registry, they would have found no information guiding them to its true owner.

The company in question was a local one, but it disguised the owner of this property just as well as the British and Liechtenstein structures disguised Yanukovich. If Manafort's neighbors had sought to ask questions about the origin of the funds used to buy the properties, or to improve them, or to buy the smart clothes, the hi-fi systems and the antique rugs, they would have found the names of companies in Cyprus, St. Vincent and the Grenadines, or the UK. When one contemplates the work Mueller's team did to dig up the details of the indictment, gravity seems to intensify and the ground falls away.

It is appropriate that the trail takes us to New York, however, because this hole didn't open up in Ukraine, or in sub-Saharan Africa, or in Malaysia, but in the heart of the West. Wealthy people have always tried to keep their money out of the hands of government, and have developed clever tools with which to do so over the centuries. In Britain and America, lawyers create trusts that allow their rich clients to technically give away their riches while retaining the benefit of them and later passing them on to their children. In continental Europe, the same job is done by foundations.

Societies across the West (and particularly the United States) have become less equal in terms of both wealth and income since the 1970s. Some economists, led by Thomas Piketty, have suggested that this is because the long-term return on capital is higher than the growth rate of the economy. This means that, barring some world war–sized catastrophe, people with money earn more in interest and dividends than workers earn wages, and so Western societies inevitably become more unequal in the absence of concerted government efforts to the contrary.

That may well be so, but it is not what this book is about. I am not an economist, and am not qualified to address whether structural issues favor capital over workers. I am a journalist and, like all journalists, I am fascinated by crooks. My book, therefore, is about the people who cheat, the kind of people who doomed the country I moved to in 1999 and shattered the hopeful wave I was hoping to ride into a glorious Russian future.

You don't need to be an economist to see that rich people's ability to take advantage of offshore tricks unavailable to the rest of us is also part of the explanation for why our societies have become so much less equal. If the wealthy can dodge taxes, and even steal, with impunity, it will only expand the divide between those who own assets and those who don't.

Western governments have struggled to keep on top of these tricks, but at least they have the institutions and traditions required to keep themselves broadly honest while doing so. In newer and poorer countries, however, those institutions and traditions do not exist. Officials and politicians have been swept away by the tsunami of money. As one lawyer in Ukraine put it: "The choice isn't between taking a bribe or being honest; it's between taking a bribe or your children being killed. Of course you take the bribe."

Corruption has become so widespread that whole countries are unable to tax their wealthiest residents, meaning that only those least able to afford it are forced to support the government. This undermines democratic legitimacy and angers the people who live under these governments, often—as we have seen most recently in Brazil—provoking them to vote for politicians who have little sympathy for democracy themselves. For people who believe in a liberal world order, there is no upside to this.

Commentators from all sides of politics have expressed concerns about the effect of inequality on the fabric of society in the United States, where the share of wealth held by the richest 1 percent rose from a quarter to two-fifths between 1990 and 2012. But if you think that's bad, look what's happened to the world as a whole: in just the decade after 2000, the richest 1 percent of the world's population increased its wealth from one-third of everything to a half. The top three and a half dozen people now own as much as the bottom three and a half billion. How is democracy possible with that kind of gulf in wealth and power between citizens?

That increase is driven by places like Russia. In the fifteen years since Vladimir Putin took over in 2000, the 4 percent of Russians that Credit Suisse considers to be middle-class (worth between $18,000 and $180,000) saw their collective wealth increase by $137 billion, which looks good until you see what the country's upper class achieved over the same period. The 0.5 percent of Russians who have more than $180,000 saw their wealth increase by an astonishing $687 billion. The top 10 percent of Russians own 87 percent of everything, a higher proportion than in any other major country—and a pretty stark fact, coming as it does out of a place that was communist just three decades ago.

Which brings us back to Paul Manafort. This wholesale looting is only possible because of people like him—Western enablers: lawyers, consultants, lobbyists, accountants and others who move their clients' money and help them hide it in clever ways. If you try telling an informed Russian that the West is a principled alternative to Vladimir Putin's Kremlin, he'll likely ask why then Putin's propaganda chief was allowed to buy property in Beverly Hills on a bureaucrat's salary, or why the deputy prime minister owns an apartment within walking distance of London's House of Commons. This hypocrisy is a gift to Putin, who can not only undermine his opponents by highlighting it, but also use the West's offshore tools against it: as a conduit for money to fund his security services, to create anti-Western propaganda and to support political extremists favorable to his interests. Corruption is a force multiplier for the West's enemies, and yet the West continues to accept dirty money into its economies by the billions.

The money sucks at your feet; the ground falls away.

***

As a boy, I had jigsaw puzzles of the world, and of Britain, America and Europe, in which I could place the shapes of the counties, states and countries into the holes left by their borders. Indeed, my own children now play with them. France is a hexagon; Italy looks like a boot; Wyoming and Colorado are hard to tell apart; Chile is helpfully long and thin. This reflects an approach to the world that divides things up between countries, and in some ways that approach is correct. If discussing the number of children born each year, or the number murdered with guns, or football-playing populations, it makes sense to apportion the people involved to the countries where the relevant events take place.

Sometimes, however, that approach is less appropriate. Transparency International (TI), the anti-corruption campaign group, publishes an annual Corruption Perceptions Index, in which it rates almost all the countries of the world by how corrupt they are, from Denmark and New Zealand at the clean end, down to North Korea, South Sudan and Somalia at the other. The United States is ranked 16th, alongside Austria and Belgium and slightly higher than Australia.

The index is presented as a map, showing corruption in terms of color, with red indicating the most corrupt countries. Most of Africa is a bright red, as are South America and Asia, while Europe, North America and Australasia are various shades of yellow. This is helpful as far as it goes, and of course it's true that you are more likely to be shaken down for a bribe in Dar es Salaam than in Delaware. But what about the more sophisticated forms of corruption used by Yanukovich or Manafort?

Ukraine is a deep red on TI's map, the 131st least honest place in the world and—alongside Russia—the dirtiest place in Europe. Yet Yanukovich's property could not have been hidden without the services of his British shell companies. So why is Britain listed as an honest 10th, alongside Germany and Luxembourg? Similarly, Manafort's money was hidden by banks and companies in Cyprus and St. Vincent, and they're ranked as a relatively clean 47th and 35th.

If Ukrainian politicians couldn't be crooked without the services of other countries, why is the crookedness pinned only to Ukraine? And if British or Cypriot lawyers are looking for business from Ukrainian crooks, do their home countries have a right to their reputations? From the money's perspective, the borders are unimportant. It has been a long time since borders got in the way of money flows. When I go to Kiev, I can use my Visa card, just like I can use it in California or Cambridge or St. Kitts and Nevis. That does not mean the borders have disappeared, of course. As the Ukrainian prosecutor I quoted above made clear, it is hard for him to obtain evidence from a foreign jurisdiction, and it's the same for investigators from any country.

Money flows across frontiers, but laws do not. The rich live globally; the rest of us have borders.

I am part of a group that tries to highlight what this means in what we call the London Kleptocracy Tours (my friends Roman Borisovich and Julie and Charles Davidson came up with the idea). We fill a bus with sightseers rather as if we were taking them to Hollywood to see where Clark Gable used to live or where Scarlett Johansson gets her hair cut. Instead of showing them stars, however, we show them politicians. As our bus driver guides us through west London, our guides point out properties owned by ex-Soviet oligarchs, the scions of Middle Eastern political dynasties, Nigerian regional governors and all the other people who have made fortunes in countries that score low on TI's list, and hidden them in countries that rank high.

We can fit only fifty-odd people in a bus at any one time, but the aim is a simple one: we want to pull away the veil that hides the abuse of the global financial system. We want to stop people from saying—or, indeed, from being able to say—that they couldn't have known.

One place we often pass through is Eaton Square, now perhaps London's most prestigious address, a magnificent oblong of grand cream-painted four-square houses, all tucked behind shoulder-height black railings and looking onto private gardens. In January 2017, a group of anarchists—they call themselves the Autonomous Nation of Anarchist Libertarians, which gives them the acronym ANAL—snuck into 102 Eaton Square via an open window and opened it as a shelter for the homeless. The house is vast and stucco-fronted, with a pediment on pillars stretching from a balcony on the first floor up to the fourth. When I called out, a black flag was flying from one of its flag-poles, and a bearded man was leaning on the balustrade smoking. He shouted down to ask what I wanted and promised to be out in a second.

A middle-aged man in purple corduroys and a waxed jacket had witnessed our exchange, and crossed the road with his wife to inform me, with the limited fury a polite English accent can muster, that I was the "scum of the earth." The bearded anarchist, a Hungarian, emerged onto the pavement, caught the tail of this and grinned at me. He led me down a flight of stairs into the basement, through a fire exit and into what had once been a cinema. He explained that his group had just lost a court battle against eviction and would be moving out, but that I was free to explore. The floor was parquet, and the stairwells extended up to lanterns cut into the roof. Rooms led into rooms led into rooms. Scribbled graffiti on the walls did nothing to detract from the fact that this would make someone a glorious house.

That someone was Andrei Goncharenko, a manager of a subsidiary of Russian gas giant Gazprom, who from 2010 through 2013 had bought a string of properties in west London. This one was the cheapest, at a mere £15 million, which is perhaps why he had left it empty. "Our main priority is to highlight the large number of empty buildings in London and to try to ensure they don't go to waste when there are so many homeless people," Jed Miller, one of the anarchists who appeared in court to argue against the eviction, told journalists. "These offshore companies which own so many empty buildings in London are using them to minimize their tax liability. That is diverting money away from crucial services."

You don't have to agree with squatting in empty buildings to recognize that he has a point. Goncharenko's mansion is one of eighty-six different properties on this one square alone that are held via the kind of anonymous structures that can stop anyone, including the tax man, from finding out who the true owner is. Some thirty of them are held in the British Virgin Islands; thirteen are in Guernsey; and sixteen are in Jersey. Others are in Panama, Liechtenstein, the Isle of Man, Delaware, the Cayman Islands, Liberia, the Seychelles, Mauritius and—Manafort's favorite—St. Vincent and the Grenadines. Goncharenko himself preferred Gibraltar as home for his company MCA Shipping. Across England and Wales, more than 100,000 properties are owned offshore, just like Yanukovich's and Manafort's properties were. It is impossible to say how many are empty, but perhaps as many as half of the new builds at the top of the market are barely used, according to one study. These are not houses for living in, but house-shaped bank accounts.

If the time ever comes when someone asks Londoners how they could not have known what was going on, they'll reply that it was hidden from them, just like Manafort's ownership of his brownstone in Brooklyn was hidden from his neighbors. Any of these Eaton Square properties could be owned by a crook, but it's impossible to pick out which ones. One apartment stretches across a single floor of two adjoining properties, and cost Cane Garden Services Limited, a company registered in the British Virgin Islands, almost £13 million. This luxury-loving and profligate shell company is registered at a betting shop on the Caledonian Road, an unlovely thoroughfare in north London where you'd be far more likely to find amphetamines than a top-notch lawyer. Is that a red flag? Perhaps, or perhaps not.

It's that dizzy feeling again. Once you start looking for red flags you see them everywhere. Houses number 85 and 102 are both owned by offshore companies registered to the same address in Hong Kong. The Liberian company that owns number 73 is registered in Monaco. One flat in number 86 is owned by Panoceanic Trading Corporation, a Panamanian company with a name that appears to have dropped out of a 1960s thriller. Surely a crook wouldn't be that obvious? Or is it a double bluff?

On our Kleptocracy Tours, we habitually describe six or seven properties in an afternoon. This means that if we wanted to explore the provenance of all the offshore-owned properties on Eaton Square, it would take us around two weeks. Then we would have to start on the neighboring roads. Every adjoining street has as many offshore properties, all intermeshed in a great web of confusion and deceit that extends as far as Britain does, and then some more. Before our grand tour had ended, it would be time to begin again at the beginning. Even those of us who like to think we know what's going on have no idea what's going on.

These wealthy nomads are taking advantage of the way money moves across borders but laws stay put in order to pick and choose which laws to obey. Under British law, you have to declare who owns a property. If you own that property in Mauritius, you do not. It will cost you money to structure your holdings that way, but if you can afford it, you have access to privacy denied to everyone else in the country.

The more I researched this, the more I realized it applies far beyond just property ownership. If you are a Syrian refugee, global visa restrictions severely limit your ability to travel. If you are a wealthy Syrian citizen, however, you can buy a passport from St. Kitts and Nevis, Cyprus or half a dozen other countries, and suddenly you have access to a world of visa-free travel denied to your compatriots. If you are an ordinary Ukrainian, you are at the mercy of your country's corrupt and inefficient court system. If you are a wealthy Ukrainian, however, you can arrange all of your business dealings so they are governed by English law, and enjoy the services of honest and effective judges.

It goes on and on. If you are Chinese and want to visit the United States, you must undergo the indignities of the visa application process; if you are a rich Chinese, however, you can invest in the EB-5 program, ostensibly designed to create jobs and attract investment into the US economy, and purchase a green card for as little as $500,000. If you are an ordinary Nigerian, you must suffer what the country's newspapers might say about you. If you are rich, however, you can hire London lawyers and sue your country's journalists based on the fact that their online articles have been read in the UK. Most important, if you can structure your assets so they are held in the United States, your government will never find out about them, whereas they will know about everything owned at home. There will be plenty more about this pick-and-mix approach to legislation later: it's the subject of this book.

***

The physicist Richard Feynman supposedly once said: "If you think you understand quantum mechanics, you don't understand quantum mechanics." I feel the same about the way offshore structures have warped the fabric of the world. But if this dizzying realization sends me out of the house and away from my computer screen, there's no escaping it. The building where I buy my morning coffee is owned in the Bahamas. The place I get my hair cut is owned in Gibraltar. A building site on my way to the train station is owned in the Isle of Man. If we spent all of our time trying to puzzle out what was really happening, we'd have no time to do anything else. It's no wonder most sensible people ignore what the superrich get up to. You follow a white rabbit down a hole, the tunnel dips suddenly and, before you know it, you find yourself falling down a very deep well into a new world. It's a beautiful place, if you're rich enough to enjoy it. If you're not, it's inaccessible.

This is the place that I call Moneyland—Maltese passports, English libel, American privacy, Panamanian shell companies, Jersey trusts, Liechtenstein foundations, all added together to create a virtual space that is far greater than the sum of its parts. The laws of Moneyland are whichever laws anywhere are most suited to those wealthy enough to afford them at any moment in time. If a country somewhere changes the law to restrict Moneylanders in any way, they shift themselves or their assets to countries with more generous laws. If a country passes a law that offers new possibilities for enrichment, then the assets shift likewise.

It is as if the very wealthiest people in countries like China, Nigeria, Ukraine and Russia have tunneled into this new land that lies beneath all our nation-states, where borders have vanished. They move their money, their children, their assets and themselves wherever they wish, picking and choosing which countries' laws they wish to live by. The result is that strict regulations and restrictions do not apply to them, but still constrain the rest of us.

This is a phenomenon with novel consequences that go to the heart of what a government is supposed to be for. The American economist Mancur

Olson traced the origin of civilization back to the moment when prehistoric "roving bandits" realized that, instead of raiding groups of humans and moving on, they could earn more by staying put and stealing from their victims all the time. Early humans submitted to this because, although they lost some of their freedom when they submitted to these "stationary bandits," they gained in return stability and security. The bandits' interests and the community's interests became aligned. Without bandits constantly raiding them and stealing their property, groups of humans built increasingly complex communities and economies, becoming prosperous, which led eventually to the birth of the state, to civilization, and to everything we now take for granted.

"We see why the warlord's subjects, even though he extracts tax theft from them year by year, prefer him to the roving bandits that rob sporadically. Roving banditry means anarchy, and replacing anarchy with government brings about a considerable increase in output," Olson wrote.

Stable government aligns the interests of the strong and the weak, since they both want to see everyone get wealthy. The weak want to be wealthy for their own sake, while the strong want the weak to be wealthy so they can take more from them as taxes. Olson used the parallel of a mafia protection racket. If the mafia's grip on a community is complete there will essentially be no crime, since it is in the boss' interests for local businesses to make as much money as possible, so the amount of it he extorts will be greater. Crime is, for a society, an unproductive activity that forces people to spend money on guards and fences and locks, rather than on things that lead somewhere useful. It is therefore in all our interests to be governed.

But Olson had a caveat: the argument only works if everyone is thinking in the long term, which is why Moneyland changes everything. The nomad citizens of Moneyland turn Olson's calculation on its head. Because they are able to keep their assets outside the communities they steal them from, they don't care what happens in the long term. The more they steal now, the more they and their children get to keep. In fact, they make money from instability: the more disputes there are, the more they can cream off as the price of resolving them.

These "offshore bandits" combine the worst features of the old roving bandits with the worst features of their stationary successors. Thanks to the magic of the modern financial system, and the anonymity provided by offshore jurisdictions that accept money whatever its provenance, they are oppressing their subjects without contributing to increased security and prosperity.

These last few years, we have got used to criticizing globalization for the way it has stripped jobs from Western countries and relocated them elsewhere, with no concern for those left behind. Globalization's defenders counter by arguing that by allocating capital to where it can work most efficiently, it has lifted more people out of poverty in China, India and elsewhere than any other movement ever. In Moneyland, however, globalization acts differently. It is not a function of capital being allocated efficiently to garner the greatest return for its owners, but of capital being allocated to gain the greatest degree of protection. This is the dark side of globalization, and there is no positive case to be made for it, unless you yourself are a thief or a thief's enabler.

Moneyland is not an easy place to confront, however. You can't send an army against it, since it doesn't appear on any maps. Nor can you implement sanctions against it, or send diplomats to talk it round. Unlike conventional countries, it has no border guards to stamp your passport, no flag to salute and no foreign minister to talk to on the phone. It has no army to protect it, because it doesn't need one. It exists wherever there are people who want to keep their money out of the reach of their country's government, and who can afford the lawyers and financiers required to do so. If we wish to preserve democracy, however, we must confront Moneyland's nomad citizens, and must find a way to dismantle the offshore structures that make it so easy for them to hide their money from democratic oversight. They are at least as significant a threat to the rules-based order that we've created to make the world safe as the terrorists and dictators we read about every day.

I have structured this book both chronologically and thematically, picking and choosing illustrative examples from as much of the world as I can to reveal quite how widespread Moneyland is. I begin by describing how Moneyland works, how it *conceals* wealth and how small jurisdictions have made a living from crafting their laws to facilitate the process. Then I describe what it means when the powerful take advantage of Moneyland to *steal*, starting with the story of one Ukrainian hospital, then showing how that one hospital is representative of much of the world.

Next, I describe how Moneyland *defends* both its citizens and their wealth: how it sells them passports; how it protects their reputations from journalists; how it prevents their stolen wealth from being recovered by its true owners. Moneyland can let you get away with murder, and indeed it has. I lay out how the citizens of Moneyland like to *spend* the cash they hide in it—the clothes, the property, the art, the rest—and what their increasingly outrageous spending habits are doing to the world. The effects of this spending are so extreme that there is now a whole field of study called "plutonomy" devoted to it.

Finally, I describe how governments have tried to *fight back*, focusing on the way the United States targeted Swiss banks, and then how clever lawyers and bankers used that opportunity to make Moneyland stronger and safer than ever. This may not seem a hopeful prospect, but if the first step to solving a problem is recognizing its existence, then we are perhaps now on our way.

Researching this book has not been easy. Moneyland is well guarded, and does not give up its secrets without a tussle. It also challenges everything we think we know about how the world works. You may find that, as with me, Moneyland induces vertigo to such an extent that once you see it, it is all around you. Why do so many ships fly the flags of foreign countries? Moneyland allows their owners to undercut their home nations' labor regulations. Why do Russian officials prefer to build billion-dollar bridges rather than schools and hospitals? Moneyland lets them steal 10 percent of the construction cost and stash it abroad. Why do billionaires live in Monaco? Moneyland lets them dodge taxes. Why do so many corrupt foreigners want to invest their money in New York? Moneyland protects their assets against confiscation.

This means Moneyland has neutered the core function of democracy—taxing citizens and using the proceeds for the common good—which in turn has disillusioned many people with the democratic experiment altogether. In despair, they have turned to strongmen like Yanukovich, who have further undermined democracy in a vicious cycle that benefits no one but the already rich and powerful.

One point that needs to be made firmly and repeatedly, however, is that I am not describing a conspiracy. Moneyland is not controlled by an arch-villain, stroking a white cat on the arm of a leather chair. If there was a controlling brain behind Moneyland, it would be easy to deal with. Moneyland is something far more complex, and far more insidious: it is the natural result of a world where money moves freely and laws do not, and where a good living can be made from exploiting the mismatches that result. If a tax rate is low in Jersey and high in Britain, there's money to be made for anyone who can move her clients' assets out of Britain and into Jersey, and the same goes for jurisdictions all over the world: they all have subtly different rules and regulations.

Moneyland is more like an anthill than a traditional organization. In an anthill, the individual ants are not obeying instructions. There aren't middle manager ants directing them to go out and pick up grass seed. There aren't police ants arresting wrongdoers who keep grass seeds for themselves, or judge ants sentencing them to terms in ant prison. The ants are responding in a predictable manner to external stimuli. In Moneyland, the individual lawyers, accountants and politicians are also responding in a predictable manner. If a law is helpful to any aspect of a rich person's existence, Moneyland's enablers make sure the rich person can enjoy the benefits of that law, wherever and whatever it is, to the greater good of the rich person, and the greater bad of the rest of us. If you squash one ant, or arrest one crooked lawyer, the activities of the rest will continue unaffected. It is the whole system that must be changed, and this is hard.

That is why I begin by describing how Moneyland came into existence, and how it defeated an attempt to make the world safe for democracy. In the dark days of the Second World War, the Allied powers confronted a threat to open societies more severe than any before or since. In response, they crafted a global financial architecture intended to give primacy to democracy in perpetuity. Never again, they hoped, would democratically elected governments be threatened by any rival. Their attempt failed, and the story of how it failed is the story of the birth of Moneyland.

2

PIRATES

In the years after the First World War, the world worked like it does now, although in a less technologically sophisticated way. Money flowed between countries pretty much however its owners wished, destabilizing their currencies and economies in pursuit of profit. Many of the wealthy got wealthier even while economies fell apart: which is why the 1930s gave us *Tender Is the Night* and *The Grapes of Wrath*, *Vile Bodies* and *The Road to Wigan Pier*. The chaos ultimately led to the election of extremist governments in Germany and elsewhere, to competitive devaluations and beggar-my-neighbor tariffs, to trade wars, to diplomatic repercussions, to border clashes, to conflict, and thence to the horrors of the Second World War, with its tens of millions of dead.

The Allies wanted to prevent this from ever happening again. So, at a meeting at the Bretton Woods resort in New Hampshire in 1944, they negotiated the details of an economic architecture that would—in perpetuity—stop uncontrolled money flows. This, they hoped, would keep governments from using trade as a weapon to bully neighbors, and block bankers from making a profit by undermining democracy. This enforced stability should stop the march to any new war before it began and create a new system of peace and prosperity. They looked back on the years before the First World War, at the way trade had flowed freely and the global order (at least for rich Western countries) had been stable. That system had been underpinned by gold. The value of a country's currency was determined by the size of its gold reserves, which rose and fell as trade expanded or contracted, and therefore acted as an automatic accelerant or dampener on money supply and thus prices, keeping everything in balance.

The old Gold Standard could not be resurrected, however. By 1944, almost all the gold in the world belonged to the United States. The delegates would have to think of something else. Britain's representative, John Maynard Keynes, argued for a new international currency against which all other currencies would be pegged. His US counterpart, Harry Dexter White, was unconvinced. He could not countenance the dollar losing its hard-won position as the world's dominant monetary force. Since the United States was the only solvent country at the meeting, he got his way: all currencies would be pegged to the dollar, which would in turn be pegged to gold. An ounce of gold would cost $35.

That was the fundamental underpinning of the system. The US Treasury pledged that, if a foreign government turned up with $35, it could always buy an ounce of gold. The United States was promising to keep everyone supplied with enough dollars to fund international trade, as well as to maintain sufficient gold reserves for those dollars to be inherently valuable. You didn't need precious metals if the dollar was as good as gold.

The other countries made commitments, too. If they wished to change the value of their currency by a significant amount, they promised that they would only do so with the approval of a new body called the International Monetary Fund. This would stop dictators from manipulating currencies to ruin their neighbors and stoke conflict. To prevent speculators from trying to attack this system of fixed currencies, cross-border money flows were severely constrained. Money could move overseas, but only in the form of long-term investments, not to speculate short term against currencies or bonds.

To understand how the system worked, imagine an oil tanker, a ship full of oil. If a tanker has just one huge tank, then the oil that fills it can slosh backward and forward in ever greater waves, until it destabilizes the vessel, which overturns and sinks. That was the system after the First World War, when the waves of speculative money capsized democracy. At Bretton Woods, the delegates designed a new kind of ship, where the oil was divided up among many smaller tanks, one for each country. The ship held the same volume of oil, but in a different way. The liquid could slosh back and forth within its little compartments, but would not be able to achieve enough momentum to damage the integrity of the entire vessel. And if one compartment sprang a leak, then it wouldn't threaten the whole cargo. It was possible to move oil from one compartment to another but (at the risk of pushing this metaphor to the point of absurdity) you needed permission from the captain, and the money had to go through the ship's official plumbing.

This is hard to imagine for anyone who has only experienced the world since the 1980s, because the system now is so different. Money flows ceaselessly between countries, nosing out investment opportunities in China, or Brazil, or Russia, or wherever. If a currency is overvalued, investors sense the weakness and gang up on it like sharks around a sickly whale. In times of global crisis, the money retreats into the safety of gold or US government bonds. In boom times, it pumps up share prices elsewhere in its restless quest for a good return. These waves of liquid capital have such power that they can wash away all but the strongest governments. The prolonged speculative attacks on the euro, or on the ruble, or the pound, which have been such a feature of the last few decades, would have been impossible under the Bretton Woods system, which was specifically designed to stop them from happening.

Strangely, one of the best evocations of this long-gone system is the 1959 James Bond thriller *Goldfinger*, written by Ian Fleming. The film of the same name has a slightly different plot, but they both feature a Soviet agent trying to undermine the West's financial system by interfering with its gold reserves. In the book, "M"—the boss of the British secret service—sends Bond to the Bank of England, where he finds a Colonel Smithers ("Colonel Smithers looked exactly like someone who would be called Colonel Smithers") whose job it is to watch for any leakage of gold out of Britain.

"Gold and currencies backed by gold are the foundation of our international credit," Smithers explains to 007. "We can only tell what the true strength of the pound is, and other countries can only tell it, by knowing the amount of valuta we have behind our currency." The trouble is, the colonel continues, that the bank is only prepared to pay a thousand pounds for a gold bar, which is the equivalent of the $35 per ounce price paid in America, whereas the same gold is worth 70 percent more in India, where there is a high demand for gold jewelry. It is thus highly profitable to smuggle gold out of the country and sell it overseas.

The villain Auric Goldfinger's cunning scheme is to own pawnbrokers all over Britain, buy up gold jewelry and trinkets from ordinary Brits in need of a bit of cash, then melt them down into plates, attach the plates to his Rolls-Royce, drive them to Switzerland, reprocess them and fly them to India. By doing so, Goldfinger will not only undermine the British currency and economy, but also earn profits he could use to fund communists and other miscreants. Fully one-sixth of the Bank of England's 3,000 employees are engaged in trying to stop this kind of scam from happening, Smithers tells 007, but Goldfinger is too clever for them. He has secretly become Britain's richest man, and has £5 million worth of gold bars sitting in the vaults of a bank in the Bahamas.

"That gold, or most of it, belongs to England. The Bank can do nothing about it, so we are asking you to bring Mr. Goldfinger to book, Mr. Bond, and get that gold back. You know about the currency crisis and the high bank rate? Of course. Well, England needs that gold, badly—and the quicker the better."

In this dull but important introductory section (spoiler alert: Bond does succeed in defeating Goldfinger, but not before he gets entangled with the Chicago mob, foils a daring raid on Fort Knox and seduces a lesbian who has "never met a man before"), Colonel Smithers dissects the philosophical question at the heart of the Bretton Woods system. By modern standards, Goldfinger wasn't doing anything wrong, apart perhaps from dodging some taxes. He was buying up gold at a price people were prepared to pay for it, then selling it in another market, where people were prepared to pay more. It was his money. It was his gold. So what was the problem? He was oiling the wheels of commerce, efficiently allocating capital where it could best be used, no?

No, because that wasn't how Bretton Woods worked. Colonel Smithers considered the gold to belong not only to Goldfinger, but also to Great Britain. The system didn't consider the owner of money to be the only person with a say in what happened to it. According to the carefully crafted rules, the nations that created and guaranteed the value of money had rights to that money, too. They restricted the rights of money-owners in the interests of everybody else. At Bretton Woods, the Allies—desperate to avoid a repeat of the horrors of the inter-war depression and the Second World War—decided that, when it came to international trade, society's rights trumped those of money-owners.

This was just one element of a whole series of measures created in the 1930s and 1940s to provide full employment and better services in the interests of stability and prosperity. The New Deal legislation in the United States severely limited the rights of banks to speculate, while the Welfare State in Great Britain provided universal healthcare and free education. The innovations were remarkably successful: economic growth in most Western countries was almost uninterrupted throughout the 1950s and 1960s, with massive improvements in public health and infrastructure. All of this did not come cheap, though, and taxes had to be high to pay for it: Beatles fans will remember George Harrison singing on "Taxman" about the government taking nineteen shillings for every one he could keep, which was an accurate reflection of the amount of his earnings that was going to the Treasury. Rich people struggled to move their money out of the taxman's reach—thanks to the separate compartments in the oil tanker. Taxes were hard to avoid, unless you physically relocated (like the Rolling Stones, who moved to France to record *Exile on Main Street*).

What you thought about this innovative bit of tanker design depended on whether you were one of the people being taxed, or one of the people enjoying unprecedented improvements in your standard of living. The Beatles and the Stones clearly hated it, as did Rowland Baring, scion of the Barings Bank dynasty, Third Earl of Cromer and—between 1961 and 1966—the governor of the Bank of England. "Exchange control is an infringement on the rights of the citizen," he wrote to the British government in 1963. "I therefore regard [it] ethically as wrong." He thought the owner of money should be able to do whatever he (and it was almost invariably a he) wanted with it, and that governments shouldn't be able to limit his opportunities by stopping that money flowing overseas. Baring thought this new kind of oil tanker was wrong. Captains shouldn't be allowed to stop oil from sloshing wherever its owner wanted it to, no matter how much damage it might do to the ship.

Funnily enough, "M" thought so, too. In *Goldfinger*, he told Bond he couldn't really understand what Colonel Smithers was talking about. "Personally I should have thought the strength of the pound depended on how hard we all worked rather than how much gold we'd got," he said, with the kind of bluff common sense of someone who insists their views are above politics. "However, that's probably too easy an answer for the politicians—or more likely too difficult." That viewpoint was very widely held in the City of London, where the bankers believed that the valuing of assets should be left to the markets with no political interference.

One of the main reasons why the viewpoint was so widespread in the City was probably that the new Bretton Woods system severely restricted its ability to make a living. Before the First World War, Britain's pound sterling had been the world's most important currency, and the bankers of the City had done very well out of financing the world's trade. Vast fortunes were made by those who worked hard, who hustled and who had the right connections. With Britain beggared by two world wars, however, and the dollar now the world's preeminent currency, the bankers had precious little to do.

"It was like driving a powerful car at twenty miles an hour," lamented one banker of his spell in charge of a major British bank. "The banks were anesthetized. It was a kind of dream life." People arrived at work late, left early, and frittered away much of the time in between having boozy lunches. One banker remembers spending his lunch breaks on the water. He would set off downriver to Greenwich on a scheduled service, eat his sandwiches and drink beer, then get the boat back again, drink more beer, and return to work. The whole pointless round trip would take as much as two hours, but no one particularly cared, because there wasn't anything to do anyway. At least he got lots of fresh air. City workers weren't very well paid, but then their jobs weren't very demanding. The banks considered it wrong to poach each other's clients, and the clients they had weren't doing very much. Well into the 1960s, tracts of the City bore the scars of the German bombs that had fallen on London two decades earlier. Shattered buildings that once housed hubs of trade and commerce grew abundant crops of rosebay willowherb and provided playgrounds for feral children. Why bother rebuilding them when there was nothing for the buildings to do?

For anyone with any understanding of London's long history, this felt wrong. There was a trading station on this hill on the north bank of the river Thames before even the Romans arrived. Rome simply formalized the situation by putting its capital here and calling it Londinium (you can still go and see a Roman amphitheater in the basement of the Guildhall, if you're sufficiently interested in all this and it's a rainy afternoon). And it's easy to see why they did so; London is perfect for trade. It is well drained, defensible, and as far inland as a ship can sail up the Thames. It looks out to sea, to the world; not upriver toward England. You can offload your cargos here and sell them to locals coming from the hinterland; or keep them in London before selling them on to other foreign traders. The City is the interface between Britain and the rest of the world; the river Thames and the oceans made London rich, and getting rich was London's purpose. London isn't technically even the capital of England; that is Westminster, a different city just upriver, which has merged with London physically but not philosophically. Westminster obsesses over the minutiae of British life, but London has always had its own politics, dominated by the great finance houses, more interested in Manhattan or Mumbai than in Machynlleth or Maidenhead.

It was London companies that first conquered India, and Africa, and North America, not the British state. They funded the railways and the steamships that bound the continents together, and insured the cargos that traveled on them. And if, under Bretton Woods, the City wasn't allowed to finance trade, to hustle, to compete for business wherever it wanted—as it wasn't post–Second World War—then what really was the point of it?

And what was particularly vexing about all this was that New York was booming. Much of the business that once flowed through London—the trade financing, the bond deals, everything London saw as its birthright—was being conducted by those pesky parvenus on Wall Street. London was reduced to acting as a financial center just for Britain, and for the shrinking band of colonies and ex-colonies so conservative that they clung to the pound. That was no fun at all.

The fact that London almost died as a financial center is hard to imagine for anyone who now sees its gleaming glass-and-steel canyons, or who joins the teeming army of commuters crossing London Bridge in the half-light of a weekday dawn. But in the 1950s and 1960s, the City was almost entirely absent from the national conversation. Fat social histories of the Swinging Sixties don't even mention what was happening in the old Roman trading post, which is strange because something very significant was brewing, something that would change the world far more than the Beatles or Alan Sillitoe or David Hockney ever did, and which would shatter the high-minded strictures of the Bretton Woods system. This is where the tunnel into Moneyland first opened up, and where the first people discovered the profits to be made from seeing where that tunnel led.

By the time Ian Fleming published *Goldfinger*, there were already some leaks in the supposedly impermeable compartments of the great oil tanker of the world economy. The problem was that not all foreign governments trusted the United States to honor its commitment to use the dollar as an impartial international currency; and they were not unreasonable in doing so, since Washington did not always act as a neutral umpire. In the immediate post-war years, the US government had sequestered communist Yugoslavia's gold reserves, and the rattled Eastern bloc countries then made a habit of keeping their dollars in European banks rather than in New York. The International Monetary Fund, which was and is based in Washington, and was and is dominated by its largest shareholder, refused to help communist Poland to rebuild. Similarly, when Britain and France attempted to regain control of the Suez Canal in 1956, a disapproving Washington froze their access to dollars and doomed the venture. These were not the actions of a neutral arbiter.

Britain at the time was staggering from one crisis to another. In 1957 it raised interest rates sharply and restricted the use of sterling in an attempt to protect the pound (this was the "currency crisis and the high bank rate" that Colonel Smithers told James Bond about). City banks, cut off from sterling, began to use dollars instead, and they obtained those dollars from the Soviet Union, which was keeping them in London and Paris so as to avoid becoming vulnerable to American pressure. This turned out to be a profitable thing to do. In the United States, there were limits on how much interest banks could charge on dollar loans—but not so in London. In the United States, banks had to retain some of their dollars in reserve in case loans went wrong—but not so in London. The banks had discovered a hole in the compartments of the Bretton Woods oil tanker: if they used dollars outside the United States, then US regulators couldn't touch them, and British regulators didn't care. These stateless dollars—they became known as "eurodollars," perhaps because of the "Euro" telex address used by one of the Soviet-owned banks—could flow between countries unhindered, just like in the old days. And the laws could not follow them.

US officials tried to put a stop to this, and the comptroller of the currency (who administered the federal banking system) opened a permanent office in London to inspect what the British branches of American banks were up to. But the Americans had no power on the far side of the Atlantic, and got no help from the locals. "It doesn't matter to me," said Jim Keogh, the Bank of England official responsible for monitoring these banks, "whether Citibank is evading American regulations in London. I wouldn't particularly want to know. If the Comptroller's people feel they can make their jurisdiction run in London, I say, 'Good luck to 'em.'" He told a foreign banker, only half-jokingly, that he could do whatever he liked in London, provided he didn't "do it in the streets and frighten the horses." The total sum of money involved wasn't enormous, compared to the amount being moved around in New York by American banks, but it was growing by a third a year, and London had finally found a new revenue stream.

Almost simultaneously (and entirely unconnectedly, except perhaps that rebellion was just generally in the air in those days), British radio listeners gained some new stations to listen to. At the time, only the BBC could legally broadcast in the UK, and it was backward when it came to sharing new pop artists with its listeners. Teenagers wanted to hear exciting new acts like Nero and the Gladiators or B. Bumble and the Stingers, and found the BBC's reluctance to play their tunes frustrating. Entrepreneurial shipowners saw an opportunity. They moored their vessels outside Britain's territorial waters, set up radio equipment, and broadcast pop music back into the UK.

Many people called these radio operators pirates, but others called their stations something else: offshore, which was less amusing but more literally accurate. The ships were situated just off Britain's shoreline, and thus outside of UK authorities' jurisdiction. Offshore radio stations were as physically present as any other broadcaster, in that you could easily find their broadcasts on your wireless, yet they were legally absent, and very difficult to deal with.

This concept of "offshore"—of being legally absent while physically present—was a useful one, and the term started to be employed to describe financial transactions as well. The banks moving the unregulated eurodollars kept two sets of accounts. One set told of the usual boring transactions, all the pounds that obeyed the exchange controls and so on. These transactions were referred to as onshore. The other described the swashbuckling, piratical new eurodollar market, the oil that had leaked out of the compartments and which was now sloshing around in the bilges of the Bretton Woods tanker. These transactions were referred to as offshore—as if they were conducted outside of British territorial waters, and Britain had no jurisdiction over them. The two sets of transactions took place in the same geographical location— the City of London—but legally one of them was elsewhere, somewhere rules did not apply. And this concept, the idea of offshore, the idea of an asset being legally outside the jurisdiction that it is physically present in, is absolutely central to our story. Without it, Moneyland could not exist.

This offshore eurodollar market gave a bit of life to the City of London in the late 1950s, but not much. The big bond issues were still taking place in New York, which was annoying. It was especially annoying because often the companies borrowing the money were European, and the people lending the money were European, too, yet it was American banks that were earning the fat commissions for setting up the deals. European governments and companies were very keen to borrow money, since there was so much war damage to repair, and the economies were growing so fast, but it didn't seem right to bankers in London that Europeans were not getting a cut of the business. One banker in particular was very annoyed about it: Siegmund Warburg.

Warburg was an outsider in the cozy world of the City. For one thing, he was German. For another, he hadn't given up on the idea that a City banker's job was to hustle for business. He wasn't prepared to sit back and accept a subordinate place in the cartel of big City banks; he lived for deals. He famously didn't consider one lunch to be enough for all the networking he wanted to do in a day, so he sometimes dined twice, with different sets of guests each time. It was Warburg who introduced the idea of hostile takeovers to Britain, despite the disapproval of the City establishment. He traveled widely, networked ceaselessly, and learned from a friend at the World Bank in 1962 that some $3 billion was circulating outside the United States—sloshing around in the bilges of the tanker, ready to be put to use. Warburg decided to get involved. He had been a banker in Germany in the 1920s, and remembered arranging bond deals in foreign currencies. Why couldn't his bankers do something similar again?

Bond deals are long-term financing arrangements, in which a borrower borrows a fixed amount of money in exchange for promising to pay a fixed interest rate and to repay the money at the end of a fixed term. Bonds are absolutely crucial to how companies and countries fund themselves. Up to this point, if a company wanted to borrow dollars, it would have to do so in New York. Warburg, however, was pretty confident he knew where he could find a significant chunk of that $3 billion—Switzerland—and he wondered if he couldn't find a way to put it to work.

There was a lot of money in Switzerland. The Swiss had been in the business of hoarding cash and assets on behalf of scrutiny-evading foreigners since at least the 1920s, when France raised the top rate of tax to 72 percent. In the years between then and the Second World War, the amount of money held in Switzerland increased tenfold, eventually making up around 2.5 percent of all household wealth in continental Europe (at a time when the continent's economy in general was stagnant). These customers were overwhelmingly Frenchmen and Italians who didn't want to pay tax. After the Second World War, the good times continued and, by the early 1970s, some 5 percent of Europe's household wealth was deposited in Switzerland. You loaded up your car with cash, drove it to Zurich or Geneva, deposited the banknotes with a discreet cashier, and went on your way. "For rich Europeans that wanted to evade taxes, the situation was the same as it was during the 1920s: the country that offered the protection of banking secrecy was Switzerland," writes French economist Gabriel Zucman in his 2015 book *The Hidden Wealth of Nations*, which delves into the Swiss role in creating Moneyland.

This wasn't exactly a secret. In the Tintin story *Flight 714 to Sydney*, published in 1968, mega-villain Roberto Rastapopoulos kidnaps a millionaire and then tries to force him to divulge the details of his secret Swiss bank account. "I know the name of the bank: I know the name in which you hold the account; I have some magnificent examples of the false signature you use," Rastapopoulos tells his captive. "In fact, the only thing I don't know is the number of the account, and that you are now going to give me." Thence follows perhaps the most madcap adventure of the whole Tintin canon, involving truth serum, a volcanic eruption, extraterrestrials and telepathy. Appropriately enough, however, throughout all this lunacy, the number of the account is never revealed. That would have been too far-fetched; this was Switzerland, after all, where banking secrecy had been legally guaranteed since 1934. Swiss bank accounts were so well guarded that only three people knew their true owners: two bankers and the owner him- or herself. And if news of the existence of great pools of cash owned in Switzerland by tax-dodging crooks had even filtered down to the authors of children's books, it was certain to be well-known to London's most ambitious financiers.

"The rich and famous, the bad and ugly, intelligence agents and Mafiosi used their numbered accounts to hide money from wives, husbands, and business partners; to embezzle company profits; to fund small wars and finance drug cartels," wrote Bradley Birkenfeld, a one-time Swiss banker we shall hear more from later in this story. "Never mind that if you held a numbered account, you actually paid the Swiss a small flat fee for the privilege and never received a penny of interest. The balance was yours to dream about, tucked safely under your Swiss steel mattress."

For the London bankers of the early 1960s, this was tantalizing: there was all this money squirreled away in Switzerland, doing nothing much, and it was exactly what they needed in their quest to start selling bonds again. As Warburg saw it, if he could somehow access the money, package it up, and lend it, he would be in business. Surely he could persuade the people who were paying Swiss bankers to look after their money that they'd rather earn an income from it by buying his bonds? Particularly if that income was tax-free. And surely he could persuade European companies that they'd rather borrow this money from him than pay the steep fees demanded in New York?

Not so fast. One thing stood in his way: the post-war system, whereby all the compartments of the oil tanker stopped speculative money from flowing seamlessly between different European countries. How could Warburg find a way to move that money from Switzerland to clients who wanted to borrow it, whatever countries they happened to be in? He took two of his best men and told them to get it done.

They began their negotiations in October 1962, the same month that the Beatles released "Love Me Do," which reached number 17 in the UK music charts—respectable for a band's first single but hardly spectacular. The bankers signed their contract on July 1 the following year, the same day that the Fab Four recorded "She Loves You," the song that sparked global Beatle-mania. Those extraordinary nine months revolutionized not only pop mu-sic, but also geopolitics, since they included the Cuban Missile Crisis and President John F. Kennedy's "Ich bin ein Berliner" speech. In the circum-stances, it is understandable that a simultaneous revolution in global finance passed little remarked.

Warburg's new bond issue—these bonds became known as "eurobonds," after the example set by eurodollars—was led by Ian Fraser, a Scottish war hero turned journalist turned banker. His elegantly written autobiography, *The High Road to England*, lays out in remarkable detail quite how many bureaucratic obstacles he overcame to realize his boss' vision. He and his col-league Peter Spira had to find ways to defang the taxes and controls designed to prevent hot money from flowing across borders, and to find ways to pick and choose different aspects of different countries' regulations for the vari-ous elements of their creation.

If the bonds had been issued in Britain, there would have been a 4 per-cent tax on them, so Fraser formally issued them at Schiphol Airport in the Netherlands. If the interest were to be paid in Britain, it would have attracted another tax, so Fraser arranged for it to be paid in Luxembourg. He man-aged to persuade the London Stock Exchange to list the bonds, despite their not being issued or redeemed in Britain, and talked around the central banks of France, the Netherlands, Sweden, Denmark and Britain, all of whom were rightly concerned about the eurobonds' impact on currency controls. The fi-nal trick was to pretend the borrower was Autostrade—the Italian state mo-torway company—when really it was IRI, a state holding company. If IRI had been the borrower, it would have had to deduct tax at source, while Au-tostrade did not have to.

(City bankers got so good at playing jurisdictions off against each other that, two years later, they even succeeded in persuading the Belgian tax authorities that closing a deal was just a formality. This meant they did not need to travel to Luxembourg to sign the final papers, and could hold the cele-bratory dinner in Brussels—where the restaurants were acceptable—rather than in the gastronomic wasteland that was Luxembourg at the time.)

The cumulative effect of this game of jurisdictional Twister was that Fraser created a highly convenient bond paying a good rate of interest, on which no one had to pay tax of any kind, and which could be turned back into cash anywhere. It was the ultimate expression of offshore. "The secret . . . was that the bonds must be totally anonymous, coupons must be paid without any deduction of tax and the bonds at maturity paid off in full without any questions asked," he wrote. These were what are known as "bearer bonds." Whoever possessed the bonds owned them; there was no register of ownership, or any obligation to record your holding, which was not written down anywhere. Fraser's eurobonds were like magic. Before eurobonds, hidden wealth in Switzerland couldn't really do much; but now it could buy these fantastic pieces of paper, which could be carried anywhere, redeemed anywhere, and all the while paid interest to their owners, tax-free. Dodge taxes *and* make a profit: they were like $1,000 interest-paying travelers' checks.

A deal as ambitious as this hadn't been done in the City of London for almost half a century, and it briefly looked like it might fail for the most mundane of reasons: no one could remember how to engrave the detailed plates needed for printing the bonds. Mercifully, two ancient Czechs turned up who had retained the skills, and all that remained was for bank directors to sign the pieces of paper. "There was one signing-machine in Brussels which could sign twelve certificates at a time, with twelve pens attached to it," remembered Spira, decades later. "But basically the company had to send a team of three or four people to Luxembourg for a week to sign pieces of paper. That shows you the idiotic bureaucracy that existed."

So, who was buying Fraser's magical invention? Well, this was a bit of a secret, since the sales were largely handled by Swiss bankers, who didn't let on who their clients were. But Fraser had a pretty good idea. "The main buyers of these bonds were individuals, usually from Eastern Europe but often also from Latin America, who wanted to have part of their fortune in mobile form so that if they had to leave they could leave quickly with their bonds in a small suitcase," Fraser wrote. "There was still a mass migration of the surviving Jewish populations of Central Europe heading for Israel and the West. To this was added the normal migration of fallen South American dictators heading East. Switzerland was where all this money was stashed away."

Later historians tried to downplay Fraser's account a little, and to claim that corrupt politicians—"fallen South American dictators"—made up just a fifth or so of the demand for these early bond issues. But Fraser was already downplaying it; these fallen dictators may have been living in South America but they weren't all locals. In the early 1960s, there were plenty of people still alive who had looted Europe in the Second World War, parked the proceeds in Switzerland, and skedaddled to Argentina. It must have been very frustrating for Nazi war criminals to have money sitting in Switzerland and no prospect of a decent return. Finally, thanks to Ian Fraser and his team, they had a risk-free and tax-free method to make their secret stash earn a living.

As for the remaining four-fifths of the money that bought up the bonds, this came from standard tax dodgers—"Belgian dentists," the bankers called them—high-earning professionals who steered a chunk of their earnings to Luxembourg or Geneva, and who welcomed this lovely new investment. Fraser could hardly claim to have been surprised by this. In his memoir, he records how "Uncle Eric"—Eric Korner, one of the senior Warburg's bankers—had a broker in Zurich he called whenever a client company was about to announce better-than-expected news. Korner would get into the trade before the rest of the market knew about it, which earned him secret, tax-free cash at his clients' expense, while simultaneously building up the pot of money in Switzerland that could be spent on the new bonds.

This is the first glimpse of the tunnel into Moneyland. It works as follows: first, you obtain money (you might have stolen it, or avoided taxes on it, or simply earned it); then you hide it; then you spend it. Previously, you could take two of the three steps, but never all of them together. You could obtain money, then spend it, but that was risky. Or you could obtain money, then hide it, but that meant it was stuck in Switzerland, and you never got to enjoy it. Moneyland set wealth free, and it didn't care where that wealth came from: steal, hide, spend, in perpetuity. This is the dirty secret at the heart of eurobonds. It was all made possible by modern communications—the telegram, then the phone, then the telex, then the fax, then the email—and this is the dark side of the revolution of convenience that we call globalization.

I am not saying there was no one with a legitimate desire for privacy. As Fraser made clear, among the first clients were European Jews who had hidden their money in Switzerland from the Nazis, and who had finally found a way to make a living from it. The problem was that the privacy, the portability and the convenience that attracted Holocaust survivors moving to Tel Aviv also attracted dentists in Antwerp, insider-trading bankers in London and Nazis in Buenos Aires. In Switzerland, the legitimately scared money mixed with the naughty tax-avoiding money, which mixed with the evil looted money. The eurobond was convenient to anyone with cash to hide, wherever it came from.

This, then, was the moment when the first rich people unlocked the door to Moneyland's magic garden; the moment when clever London bankers conjured into existence a virtual country where, if you were rich enough, whoever you were, wherever your money came from, the laws did not apply to you. Ordinary Belgians paid taxes on their paychecks, while dentists who could afford to maintain Swiss bank accounts not only avoided those taxes, but earned profits from doing so. The looted residents of Eastern Europe worked to rebuild their shattered countries, while the Nazis who looted them not only kept the proceeds of their crimes but earned a tidy living doing so.

As we will see, the fact that First World tax avoiders and Third World kleptocrats both inhabit Moneyland is central to why it is so hard to do anything about it. We can thank Ian Fraser and his Warburg's colleagues for that.

That first deal was for $15 million. But once the way to sidestep the obstacles that stopped cash flowing offshore had been flagged, there was nothing to stop more money from following its path. In the second half of 1963, $35 million of eurobonds were sold. In 1964, the market was $510 million. In 1967, the total passed a billion dollars for the first time, and it is now one of the biggest markets in the world. Even American companies abandoned New York, with its tiresome regulations, and started issuing eurobonds, though this meant new moves in the game of Twister required to dodge government attempts to keep some kind of control on the surges of hot money. Fortunately, a favorable Dutch–US tax treaty allowed American corporations to borrow money through specially created and otherwise unneeded subsidiaries in the tiny Caribbean islands called the Netherlands Antilles, so they didn't have to pay any tax.

And what did this mean for the compartmentalized oil tanker created at Bretton Woods? It was as if the cargo's owners had created their own plumbing system, allowing them to move their oil from tank to tank without the captain's permission or knowledge. But here the metaphor breaks down, because of the nature of money. These dollars escaped offshore, where they avoided the regulations and taxes imposed upon them by the US government. But they were still dollars, and thus thirty-five of them were still worth an ounce of gold. The trouble that followed stemmed from the fact that dollars don't behave like oil. Unless you use it for something, oil is oil; it just sits there, doing nothing. Dollars, however, multiply.

If you put a dollar in a bank, the bank uses it as security for the money it lends to someone else, meaning there are more dollars—your dollar, and the dollars someone else has borrowed. And if that person puts the money in another bank, and that bank lends it, there are now even more dollars, and so on. And since every one of those dollars is nominally worth a fixed amount of gold, America would have needed to have kept buying ever more gold to satisfy the potential demand. If America did that, however, it would have to have bought that gold with dollars, meaning yet more dollars would exist, which would multiply in turn, meaning more gold purchases, and more dollars, until the system would eventually collapse under the weight of the fact that it didn't make sense; it couldn't cope with offshore. It's as if the oil in the tanker wasn't just moving covertly from tank to tank, but doubling in volume every time it did so.

Perhaps you've already worked out what this means. Foreign governments had the right to buy gold at $35 an ounce, yet there were more and more dollars, and still only a fixed amount of gold. The simple rules of supply and demand insist that a black market would have appeared sooner or later, in exactly the same way that unofficial exchange rates always spring up in dictatorships that try to control the dollar price. A foreign government could buy gold at $35 an ounce from the United States, then sell it on the open market for eurodollars. It could then use those eurodollars to buy more US gold for $35 an ounce, which it would sell at a profit, and so on. It would basically be the Goldfinger scam, but vastly more profitable, without the need to smuggle bullion disguised in the armor plating of a Rolls-Royce or play 007 at golf, and limited only by the amount of money Washington was willing to lose. The scam was prevented only by the participants' willingness not to profit from such an obviously flawed system.

The US government tried to defend the dollar/gold price, but every restriction it put on dollar movements just made it more profitable to keep your dollars in London, leading more money to leak offshore, and thus more pressure to build up on the dollar/gold price. And where the dollars went, the bankers followed. For American banks, Britain began to play a role loosely akin to that played by China for American manufacturers today. The City had looser regulations and more accommodating politicians than Wall Street, and the banks loved it. In 1964, eleven US banks had branches in the City of London. In 1975, fifty-eight did. By that time, however, Washington had bowed to the inevitable and stopped promising to redeem dollars for gold at $35 an ounce. It was the first step in a steady dismantling of all the safeguards created at Bretton Woods.

The philosophical question over who really owned money—the person who earned it, or the nation that created it—had been answered. If you had money, thanks to the accommodating bankers of London and Switzerland, you could do what you wanted with it and other governments could not stop you. If they tried, they just made the situation worse, like trying to firm up a leaky inner tube by squeezing it. Money kept heading offshore, however officials tried to stop it. As long as one country tolerated offshore, as Britain did, then the efforts of all the others came to nothing. (If only everyone had listened to Keynes and created an international currency at Bretton Woods, this would not have happened.)

This, then, is the origin of the inevitable tension between borderless money and bordered states. If regulations stop at a country's borders, but the money can flow wherever it wishes, its owners can outwit any regulators they choose. If one boxer has to stay within the ropes of the ring while his opponent can jump out at any time, ducking back in from any direction undetected and without warning, it's clear whom the smart money favors.

The developments that began at Warburg's did not stop with simple eurobonds. The basic pattern was endlessly replicable. You identified a line of business that might make you and your clients money. You looked around the world for a jurisdiction with the right rules for that business—Liechtenstein, the Cook Islands, Jersey—and you used it as a nominal base. If you couldn't find a jurisdiction with the right kind of rules, then you threatened or flattered one until it changed its rules to accommodate you. Warburg himself started this off, by explaining to the Bank of England that, if Britain did not make its rules competitive and its taxes lower, then he would take his bank elsewhere, perhaps to Luxembourg. Hey presto, the rules were changed, and the tax—in this case, stamp duty on bearer bonds—was abolished.

The world's response to these developments has been entirely predictable as well. Time after time, countries have chased after the business they have lost offshore (as the United States did by abolishing the regulations the banks were dodging when they moved to London), thus making the onshore world ever more similar to the offshore piratical world that Warburg's bankers created. Taxes have fallen, regulations have relaxed, politicians have become friendlier, all in an effort to entice the restless money to settle in one jurisdiction rather than another. The reason for this is simple. Once one jurisdiction lets you do what you want, the business flows there and other jurisdictions have to rush to change, too. It is the Moneyland ratchet, always loosening regulations for the benefit of those with money to move around, and never tightening them.

***

Moneyland may not have an army, or a flag, or a border, or any of the attributes of statehood, but it does have a language: the language of euphemism. Anyone who spends any time among the lawyers and accountants who are the legal guardians of Moneyland will hear mention of—on a sliding scale of increasing illegality—"fiscal friction," "succession planning," "tax neutrality," "commissions" and "facilitation payments." After a while, you will find yourself speaking this way yourself.

So, how much money is there out there, hiding behind this palisade of circumlocution? This is a difficult question to answer: the money is invisible, and kept invisible by well-paid, imaginative and highly intelligent people. It is dark matter and, like dark matter, it can only be studied by recording its effect on things that we can see.

Gabriel Zucman, the French economist who has studied Swiss banking, has tried to make these calculations. By analyzing the statistical anomalies that banking secrecy creates, he estimates that 8 percent of all the world's financial wealth was held in tax havens in 2014: $7.6 trillion, out of a total of

$95.5 trillion. Around a third of that was registered in Switzerland, and the rest in Singapore, Hong Kong, the Bahamas, Jersey, Luxembourg, and various other places. And that does not include all the non-financial assets that are owned offshore—artworks, yachts, real estate, jewelry—which he thinks may add up to another $2 trillion. (This does not mean the assets are necessarily in Switzerland, Hong Kong, the Bahamas, etc. They are legally present in those jurisdictions, while being physically present somewhere else. There isn't much to buy in Jersey after all, unless you have a passion for fudge.)

When I visited his office at the University of California, Berkeley, Zucman explained to me that the anomalies are caused by the fact that countries are good at reporting when foreign money has invested in them—houses in London, condos in New York, villas on the Riviera—but bad at reporting when money has left. This means that the amount of money that has entered countries does not match the amount that has left them. "Our planet as a whole has a net debt, a net financial debt, which of course is not possible at a global level," he said. If you put the inflows and outflows of all the countries in the world into a spreadsheet, the sums should add up—all outflows are just someone else's inflows—but they don't. It's like the list of countries' foreign investment positions is missing an entry. One more country is needed in the spreadsheet to make the columns match: let's put it between Monaco and Mongolia. That seems apt.

Zucman is not the only person who's tried to map Moneyland. James Henry, an American economist, came up with a far higher number for the volume of cash it is hiding; he thinks it was $21–32 trillion in 2010. He grasped for astronomical metaphors to explain the sheer bewildering complexity of his task. "The subterranean system we are trying to measure is the economic equivalent of an astrophysical black hole. Like those black holes, this one is virtually invisible and can be somewhat perilous to observers who venture too close," he wrote in a 2012 paper on the subject. "We are up against one of society's most well entrenched interest groups. After all, there's no interest group more rich and powerful than the rich and powerful."

Different nations are affected by Moneyland in different ways. Wealthy citizens of the rich countries of North America and Europe own the largest total amount of cash offshore, but it is a relatively small proportion of their national wealth, thanks to the large size of their economies. Zucman estimates it to be just 4 percent for the United States, around 10 percent for Western Europe. For Russia, however, 52 percent of household wealth is offshore, outside the reach of the government. In Africa (taken as a whole), the total is 30 percent. In the Gulf countries, it is an astonishing 57 percent. "It's very easy for oligarchs of developing countries, non-democratic countries, to hide their wealth. That provides them with huge incentives to loot their countries, and there's no oversight," Zucman explained.

So, that is how Moneyland came into being: how the careful safeguards against it were destroyed, setting it free to spread around the world. Now, let's pay some of its gatekeepers a visit.

3

QUEEN OF THE CARIBBEES

Nevis (pronounced "knee-vis") is a forest-covered, cloud-topped nipple protruding from the water where the Atlantic Ocean meets the Caribbean Sea. By surface area, it is barely bigger than Manhattan, and its population is just 11,000. When it won independence from Britain in 1983—as the junior half of the Federation of St. Kitts and Nevis—its economic prospects looked grim.

Simeon Daniel was head of the Nevis government at the time, and it was his job to provide for his people, but the cupboard was worryingly empty. "There were not," he reflected years later, "many opportunities to earn a decent living." Yet Daniel did have one good card to play.

During the independence negotiations, he had insisted on the fullest possible autonomy. Small his island might have been, but the federal constitution gave it almost complete control over its own affairs. And it so happened that a coup in Liberia had recently created a potentially lucrative gap in the market for a nation with the right get-up-and-go. American shipowners would pay handsomely for a "flag of convenience" for their vessels to sail under when they wanted to dodge US regulations, and they feared the Liberian flag might be taken off the market.

It was an American lawyer named Bill Barnard who first invited Daniel to consider the possibilities. "Mr. Barnard and his team set up the entire infrastructure," Daniel recalled. "They drafted and prepared the text for the relevant legislation which we then passed in the Nevis House of Assembly."

Having discovered how pliable the government was, Barnard developed grander ambitions for Nevis than a mere ship registry. Why only help shipowners dodge the rules, when you can help everyone? Barnard was taking Nevis into the secrecy business. His company, later named Morning

Star, gained an exclusive monopoly over the island's products. Barnard imported American lawyers to cook up a delicious spread of financial goodies, which Nevis dutifully copied onto its legal menu. Barnard has not returned my calls, texts or emails, but it appears that his team borrowed most of their initial raft of legislation from the US state of Delaware. It passed in 1984. A year later came a confidentiality ordinance, which banned anyone from giving financial information to anyone not entitled to hear it, and the island was good to go—not that it stopped there.

David Neufeld is one of the many US attorneys who have helped build ramparts around the island's financial system over the years. In 1994 he wrote Nevis a law that introduced a version of Wyoming's innovative limited liability companies (LLCs), which he improved by adding aspects of other laws that he felt his clients would like. "We cherry-picked," he told me. "It was a way of, you know, playing God with Creation, not to be too obnoxious about it. Obviously, my creation is somewhat less ambitious than Creation. I didn't take the seventh day off. That's a distinction between me and God: He works faster."

The ideas that Neufeld and others have brought to Nevis have made it a formidable fortress for anyone seeking to protect their assets. Nevis doesn't recognize foreign court judgments, so you have to bring any legal claim in the island's court. But in order to bring that case, you must post a $100,000 bond up front as proof of your good intentions. If the abuse you're complaining about happened more than a year before you file the papers, your case will be automatically dismissed. And even if you succeed, there is limited information to find. Nevis doesn't require its registered structures to keep any financial documents on the island, and they face no reporting, auditing or accounting requirements. A foreign company can relocate to Nevis anytime its owner likes; or a Nevis company can move elsewhere. Either way, it doesn't have to inform the island's registry who owns it: that information is between the shareholders and the registered agent, and can't be shared without a court order.

The lawyers who crafted these barriers have made a decent living out of their innovations, and are rather proud of them. "We put together a group of maybe ten people or so, from all around the United States, and we essentially got together once every other week for an hour and a half. We literally started at the beginning of the code, and we worked our way through every word," Shawn Snyder, a Florida trust specialist who chaired the most recent re-examination of the island's laws, told me. "When I work with my clients, I always tell them there's a new golden rule for asset protection: he who has the gold, wins."

Lobbying takes place everywhere, but here it is stripped down to its barest essentials. American lawyers write bills that the Nevis assembly turns into law, so the American lawyers can make money and Nevis can levy fees. It is a purely transactional relationship. It goes without saying that Nevis charges no tax on the companies it hosts (unless you want it to; there can be advantages), but the island is much more than just a tax haven. It is an everything haven, a miniature exemplar of the dozens of jurisdictions that have sprung up to service Moneyland, to shelter the assets of anyone rich enough to afford their services.

There are now approximately 18,000 corporate structures based on the island, a significantly higher number than Nevis has people. The industry brings in almost $5 million a year in revenues, while the government makes another $5 million a year in fees, plus all the taxes paid by the lawyers, accountants and others that the industry employs. That may not sound like much, but for an island with the population of a small town, it's a good living. It's no wonder ex-premier Daniel was so pleased about the acorn he planted. "The financial services industry has helped to provide the economic resources to allow Nevis to grow and its people to prosper," he wrote.

Nevis prospers by renting its sovereignty to rich people who believe America is over-litigious, that women get too much money in divorce settlements, and that lawyers lie in wait for the successful. These beliefs are widespread among the rich, and Moneyland has given them the power to do something about it.

Once upon a time, if wealthy Americans felt their country was over-litigious, they would seek to influence a political party to change the laws. If they felt their spouses' divorce settlements were too generous, they could argue for legislation to be passed to change that. It might have taken a while, and it might have been imperfect, but that's democracy for you.

That process of messy compromise, of back-and-forth, has been replaced by asset protection. Instead of campaigning to change the laws, they have opted out of them altogether. If you're an ordinary person, you still face the risk of litigation and divorce settlements, as American law demands. But if you're rich enough, you can avoid US jurisdiction and tunnel into Moneyland, where your money is hidden from the rest of us.

"I don't like the word hidden. It's protected, not hidden, there's nothing to hide. Look at it from the other way, a lot of females are gold-diggers. You are married to a man, you don't really love him, but he has money. People find ways and means to protect their assets," Laurie Lawrence, financial adviser to the Nevis government, and before that permanent secretary of finance for more than two decades, told me. "If you are a doctor in the US, you know that you could get a malpractice suit that could destroy you financially. So you take some steps to protect your assets, so that if something were to happen, then you're not broken by it."

The lawyers who wrote the Nevis laws are delighted with their work, but those who come up against the island's structures from the other side are significantly less impressed. Back in 2013, a Russian woman won what was up to that point the biggest divorce settlement in British history (£53 million), after her lawyers managed to unpick the complex web of offshore structures her husband had created to try to deny her access to the assets they had accrued over seventeen years of marriage.

The couple's names were withheld by the court, as is standard practice in most family cases in the UK, but the details of the husband's offshore schemes were made public—he used three Nevis companies to conceal his ownership of four expensive London properties, among other things. "The case has been a fantastic charade with the husband a shady puppet master in the background. At fabulous cost (£1.4 million and counting), those representing the wife have crossed and re-crossed the globe in an attempt to trace the husband's assets, every penny of which has been acquired during the course of the marriage," Justice Eleanor King wrote in her ruling. The wife won in the end, but is it really justice if it's only available to someone who can afford to spend £1.4 million getting it?

Even bigger was a Florida divorce battle between Finnish-born tech millionaire Robert Oesterlund and his Welsh-born wife, Sarah Pursglove, which was revealed in detail in a lengthy 2016 article in the *New York Times*. Oesterlund had, according to the paper, hidden his substantial fortune in what amounted to "a worldwide financial system catering exclusively to the wealthy ... [which] has one main purpose: to make the richest people in the world appear to own as little as possible." Fortunately for Pursglove, she was able to hire Jeffrey Fisher, a highly skilled attorney who assaulted Oesterlund's protective ramparts from angles no one else would have thought of. The article is a fascinating dive into the realities of asset protection; inevitably, the case involved shell companies in Nevis.

"They started coming up around twelve years ago; I would say around 2005. And they're coming around with increasing prevalence," Fisher told me, by telephone from West Palm Beach. "I've been doing this a long time now— I'm a former prosecutor, and I know about the ways people hide money, and what they'll do. My approach to getting assets that are in asset protection entities like a Nevis LLC is that you don't go to Nevis and try to get the money out; that is a foolhardy enterprise. They passed laws and they set up structures to stop us and to make it expensive and to make it take years and years and years. What we do here is we use some more creative approaches to, for lack of a better term, make them cough up the dough."

The trouble is, if you can't afford to hire someone like Jeffrey Fisher, who has been repeatedly listed among the top divorce lawyers in America, you don't stand a chance. "Most of these cases, if you don't know what you're doing, you're going to lose. And if you don't have adequate resources to undo the insidious structure that they set up, you're going to lose," he said. "You've got to realize that the asset protection industry is trillions of dollars, not billions of dollars; it's trillions of dollars. Essentially, it's: we're going to find a way to screw legitimate creditors out of collecting a legitimate debt; that's the business these people are in, but they call it something different, and they throw a lot of money at it and they're able to propagate it that way."

This might not be such a problem if the only takers for Nevis' services were rich Americans keen to hide their wealth from their fellow citizens. However, just as with Warburg's eurobonds, the island's peculiar trade draws in crooks and tyrants from all over the world. The evil money always mixes with the naughty money. Name a scam, any scam, as long as it's complex and international, and it will involve somewhere like Nevis.

Navinder Sarao, the British day trader convicted in 2016 for "spoofing" the US markets in the "Flash Crash" of 2010 (when the Dow Jones Industrial

Average lost more than 600 points in minutes, at least partly because Sarao sent fake orders to drive down prices, temporarily wiping trillions of dollars off the value of US shares), diverted his profits into two Nevis-registered trusts, one of which he called the NAV Sarao Milking Markets Fund. In Britain's biggest ever tax fraud, a group of conspirators made £100 million by duping celebrities into investing in bogus green technology. The cash was cycled through structures in Nevis. "This case involves a scheme whose chief characteristics were utter dishonesty, sophisticated planning, and astonishing greed," said the judge at the fraudsters' sentencing in late 2017. "The time taken to investigate and charge these defendants was entirely due to the sophistication and complexity of the fraud."

A securities fraud prosecuted in New York in 2015 sent money via Nevis, as did a day-trading scam tried in New Jersey in 2017. A particularly egregious con man took $161 million from 620,000 vulnerable Americans in a payday lending scheme that ran for a decade until 2014, charging up to 700 percent in interest, which was hidden for part of its life span behind Nevis structures. "The Hydra Lenders' purported 'offshore' operation consisted of little more than a service that forwarded mail from addresses in Nevis or New Zealand to the Kansas City, Missouri, office," the office of the US Attorney for the Southern District of New York reported.

Search for "Nevis" on the Department of Justice (DoJ) website, and the examples pile up. There's a $250 million money-laundering scheme used by someone who illegally manipulated the price of US shares, and who hid his ownership of his company behind Nevis structures. There's a civil recovery case against a Nigerian businessman accused of embezzling hundreds of millions of dollars, laundering it through the United States and using it to buy an $80 million yacht called the *Galactica Star*. He used Nevis companies to obscure ownership of his private jet (the criminal case is ongoing in Nigeria, where he is accused of stealing $1.7 billion; he denies any wrongdoing). Back in 2012, the DoJ seized a Manhattan condominium and a Virginia property, which had been bought with bribes paid to the family of the former president of Taiwan, whose ownership of them had been obscured behind a Nevis structure.

Outside the United States, justice departments are not as good at publicizing their achievements, but news archives reveal similar accusations made all over the world. Thanks to the documents fished out of the Dnieper River in 2014, we know that Ukraine's ex-president Viktor Yanukovich hid his ownership of coal mines behind Nevis companies. Money stolen from the Russian budget by corrupt policemen, in a crime exposed by the anti-corruption lawyer Sergei Magnitsky, who later died in jail when denied medical treatment, passed through Latvian bank accounts owned eventually in Nevis. Members of the ruling family of Azerbaijan, according to articles by the fearless investigative journalist Khadija Ismaylova, owned mobile phone and gold-mining companies at least partly via Nevis. It is hardly surprising that bloggers who sought to damage the reputation of French presidential candidate Emmanuel Macron when he ran for election in 2017 did so by inventing a company in Nevis—La Providence LLC, purportedly named after the school he attended—and claiming it was where he hides his cash. The accusation was false, but gained publicity because having a company in Nevis is precisely the kind of thing a crooked politician would do.

Jack Blum is a veteran investigator of corruption who spent fourteen years as the in-house attorney at the Senate Antitrust Subcommittee, and he is wearily familiar with the island. "The directors and officers have no fiduciary responsibility, and there's no requirement that such minimal records as may exist be kept in the place of incorporation. So, if somebody finds out that there's a Nevis company involved and you go to Nevis, you could waterboard the entire board of directors and nobody would know anything," he told me over coffee near his house in Annapolis, Maryland. "You're wasting a whole lot of time if you go there, because you won't find much." He said it again, to underline the point: "You ain't going to find anything there."

Still, one of the few advantages of being a freelance writer is that my time is my own to waste. I love a challenge, so I bought a ticket, and went to see for myself. Perhaps I might find something where others had failed?

Flying to St. Kitts from Miami takes three hours; then the taxi ride to its capital, Basseterre, is about ten minutes. Basseterre is an unhurried low-rise town where neighbors gossip across the road to each other, chickens peck in side streets, and hawkers sell Bob Marley T-shirts or little bags of peeled sugar cane to the passengers who swarm down from the giant cruise liners.

From there, you take a little ferry along the island's southern shores, where the waves roll in unimpeded from the Atlantic and things get bumpy, until you arrive in the shelter of your destination and the water calms once more. Nevis is a gorgeous island to look at from the water, its gentle slopes rising ever more steeply toward a peak that is almost always hidden by white cloud. It looks snowcapped, which may be why the first Spaniards to see the island named it Nuestra Señora de las Nieves (Our Lady of the Snows), the term that was eventually shortened to Nevis.

In the eighteenth century, this was a major sugar-growing and slave-trading center for the British Empire. It was also the birthplace of Alexander Hamilton, first US secretary of the Treasury turned unlikely modern-day pop-culture icon. During the nineteenth century, when bigger colonies had easier transport links and larger populations, Nevis lost its prominence, which is when it was subordinated to St. Kitts. By the time of its independence, it was barely a backwater, and it is something of an achievement that Barnard and his offshore lawyers found it at all. North of Charlestown, Nevis' Lilliputian capital, is the Four Seasons, a luxury resort that helped introduce Nevis to high-end tourists when it opened in the early 1990s. There is now a significant overlap between the kind of wealthy customers who visit the island's five-star hotels and the people who make use of its asset protection products.

Charlestown is a strange town to walk around if you have been studying Nevis-related business, since so many of the companies involved are nominally headquartered within such a small area. The companies that hid the involvement of Azerbaijan's ruling family in the country's gold and telecoms industries were housed in the building directly in front of you when you get off the ferry. Ten meters or so up the road, you will find the Edith L. Solomon Building, which has lost several of the letters from its name: it was home to a scandal-hit payday loan company in Idaho. Thirty meters north is the Morning Star office, which is the nominal home of companies owning thirty-six houses in Britain, including one in Mayfair with a view over Hyde Park. In total, more than 300 properties in England and Wales are owned via Nevis companies, almost all of them headquartered in an area little bigger than a football pitch.

I was particularly keen to investigate two companies that featured in the ownership structures of some Latvian bank accounts used to launder billions of dollars from Russia. The scheme was exposed in 2014 by investigative journalists from the Organized Crime and Corruption Reporting Project (OCCRP), who dubbed it "the Russian laundromat." The companies' home address was Suite B, Hamilton Development, Charlestown, which is also the headquarters of the Nevis International Trust Company (NITC). But no one in the town appeared to know where that was. At a loss, I inquired at the Financial Services Regulatory Commission (FSRC), where the receptionist informed me I needed to trek up the hill.

It was a thirsty hour's walk up the slope of the dormant volcano that is Nevis Peak, a journey enlivened only by an occasional monkey stopping to stare at me as I passed by. Unfortunately, when I reached the location the receptionist had identified, the people there had no idea what I was talking about and told me I was in the wrong place entirely. I needed to go back down the hill, they said, then along the coastal road past the Four Seasons, and I would see the Hamilton Development on my left. There, too, however, my inquiries proved fruitless. The receptionist kindly dialed the number given for the NITC in the Yellow Pages. The employee who picked up the phone refused to tell me where the NITC was located, or to give me any information about the companies I was inquiring about.

"I'm not a robber," I said, at last.

"I don't know that, do I?" she replied. And that was that.

In search of answers of a more general kind, I went to meet Heidi-Lynn Sutton, regulator at the FSRC. She is the person whose job it is to make sure the island's structures are not abused by criminals, corrupt officials or tax dodgers: an important responsibility. She brought along three colleagues. The four of them sat across from me at the conference table in their offices as if they were interviewing me for a job.

I asked why the US State Department had been so critical of Nevis in its latest assessment. The Bureau for International Narcotics and Law Enforcement Affairs gives a yearly report on different jurisdictions' efforts to combat money laundering and financial crime. In 2017, it said that Nevis was "a desirable location for criminals to conceal proceeds," and specifically criticized the island for allowing anonymous bank accounts, having strong bank secrecy laws, and obscuring the true ownership of its companies and other corporate structures.

Sutton, sounding rather like a schoolteacher failing to disguise her contempt for a particularly dim pupil, said the US government's information was out of date. This surprised me, since I imagined it was commonly accepted that the ownership of Nevis companies is non-transparent. To make my point, I recounted my own experience of trying to find the shareholders of the firms involved in the Russian laundromat scandal. She appeared to find it very funny that I had gone to such lengths to try to find an office building. "For what purposes will you need the information?" she asked. When I explained about the laundered billions, she laughed at me. "I cannot speak to that. I really cannot speak to that."

For the next half hour, Sutton maintained a policy of blanket denial to every criticism about Nevis that I passed on to her. The complaints that American lawyers had made about the futility of bringing legal proceedings in Nevis were incomprehensible, she said. "US lawyers were involved in the drafting of our legislation, so it's most surprising. Most surprising."

Didn't some of the island's provisions make it hard for women to get a fair divorce settlement, or for victims of medical malpractice to seek recompense? I continued. Wasn't it disproportionate to expect people to front up a $100,000 bond just to bring a case in the Nevis court? "Some countries are very litigious. If you can get a little burn on your hand, because you spill a McDonald's coffee, somebody will sue you, so this was there to make sure that persons are protected, and we do not have the jurisdiction of our court being bombarded with frivolous lawsuits," she said. I noticed one of her colleagues passing another a note under the table.

I was beginning to feel annoyed by their indifference, so I asked whether Sutton was aware that corrupt foreign officials had abused Nevis structures ("You saying it doesn't mean that it's true"). I listed specific examples: the ruling family of Taiwan ("That's an allegation"); the former president of Ukraine ("I can't speak to that"); the Russian laundromat ("Is there an investigation by a law enforcement body?"). She seemed so uninterested in the fact that multiple large-scale thefts had been facilitated by companies based within a few feet of her office that I began to feel as if I had gone slightly mad.

"It's not something you can hang on Nevis. This happens all over the world," she said, confidently. "I can't tell you that I accept that there have been multiple usages of our structures to facilitate whatever. I can't accept hearing it from you. I won't be able to speak to that."

If everything is so fine here, I asked, why did people invent a Nevis company to make the French presidential candidate Emmanuel Macron look like a crook during his election campaign? "I have no idea. I can't go into the minds of anybody," she said. "People make things up all the time."

I had spoken to many regulators and investigators over the years, but I had never met anyone like Heidi-Lynn Sutton before. In every previous instance, my interlocutors had shown at least polite interest in my concerns, and sometimes even shared them. Sutton literally laughed in my face. She insisted that the island's mechanisms were stringent, its regulatory process robust, and that it met international standards in all that it did, despite every piece of evidence to the contrary. "Once you are an international financial center, and provide certain services, you will always be a target. It doesn't mean that it's true," she said.

It is possible that she is right, and that the examples I mentioned to her are simply isolated and sporadic cases. We have no independent assessment of the competence of her regulators, or any way of knowing the extent of criminal penetration of the structures that she and her subordinates oversee. It is possible that Nevis' minuscule police force is more than capable of cracking down on financial crime, and winding up the firms that facilitate it, rather than ignoring it to attract more business to the island. It would be nice to think so.

If the experience of another financial center is anything to go by, however, we should not be too sanguine.

Jersey is an island in the English Channel. Though it is just off the coast of France, it is part of the British Isles, more or less. From the 1960s it used its autonomy to establish an offshore industry, which, in what will now seem a familiar pattern, began as a means to help Brits hide their money and soon became a financial center in its own right. Jersey has ten times the population of Nevis, is far richer, and its offshore center is decades older. Age has not brought respectability, however. When outsiders have dug into its secrets, what they have found has appalled them.

Jersey's specialty is the trust. Trusts are said to date back to the Middle

Ages, when knights went away on a crusade and wanted to preserve control of their property for their wives and children. The knights gave their assets to a trusted retainer on the condition that any income they generated would continue to flow to their children. This principle has multiple applications in all legal systems based on Britain's, including one of the great offshore tricks, since it separates the legal ownership of something from the benefits it provides. A condo may be in New York, and you may live in it, but you do not own it; it is owned by a trust company in Jersey that has a legal arrangement to pass it on to your grandchildren. The advantages of this from the perspective of a potential Moneylander are clear: if you no longer own something, you cannot be taxed on it, only on the revenue that it generates. Trusts are central to "succession planning"—the euphemism for when rich people dodge inheritance tax—and Jersey lawyers are very good at setting them up.

Like Nevis, Jersey has sought to maintain its competitive advantage by copying innovations from other jurisdictions. Members of its parliament—called the States—have traditionally been happy to go along with the professionals' wishes in order to keep them on the island. As one deputy said, during a debate in 2008: "If we do not have the money there are plenty of other people that will take it. We are not going to have much of a social service if we do not have a finance industry."

This is understandable from Jersey's point of view, but it does make you wonder who exactly is in charge: the deputies from the States, or the legal and financial firms threatening to leave the island if the deputies don't do what they want.

That was a question that troubled John Christensen, a local accountant hired as a government economic adviser in 1987. Christensen had gone to university in Britain to study economics, but he came home to Jersey to raise a family. "For me the big problem was that the lobbies for the financial industry were so strong that the only area they were really interested in growing was financial services," he told me. And he began to worry that the island was starting to ignore some very dodgy behavior as a result.

In 1996, after almost a decade in the job, Christensen got a phone call from a reporter from the *Wall Street Journal* who was interested in a Jersey-based trader. A group of mostly American investors were claiming that a man named Robert Young had lost $27 million of their money while fraudulently claiming to have made a profit, and that the Jersey authorities were refusing to do anything about it. Young had been working with Cantrade, a private bank owned by UBS.

Christiansen made some inquiries. It turned out that the chair of the committee that decided to ignore the complaints had served for four years as a director of Cantrade. The head of the island's government had previously been a senior partner at Cantrade's law firm. And Cantrade's own accountants were tasked with investigating whether it had done anything wrong. Funnily enough, they decided that it hadn't. None of this looked good. When lawyers finally raided Young's house, they found forty Gucci handbags and five Rolex watches. In December 1993 alone, he ran up an Amex bill of $144,000.

Young and his accountant were jailed in 1998, while Cantrade paid substantial out-of-court compensation to the defrauded investors. But for overseas observers, that was not good enough. John Moscow, then New York district attorney, told one journalist at the time that he was regularly frustrated in his investigations by Jersey's refusal to help. "It is unseemly that these British dependencies should be acting as havens for transactions that would not even be protected by Swiss bank secrecy laws," he fumed.

It was this case that Christensen discussed with the *Wall Street Journal* reporter. When he gave his opinion of the island's rulers, he asked not to be quoted by name. "By and large," Christensen told the journalist, "they are totally out of their depth." It didn't take long for Jersey society to discern the identity of the *Journal*'s source, and Christensen has never been forgiven. He left the island and moved to the mainland, where he eventually helped establish the Tax Justice Network, which campaigns against tax havens. Twenty years later, Jersey officials are still insisting his criticism of Jersey was a result of being passed over for a promotion. "It's baggage. He has baggage, serious baggage, talking of conflicts of interest," the director general of Jersey's financial services commission told me.

Jersey is a small place with a population of just over 100,000. Like any small place, it is prone to gossip. To an outsider, the whole Christensen/*Wall Street Journal*/Cantrade saga might sound as dull as someone else's office politics, until you consider the implications. If the people who run the financial system are the same ones who run politics, the courts and the regulators, then the potential for insider deals is clear. The legal autonomy of the island becomes a cloak for the skulduggery of the wealthy, both on the island and off it. The rule of law becomes a sham. And, according to two senior policemen who served in Jersey after long careers in the UK, Jersey's laws simply do not apply to those strong enough to ignore them.

In 2000, stung by critical reports, Jersey police hired a Scotsman called Graham Power to run the island's force. His appointment, and that of his deputy—an Ulsterman called Lenny Harper—was intended to professionalize Jersey policing and improve its image. It did precisely the opposite, dragging the issues hinted at in the Cantrade scandal into the open.

Power was suspended from his post in 2008 following an investigation into child abuse that provoked sensational tabloid headlines. His officers uncovered evidence of crimes committed in a children's home, in a youth sailing club, and by a man who was accepted into the honorary police force despite a record of child molestation. The government decided that Power and Harper had to go. They did not leave quietly: the statements they prepared for subsequent court hearings and a public inquiry revealed quite how difficult they had found it to police this small and wealthy jurisdiction. Power described something he called "the Jersey way," an incestuous practice in which closed-door deals prevented uncomfortable subjects from being discussed in public.

"There was a deep-rooted concept of doing 'favors' for one another," he wrote in one statement. "Jersey has an upper echelon of people who often rotate between positions of influence. There is an entrenched cultural resistance to 'rocking the boat.'" While his officers were trying to investigate allegations of child abuse leveled at senior members of the community, politicians were demanding that he stop doing so, since he was harming the reputation of the island. "The rules and obligations that apply to most islanders are assumed not to apply to those in positions of power," Power wrote.

The resilience of Jersey's elite is not new (Jersey is perhaps the only place in Europe that had the same government before, during and after Nazi occupation) but it had never previously been described with such forensic force. Harper, Power's deputy and the officer who led the child abuse investigation, was even more damning. He arrived in Jersey in 2002, after a long and successful career in some of Britain's toughest regions. "It's surreal in many ways.

I mean, I worked on the Falls Road, I worked in the interrogations centers in Belfast, and I worked in some of the worst areas in London and some of the worst areas in Glasgow," he told me by telephone from his home in Scotland. "And none of it really compares to those days in Jersey."

He recounted being harassed by the island's honorary police (whose officers come under a separate command), being asked to drop investigations, being unable to sack corrupt underlings, and many more incidents that seem out of place in such a neat, groomed, impeccable-looking place as Jersey. "I'm sounding like a communist now, I'm sounding like a socialist, and anybody further from a communist or socialist you couldn't find," he told me. "But this clique, this Jersey clique ... they do not want the law enforced in an unbiased and impartial manner; that is the last thing they want. They want the law enforced to benefit them."

The disdain did not flow in one direction: Jersey politicians condemned both Harper and Power. However, looking at the island's response to the media storm that surrounded the child abuse investigation, it is difficult to fault the coppers' assessment that what Jersey's elite hates is exposure. In 2008 the island's chief judge condemned the media for reporting on child abuse rather than the perpetrators for having committed it. "It is the unjustified and remorseless denigration of Jersey and her people that is the real scandal," Bailiff Philip Bailhache said at a celebration of the island's liberation from Nazi occupation. His words were heartfelt but I doubt that, after you've read the next chapter and learned how Jersey helped Russian insiders loot their homeland, you'll agree with him.

4

SEX, LIES AND OFFSHORE VEHICLES

The 1990s in Russia were disastrous. The army lost a war against Chechnya, a region with fewer people than Russia had soldiers. The economy collapsed. The government defaulted on its debt. Male life expectancy fell below sixty years. Epidemic diseases spread fast. The country was ruled by an erratic alcoholic, whose government was bullied by oligarchs and in hock to the International Monetary Fund. Still, though, a late-night news broadcast on March 17, 1999, represented a new low, even by the standards Russians were used to.

For several minutes, the state-owned RTR station broadcast grainy but unmistakable footage of a paunchy, pouchy, balding, nude man cavorting with two much slimmer, far younger, equally naked women, neither of whom was his wife. The women were not identified, but the man—the presenter said—was a "person resembling" Prosecutor General Yuri Skuratov, who was at the time clinging on to his job despite pressure from President Boris Yeltsin that he resign. RTR's implausible justification for airing this excruciating footage was that it wanted to protect the country's most senior lawman from blackmail. "The aim of the All-Russia State TV and Radio Company was to protect the interests of the state, society and the prosecutor general himself from the possibility of this material being used to the detriment of the state, society and prosecutor general," the channel said in a statement.

Skuratov's explanation for what had happened was more convincing. He said the government had attempted to blackmail him with the video, because it wanted him to stop investigating a corruption scandal that threatened to engulf everyone from President Boris Yeltsin downward, and had chosen to play dirty when he refused. Central to his investigation were kickbacks supposedly paid by a Swiss construction company for contracts to restore government buildings, including both houses of parliament. There was a subsidiary scandal, too. It attracted relatively little notice in the noise surrounding the video, but it was perhaps even more consequential, since it involved far more money and penetrated just as deeply into the heart of the state.

In February, Skuratov had told members of the Duma—Russia's parliament—that the Central Bank had passed $37.6 billion, 9.98 billion deutschmarks, ¥379.9 billion, 11.98 billion French francs and £862.6 million to an obscure offshore shell company called FIMACO between 1993 and 1998, a time when the country's finances were in free fall. Much of this money had originated in IMF loans, and FIMACO had invested it in the government bond market, which was at the time returning fantastic profits. The prosecutor accused central bankers of using the profits from these trades to live lavish lifestyles, while hiding the details from both government and legislature behind the wall of offshore secrecy that FIMACO provided.

FIMACO was registered in Jersey and had, it transpired, been quietly in existence—without staff, premises or a physical presence of any kind on the island—since November 1990, the dying days of the Soviet Union. It had been created by Bank Commerciale pour l'Europe du Nord, the same Moscow-owned but Paris-based bank whose "Euro" telex handle may have given euro-dollars their name back in the 1950s. But no one could say for certain why the bank had created it, since the explanations of central bankers kept changing. At various times, they said they had used FIMACO to check whether investment mechanisms worked as they were supposed to. At other times, they said the vehicle was useful for holding foreign reserves. At still other times, they said FIMACO provided expertise. This last explanation was absurd: FIMACO had no expertise, because it had no staff. It was as if the Federal Reserve had decided to secretly route billion-dollar transactions via a Cayman Islands shell company, then claimed that the operation was not only routine and beneficial, but actually helped it learn some new skills.

Eventually, the Central Bank's chairman, Viktor Gerashchenko, admitted that FIMACO had been used to hide Russia's assets from its many creditors, including the IMF, which expressed annoyance at having been lied to. He said he had been worried that, if Russia lost a court case, creditors would have been able to seize its assets overseas. That is why, he said, it had been useful to hide them in the black hole that was Jersey. It was not a dignified answer, since it presented Russia as little better than a cheating husband stashing his cash in Nevis so his wife couldn't find it. But it was better than the alternative explanation, which was that the bankers were on the take.

Gerashchenko's admission did not stop the alternative explanation from being widely discussed. Boris Fyodorov, who had served as finance minister in the early 1990s, said that he had raised the subject of FIMACO while in office, but had been told it was none of his business. He was sure the scheme was a way of creaming off commissions for insiders. "They were simply allowing friends to earn handsome profits," he told journalists as the scandal brewed. There was never a final resolution of the issue, however, thanks to the Skuratov sex video. Yeltsin suspended the troublesome and libidinous prosecutor from his job within days of RTR's broadcast. Parliament was then persuaded to sack him and his replacement enjoyed a long and successful career after wisely deciding to halt the probes into both the Swiss corruption scandal and the use of FIMACO. This meant the cases were never tried in court, or aired in public. The IMF did oblige Russia's Central Bank to commission an audit into FIMACO, but it was widely derided, since it relied exclusively on information provided by the Central Bank and had no independent investigatory powers.

Writers who kept looking into the case found much to trouble them, however. One noted that, in 1999, the Russian Central Bank had a staff of 86,000, as compared to 3,000 at the Bank of England and 23,000 at the Fed. On top of this lavish pot of patronage, Gerashchenko earned 70 percent more than the most important central banker in the world, the Fed's Alan Greenspan, plus extra for his role as a board member of the bank's subsidiaries. The Russian Central Bank (RCB) looked out of control, the kind of institution that might decide to trade on its own account with the government's money.

"Since the RCB did not have to obtain Duma approval each year for its budget, executives at the RCB could use the profits from their subsidiaries' trading activities in Europe and through FIMACO in any way they wanted and, apparently, they did," the American economist Marshall Goldman noted in his 2003 book *The Piratization of Russia*, on the failure of Russia's reforms. "It is not simply a case of outright theft or plundering of the state treasury that is common to some countries in Africa, Asia or Latin America, but a much more sophisticated example of the abuse of domestic and international trust involving state-sanctioned money laundering ... if the director of the RCB engaged in money laundering at the highest level, how could he be expected to serve as a role model for the rest of the country?"

The use of FIMACO may have even allowed the Russian Central Bank—part of the Russian state—to avoid paying taxes on its trades, which makes this a remarkable case study of how offshore-enabled secrecy allows even the most unlikely institutions and individuals to avoid scrutiny, dodge taxes and make profits. While ordinary Russians were waiting months for their salaries, these government employees were able to use the government's money to make money from government-issued debt, without paying taxes to the government on the profits, then were able to stash it—via FIMACO—in Moneyland. This is the kind of thing that disillusioned those naïve Westerners who had hoped that, when communism collapsed and the Soviet Union broke into fifteen republics, Russia could succeed in building a free, democratic, rules-based system for the first time. By the end of the decade, that viewpoint was confined only to the most obstinate, ignorant and/or willfully blind optimists (people like me, in fact). The wholesale looting of the country, enabled and concealed by tax havens like Jersey, doomed any prospect of development, and rewarded the very people responsible for making things worse.

In 1999, the US House of Representatives convened a series of hearings to discuss the danger of dirty cash from Russia making its way into the US banking system. This risk was real, since the Bank of New York had recently been revealed to have helped billions of Russian-origin dollars flow undetected into the country, through a labyrinthine network of bank accounts and shell companies. The House Committee on Banking and Financial Services heard from several experts, including a former KGB agent and several specialists in the mechanisms of money laundering. Perhaps the most startling testimony, however, came from Richard Palmer, who had served as the CIA's station chief in Moscow in 1992–94. He explained how the ex-Soviet elite had strategically exploited the secrecy provided by offshore centers like Jersey to seize anything they could steal. FIMACO had been one of hundreds, if not thousands, of corporate structures used to undermine Russia's sovereignty for the benefit of its rulers, he said.

"Profits from these operations were deposited in tax havens such as Switzerland, Cyprus, the Caribbean, Panama, Hong Kong, Ireland, and the British Channel Islands, where they would be ready to assist in forming 'non-attributable' companies," he wrote to the committee. "There is one constant thread throughout these steps to loot the state. The goal was to take the money outside of Russia, and keep it there, safe from any threats of retrieval attempts by subsequent Russian governments."

His evidence is extensive, is available online, and deserves to be read in full, not least because of a warning that the money that was pouring out of the ex-Soviet republics posed a long-term danger to the stability and honesty of America's political system, which looks extremely prescient in the age of Manafort, Trump and Robert Mueller. Apart from that, perhaps the most striking section of his testimony is when he rubbishes some of the more optimistic myths about the post-Soviet transition. He describes one such myth as being the belief that Russia was on the right course, that life there was broadly akin to that in Chicago under the rule of Al Capone, and that all everyone had to do was wait for Russia to sort itself out and things would be OK.

"For the US to be like Russia today," he wrote, "it would be necessary to have massive corruption by the majority of members of Congress as well as by the Departments of Justice and Treasury, and agents of the FBI, CIA, DIA, IRS, Marshall Service, Border Patrol, state and local police officers, the Federal Reserve Bank, Supreme Court justices, US district court judges, support of the varied organized crime families, the leadership of the Fortune 500 companies, at least half of the banks in the US, and the New York Stock Exchange. This cabal would then have to seize the gold in Fort Knox and the federal assets deposited in the entire banking system. It would have to take control of the key industries such as oil, natural gas, mining, precious and semi-precious metals, forestry, cotton, construction, insurance, and banking industries—and then claim these items to be their private property. The legal system would have to nullify most of the key provisions against corruption, conflict of interest, criminal conspiracy, money laundering, economic fraud, and weaken tax evasion laws. This unholy alliance would then have to spend about 50 percent of its billions in profits to bribe officials that remain in government and be the primary supporter of all the political parties ...

the US president would not only be aware of these activities but would also support them—including the involvement of his own daughters and all of his close political and financial supporters. Further, he would direct a campaign to smear and remove the Attorney General for investigating the office of the president."

And that was not all, because, of course, this dystopia was not confined within national borders.

"Most of the stolen funds, excess profits, and bribes would have to be sent to offshore banks for safekeeping. Finally, while claiming that the country was literally bankrupt and needed vast infusions of foreign aid to survive, this conspiratorial group would invest billions in spreading illegal activities to developed foreign countries."

***

As the story of FIMACO demonstrates, and as Palmer made clear, it is remarkably easy to loot a country providing you are in charge of it. And this is the true power provided by Moneyland, and which the rulers of Russia had grasped.

In the early days, the days of the pioneering eurobonds, Moneyland had been a device used by rich Westerners to shield their cash from governments wishing to take it from them. These were the wealthy Brits parking their savings in Jersey; the Belgian dentists sending their money to Luxembourg; the Americans stashing their cash in Switzerland. These tricks and ploys had been created by London's most ingenious bankers, been honed by the sharp minds of Zurich and Wall Street, had evolved in multiple tax havens, until wealthy Westerners could be confident their money was safe from the best-resourced and most diplomatically fearsome tax authorities on the planet. This was naughty, perhaps, but few would argue that it was actually evil.

The true revolution happened, however, when these tricks were deployed in countries without the rule of law, or the robust political institutions of the West.

The creation of Moneyland in the aftermath of the Second World War, when capital was hemmed in by the controls of the Bretton Woods system— the compartments in the oil tanker of the world economy—had been the result of a battle between tax authorities and the wealthy, who had already been jousting with each other for centuries. This long-running campaign for control of the wealthy's money had created an evolutionary arms race between predators and prey, who spurred one another to ever-greater feats of speed, cunning and agility. Imagine tigers and buffalo becoming ever more perfectly adjusted to each other over the millennia; this was the fiscal equivalent, except the weapons were not muscles, horns, claws and teeth, but shell companies, trusts, secret bank accounts, bearer instruments and more. Even the US Treasury struggled against this kind of opposition, but at least it understood what it was up against.

When lawyers and accountants released these predatory instruments into the ecosystems of sub-Saharan Africa, Asia and the former Soviet Union, however, the mismatch was total. It was as if tigers had been suddenly introduced to a continent inhabited primarily by large, peaceable, flightless birds. Unprepared tax authorities and underfunded investigators were being asked to resist the most skilled rules dodgers in the world. They didn't stand a chance.

Thus was unleashed the orgy of looting that led eventually to the excesses of Yanukovich and his log-built palace on the edge of Kiev. But it began long before, in the final days of Western imperialism. Offshore finance hit the weak and shambolic administrations of sub-Saharan Africa and the ex–Soviet Union with the impact of a Hellfire missile on a Napoleonic warship. Nothing and no one was safe, except the people doing the stealing.

If you look at the subsequent careers of the individuals involved in the Russian sex tape scandal, you will understand quite how unequal the battle became. Skuratov tried to resurrect his career by running for president in 2000, but he came in a disastrous ninth with just 300,000-odd votes. Thereafter, he slipped into obscurity, whence he emerges only as the occasional butt of a joke. The sordid tape of his exploits can still be found on the internet, and my generation of Moscow journalists still chuckles at the words "person resembling." To anyone younger than us, however, his name means nothing.

The man who authenticated the tape also ran for election in 2000, but did rather better for himself. Vladimir Putin headed the FSB, the main KGB successor organization, at the time of the scandal, and suspicion has long pointed to his organization for having provided the footage to Russian television in the first place. After he won the presidency in 2000, none of the individuals criticized by Skuratov for having enriched themselves at Russia's expense were prosecuted. According to Felipe Turover, a Spanish banker who advised Russia's government on debt deals and provided many of the documents used by Skuratov and the Swiss investigators, Putin himself did particularly well from equivalent scams, thanks to a role he held in the Kremlin running Russia's property portfolio.

"In 1997, all possible kinds of front companies, joint-stock companies and limited companies were created. The majority of the most expensive property and other foreign assets was registered to these structures. That means foreign property arrived in the state's hands in a thoroughly plucked form. And it was the current premier who did the plucking," Turover told a journalist from the respected Russian investigative publication *Novaya Gazeta* in late 1999, while Putin was still prime minister. When pressed further, he replied: "I am not going to answer that question for now. I think both you and I want to stay alive." (Turover later denied having mentioned Putin in the interview, but *Novaya Gazeta* has not retracted the story.)

All those assets are still safely nestled away, in Moneyland, where they have joined money that has been gathering from almost every corner of the world, for decades. This has not happened by accident. Moneyland exists because it makes money for its stewards, who are well paid for serving its wealthy citizens. They, not the Moneylanders, are the tigers whose claws and teeth are shell companies, trusts and secret bank accounts. One might be tempted to call them paper tigers, but they are truly formidable, as we shall see.

5

MYSTERY ON HARLEY STREET

A handful of addresses in London are more than just a place on the map. Fleet Street, for example, is a synonym for the newspaper industry (even though the journalists long ago moved elsewhere), just like Wall Street means finance in New York. Similarly, Downing Street means power, Savile Row means bespoke tailoring, Whitehall means administration, and Harley Street means private healthcare. For more than a century, this handsome, tree-lined road—which runs north–south from the tourists and buses of Oxford Street to the traffic-clogged artery that is the Marylebone Road—has been the address of choice for Britain's most prestigious doctors. They began to congregate here in the second half of the nineteenth century, attracted by the good housing and the convenient proximity of several large railway stations, and there were 1,500 medical professionals based on or around the street by the middle of the last century, when the National Health Service was created. Their successors still offer private healthcare to those who can afford it.

Number 29 is toward the southern end of the street, barely a five-minute walk from the Royal Society of Medicine. It is a stone-fronted terraced house, set between two redbrick properties; five stories high, with a bay window on the ground floor, beside a dark-stained wooden front door. An intricate steel balcony adorns the first floor, and a stone balustrade can be seen just below the roof. It is understated, a physical representation of the careful professionalism that Harley Street exudes. Dr. Samuel Fenwick, born in Northumberland and educated at St. Andrews University in Scotland, moved into number 29 in 1862, becoming just the second medical man on the street, and thus helping set in train the process that turned Harley Street into a synonym for the highest quality in healthcare.

Another Fenwick—Edward Henry—had already qualified as a doctor from 29 Harley Street in 1882, and he was in turn succeeded by Leslie Paton, an ophthalmologist who was recorded as living there in the early 1920s. The house came up for sale once more in 1946, and the lease was bought by Ronald Raven, a war hero, amateur theologian, surgeon, philanthropist and cancer specialist who had left the British army with the rank of colonel. Photos taken toward the end of his life show him to have been gray-haired and senior, with sharp eyes and an aquiline nose. Photographs from a memoir that his sister (herself a distinguished nurse) published after his death show a wood-paneled consulting room, its shelves lined with calfbound volumes, and adorned with fine porcelain. Other pictures in the book show Professor Raven together with the Queen, the Queen Mother, the king of Saudi Arabia and other global figures. He walked out of number 29 for the last time on July 23, 1991, to attend the inauguration of the Ronald Raven Chair in Clinical Oncology at the Royal Free Hospital, at a ceremony presided over by HRH Princess Anne, the Princess Royal. He had delivered the manuscript for his final published work, *An Atlas of Tumors*, just days previously, and died three months later, aged 87. "Ronald Raven was always impeccably dressed and friendly to all, giving total attention to each person. He had a prodigious memory, and his meticulous attention to detail evinced itself in everything he did" is how the Royal College of Surgeons remembers the former resident of number 29.

From all of this, it should be clear, firstly, that Ronald Raven was an exceptional man, and, secondly, that he and his predecessors had made number 29 distinguished even by Harley Street's standards. And that is why it was strange to learn that Viktor Yanukovich, the caricaturishly awful kleptocrat who fled Ukraine in 2014, owned his secret property empire from here. It was like discovering that the New Jersey mob was operating out of a Quaker meetinghouse.

The president's luxurious forest shag pad—the one with the heated massage table, floating duck house and televisions at sitting-down height in the toilets—was owned by the Ukrainian company Dom Lesnika. That was in turn owned by Astute Partners Ltd, registered at 29 Harley Street. That was owned by Blythe (Europe) Ltd, also registered at Ronald Raven's old home. The registered shareholder of Blythe (Europe) Ltd, meanwhile, was P&A

Corporate Services Trust Reg, of Vaduz, Liechtenstein, a central European micro-principality that has mysteriously survived into the modern age, and which does not reveal who owns its companies. The only individual named on the documents was Reinhard Proksch, an Austrian lawyer listed as the companies' director. Number 29 Harley Street may be in the very heart of London, but these companies were as offshore and anonymous as anything registered on a tropical island: they conspired to make Yanukovich's palaces physically part of Ukraine, but legally elsewhere, their ownership safely protected from scrutiny, in Moneyland.

Ukrainian anti-corruption activists started investigating this mysterious property empire toward the end of 2013, discovered its curious connections to Harley Street, and approached Proksch to find out who was the real owner of the companies he managed. Proksch denied any connection to Yanukovich. "The whole story is just another Ukrainian shit-storm . . . All companies mentioned in the shit-storm story exist, but are held and operated for UK/US and UAE based clients and foreign investors," Proksch wrote in a statement he has since scrubbed from his website.

The post-revolutionary authorities in Ukraine did not believe him, however, when he claimed that the president played no role in the companies. And when Yanukovich fled, investigations continued. A court returned the forest mansion and all of its luxurious facilities to state ownership in 2015, and prosecutors are currently investigating the Ukrainian officials responsible for transferring the property to the president in the first place. In the country's struggling efforts to restrain official corruption, this counts as a rare win, and should be celebrated. Many aspects of the case have not been investigated, however, including how it happened that the president ever came to obscure his ownership of stolen property via a stately terraced house on one of London's most prestigious streets. The appeal of 29 Harley Street to his financial advisers was clear: it gave a respectable gloss to what was essentially an act of identity fraud. Viktor Yanukovich was pretending he did not own something, by hiding behind multiple corporate vehicles, when in reality he did. And that brings us back to Moneyland, because 29 Harley Street is home to not just the two companies that owned Sukholuchya. As of April 2016, it also housed 2,157 others, many of them involved in frauds almost as egregious as those of Yanukovich. And the story of how a central London property switched from being somewhere an eminent doctor received his patients, to being somewhere seekers of anonymity could hide their ill-gotten gains, is the story of Moneyland in microcosm.

There are not actually 2,159 functioning companies inside number 29. If all of those corporate entities had employees, and filing cabinets, and water coolers, and conference rooms, then they would require most of Harley Street, rather than just one house, to contain them. The house is essentially a postbox, a registered address for companies that carry out their activities elsewhere. If you walk up to the front door, you will notice a line of nine doorbells down the left-hand side: the top one reads, in white letters on a light blue background, "Formations House." This is the real tenant. It is a company that creates companies, and has been since 2001.

There are several hundred company formation agents—companies that make companies—in the UK (the precise number is unknown—owing to a flaw in Britain's regulatory architecture, these gatekeepers don't have to register with anyone before going into business), and theirs is a high-volume, low-margin game. They do charge extra for businesses with particularly rare names—at the time of writing, Formations House had both "Apple Ltd" and "Sex Ltd" for sale at £100,000 each—but their main product is the standard limited company, which costs just £95. You have to sell a lot of those to cover the rent on a building like 29 Harley Street, and Formations House does just that: according to its website, more than 10 million companies have been conjured into existence at the address in the last sixteen years, not just in Britain, but everywhere from Delaware to the Seychelles.

That is three times more companies than are on the entire British corporate register. Even allowing for a little corporate exaggeration, it is clear Formations House has been creating companies on an industrial scale. It has 25,000 ready-made companies for sale as I write, and most of them are far cheaper than "Sex Ltd": you can buy "The Financial Corporation Ltd" for a mere £265, and "American Ltd" looks like a steal at £5,000. Some of them already have bank accounts, VAT registration and all the other things you need to go into business straightaway.

Formations House is competing not just against British formation agents, but against rivals all over the world. Its prestigious address helps it stand out from the crowd. For a monthly fee, the businesses that register here can pretend that 29 Harley Street really is their corporate headquarters. Receptionists will answer the phone in any company's name, forward mail and faxes, and provide conference facilities, which provides both the glamor and the respectability that can help a company look classy.

Take a former resident, Sherwin & Noble (S&N), for example. S&N was an investment company owned by Sir Richard Benson, a portly, balding, elderly financier, who attended a series of meetings in Las Vegas on November 10, 2003. The meetings were at the Stirling Club, a high-end private venue just off the Strip, and the other attendees had already been briefed about how to behave in the presence of a man as distinguished as Sir Richard. They must, they heard, speak only when spoken to, stand when he entered the room, and obey correct etiquette at all times. Sir Richard had won his knighthood helping the Queen of England out of a little financial embarrassment involving a trust company, so he was connected at the very highest levels of global society. The attendees were Gerry Florent, Ralph Abercia and his son, Ralph Jr. Florent wanted $55 million to buy land on which to build a hotel in Florida. The Abercias wanted $105 million for an "aquarium/entertainment complex" in Houston. They were hoping Sir Richard would put up the cash to help their dreams become reality.

"During the morning session, Benson stated that he had owned his own insurance company in the past and decided to start a company to provide funding on large projects, similar to Lloyd's of London," a later indictment stated (this is not a story that ends well, for anyone). "He joined forces with an existing company called S&N and put up $500 million, which was matched by S&N. S&N was now worth billions." As proof of its bona fides, Florent and the Abercias received glossy, spiral-bound booklets with details of projects S&N had already funded, and which laid out its impressively robust-looking balance sheet.

Sir Richard was positive about their proposals and, in order to access his money, all they had to do was pay some advance fees (two payments of $412,250 each from Florent; two payments of $787,500 each from the Abercias) to signal their commitment. There appeared to be no risk; if Sir Richard decided not to proceed, then S&N would repay them. Both Florent and the Abercias were delighted. This was the signal they'd been hoping for.

When they got back home, they wired over the first tranche of the fees, and waited for their money. They waited and they waited, until they began to get worried. They rang and faxed the S&N office at 29 Harley Street with their concerns, and were assured that all was well. Eventually Florent began to get suspicious. He held off wiring the second half of the fee and brought in a private investigator. Which was when things fell apart. The investigator rapidly discovered that S&N, far from being an investment firm worth billions, was nothing but an empty shell. The spiral-bound booklet had been copied from the banking giant HBOS, with a few details changed. The company had no physical presence on Harley Street; the phone calls and faxes were being answered by fraudsters in the United States. The Abercias, who had wired over the second tranche of the fee, were devastated. "That was a lot of money," Ralph Sr. told a local journalist. "We're still paying the damgum thing back."

It was an advanced-fee fraud of elaborate brilliance. Even the location—Las Vegas—gave it the air of *Ocean's Eleven*. Not only did S&N have no money, but Sir Richard Benson was an invention, played by a struggling actor called Henri Berger. He never rescued Buckingham Palace from foreclosure, had no knighthood, and even struggled to maintain a believable English accent. S&N's only asset was the thing that had given it credibility—its registered address on one of London's most prestigious streets—and even that was paper-thin, since S&N's only director was another company, an anonymous one in the British Virgin Islands. The various people involved in creating the fraud were jailed in September 2011 and ordered to pay millions of dollars in restitution.

It was such a dramatic scam that it could well have destroyed the reputation of 29 Harley Street altogether, but that did not happen. Just over a month after Lal Bhatia—the architect of the Las Vegas scam—and Berger were jailed, representatives of a Dutch shipping company called Allseas met a businessman called Marek Rejniak to discuss an investment proposal. Allseas had €100 million, but needed more if it was to build a vessel to dismantle oil rigs. Rejniak claimed his team could double any investment in thirty days, and expand that initial capital into €1.2 billion within three years. Presumably this sounded too good to be true, but Rejniak insisted that it wasn't. At the meeting, which took place on October 16, 2011, in Malta, he claimed to have links to the US Federal Reserve, the Vatican and the Spanish House of Aragon. This gave him access to "medium term notes," mysterious and secret financial instruments, that would be bought and sold in London by an "A1 trader" called Luis Nobre, via two companies called LARN Holdings and ERBON Wealth Management. The companies, which were named to reflect Nobre's initials and his surname spelled backward, were based at a prestigious central London location: 29 Harley Street.

It is hard now to believe that Allseas fell for such a transparent fraud, but it did. The next day, it transferred the whole €100 million to Rejniak's Maltese account, whence it moved to LARN's accounts in London, where Nobre began to spend it. The full details of Nobre's extravagance emerged during his trial for fraud at Southwark Crown Court (which ended in 2016 with him being jailed for fourteen years, though Rejniak was never found). Nobre had lived in a suite at the five-star Landmark Hotel, where he left £100 tips and used the ballroom for business meetings, before skipping out and leaving his girlfriend (and their baby) with the bill.

He is Portuguese, and at the time of his trial had long dark hair shot through with silver thread, wore beautifully tailored pinstriped suits, and made the unwise decision to defend himself. He was passionate, verbose and entirely unconvincing, much to the frustration of everyone involved. The judge frequently had to adjourn the case so Nobre could calm down, and the opposing lawyers would try to coach him a little in what he was supposed to say. It didn't help him, but did mean his trial dragged on for months longer than it was intended to. After the members of the jury found him guilty, the judge gave them a life's exemption from doing jury service again, and they gave him a round of applause.

Strange though it may sound, these two bizarre cases are just a tiny part of the criminal epidemic connected to Ronald Raven's old home: land-banking fraud, VAT fraud, timeshare mis-selling, they all trace back here. Media outlets in Norway, Italy and Romania, as well as Britain, Ukraine and the United States, have detailed crimes linking back to this one house. In one curious crime, a gang of inept crooks pretended to make a film so as to claim tax relief, then, when they were caught, actually did make a film, as if that would somehow erase their original misdeed. The film—called, improbably, *Landscape of Lies*—was shot on the cheap. Its Middle Eastern scenes were clearly filmed in southern England, and its star was ex-GMTV weather girl turned *Loose Women* presenter Andrea McLean. When the trial began, director Paul Knight, a former night club bouncer, was left without his money and turned up at Harley Street to demand payment: with predictable results.

"Lo and behold," he said over the phone to me in 2016, "you realize the swanky Harley Street address was just a building with a few letter boxes. It kind of put the final cherry on the cake." Knight never got his money, though his film did win a Silver Ace at the Las Vegas film festival (the event later rescinded the award when it realized it had essentially celebrated the product of an elaborate and unsuccessful alibi).

It should be stressed that the vast majority of companies created and registered at 29 Harley Street probably have no connection to fraud. But it still brings us to the old problem at the heart of Moneyland, which is that the same things that attract the naughty money—privacy, security, deniability—also attract the evil money. A start-up trying to fake it till it makes it would want to use 29 Harley Street for the same reason that criminals would: its address gives them a degree of prestige they could not otherwise obtain, and for a mere £50 a month.

But the prestige of the address, though no doubt useful for drumming up business, creates an unforeseen problem for Formations House (as well as an opportunity for any investigator). It all but guarantees a headline for any fraud trial connected to a company it hosts. The juxtaposition of Harley Street and embezzlement is the kind of thing that journalists find funny, and the salacious details of these cases have been written up on the crime pages for more than a decade. Simply searching for "Harley Street" and "fraud" gave me a whole list of cases, any one of which could have made it into this chapter. Formations House is probably no worse than any other British company formation agent in terms of the number of its companies that engage in fraud, but its companies and their prestigious address have left a long and conspicuous trail through the news archives, detailing their repeated and elaborate misdeeds.

I will explore the ability of companies to disguise an individual's identity more fully in the next chapter, but it is extremely potent, thanks in part to loopholes in the law that regulates them. Companies need shareholders and directors, and often have secretaries, too. In Britain, the identity of these individuals must be published, to allow outsiders to connect corporate entities to the individuals that own and control them. If the individuals involved in running a company change, its managers are supposed to inform Companies House, the UK's company registry. Companies House does not check the information, so it is perfectly possible to lie your way to anonymity. However, if you want your identity to remain secret without breaking the law, there have always been clever tricks available to those who know how to exploit them.

In February 2004, for example, Formations House created three companies: Corporate Nominees, Legal Nominees and Professional Nominees. The second company owned the other two, while itself being owned by the first company. The third company was secretary of the other two, while its own secretary was the first company. The second company was director of the other two, while its own director was the first company. It is hard to appreciate the curious symmetry of this arrangement unless you draw it out on paper, but it is marvelous, a real connoisseur's trick. Somehow the three companies managed to abide by every requirement of the law, while flouting its spirit entirely. These three companies then became directors, secretaries and shareholders of other structures, which in turn owned others. If you stopped and traced your way along the chain of ownership, you eventually ended up at the central triumvirate, with their elegant circular ownership structure, and the most you could say about them was that they all owned, controlled and managed each other.

To resolve problems like this, in 2008 Parliament passed a law demanding that companies have at least one real person as a director, so there will always be someone who can be contacted if a company is involved in fraud. In response, company formation agents signed up people who, for a fee, would declare themselves directors of hundreds of companies. Edwina Coales, a serial director for Formations House, has been at one time or another an officer at 1,560 companies listed in the UK registry. At the time of writing, her list of directorships had contracted significantly, and she remained in control of just one company. But that is still impressive. When I knocked on the door of her house in central London, the residents told me she'd been dead for five years.

It was Coales' daughter, Danielle Ardern, who created Formations House, along with her husband, Nadeem Khan. In the first companies they created, they acted as directors under their own names, with Khan occasionally hiding behind a pseudonym—Sam Soloman—under which he also blogged. Ardern always gave her address as 29 Harley Street, but she was not present when I visited.

The door buzzed open into a grand, marble-floored hall leading into the gloomy distance. A staircase rose to the left, up which presumably Ronald Raven's patients would have walked to reach his consulting chamber. A young man emerged to ask my business, then showed me into a conference room, which looked out through the bow window onto the street. Eventually, a young woman came to ask what I wanted, but declined to answer my questions when I explained that I was interested in what happened in the building. "Most publications can be not very positive, so we are careful," said the woman—whose name was Charlotte Pawar—though she agreed to write her email address in my notebook. I emailed her with questions, but she never responded, or returned my phone calls, until I published an article about her business. "We feel the article is clearly biased against Mr. Khan (when no wrong-doing was ever proven in court) and clearly biased against Formations House as one of the many formations agents in not just the UK but worldwide," she wrote.

It is true that Khan's wrongdoing was not proven in court, but that is because he died before the Nobre case ever came to trial. According to the prosecutor in that case, Khan's enabling of fraud went a lot further than just creating companies. "His actions ... were key in allowing Nobre to launder more of the stolen Allseas money," the barrister's opening note stated. According to the Crown's case against Nobre, £160,000 of the stolen money was passed to Khan, nominally to buy four companies, but really to finance pre-paid credit cards funded via a Cypriot bank, thus allowing Nobre to keep spending the money he stole while he was on police bail. If the case against him was correct, Khan was helping him to keep the cash in Moneyland, and doing his best to stop the authorities from getting their hands on it. Khan is dead, however, so no verdict was ever reached.

Without Khan, who now owns Formations House? Back in 2016, when my article came out, it was owned by Nominee Director Ltd, which was owned by another Harley Street company, Legal Nominees Ltd, one of the magical threesome at the heart of the anonymity business. Professional Nominees and Corporate Nominees were still secretary and director, but the business structure had changed since the triangle of companies had been created to guard the inner sanctum of Formations House back in 2004. In around 2014, 200,000 shares in each of the three companies had been acquired by Sigma Tech Enterprises, a company registered at a service address in Hong Kong. No such company featured on the Hong Kong corporate register, so presumably it was registered elsewhere, perhaps in the Seychelles, since the company's website announced that any disputes over its privacy policy would be decided under the law of the Indian Ocean archipelago. But that is just a guess. The corporate wizards of Formations House had saved the best tricks for themselves, and sucked their whole company down the tunnel into Moneyland, where no one could follow it.

6

SHELL GAMES

Here is the problem: someone has assets, and she wants to enjoy those assets, but she is embarrassed about how she obtained them. Perhaps they have been stolen, or they might be untaxed; it doesn't matter. In either case, if the owner were to publicly enjoy the use of them, it might prove embarrassing, and she doesn't want that. And here is the opportunity: if you can find a way to de-embarrass the assets, so she can enjoy them freely, she'll pay you. This is Moneyland's core industry, providing the middle stage in the pathway steal–hide–spend.

All around the world, highly intelligent people are earning fees by seeking new and innovative ways to make dirty property clean, hunting out the loopholes that allow their clients' stuff to slip down the tunnel and into the virtual world. The more complex the solution, the more valuable it is, and some of these solutions are imaginative indeed. In 2016, a Japanese newspaper reported that top Chinese officials were extracting eggs from their wives, fertilizing them, then having them implanted in women in Japan. The loophole here is that Japanese law does not regulate surrogacy, and lists the surrogate as mother on the child's birth certificate, thus making the child eligible for Japanese citizenship. A corrupt official can therefore transfer his wealth to an apparently unrelated Japanese child, with no one realizing that the child is his son or daughter. It works like defection, but without any of the downsides: there's no need to slip across a border at the dead of night, no need to apply for asylum. The individual has defected while still a blastocyst.

According to files reviewed by journalists from the *Mainichi Shimbun*, the Japanese newspaper that broke the story, a surrogacy broker had arranged for eighty-six Chinese children to be born in Japan. Some of their parents were directors of state-owned companies, others had connections with major universities, and some were senior figures in China's ruling Communist Party. "The main reason wealthy relatives of the Party's senior officials have children with Japanese citizenship is the anonymity it affords. Even if Chinese investigative authorities go to great pains to track the flow of assets, they end up at unrelated accounts and companies of people who are ostensibly Japanese," the newspaper said.

Its journalists interviewed a woman in her thirties who said she had undergone the surrogacy procedure on instructions from her husband's uncle, a top Party executive. They spoke in Hong Kong on the condition that she not be identified in any way. "If there's someone in the family with Japanese citizenship, it'll make it easier for us to flee there if China collapses," the woman said, before adding (with "a wry smile"): "the higher up in the Communist Party someone is, the less likely they are to be willing to sacrifice themselves for the country."

There are of course downsides for a Chinese official who chooses this method of de-embarrassing his assets. It costs ¥15 million (around $130,000) and, perhaps more seriously, may well mean having almost no contact with the child. Another Chinese parent who spoke to the paper had a son born in August 2014, who lived at a childcare center in the Kanto Region, and they only saw each other twice a month. That might be bad for the child's relationship with his parents, but it was clearly good for the family's wealth-management strategy. The journalist saw the toddler's bank statement: it contained ¥2 billion (more than $17 million), all of them embarrassment-free.

The broker was apparently surprised by the success of the service, having originally intended it only for infertility treatment, but was more than happy to continue offering it to corrupt officials or their relatives while demand lasted. "How they use surrogacy is up to the client. We ourselves are not running a defection business," the broker said.

Such dystopian de-embarrassment tools are not for everyone, of course, and there are many more low-tech techniques to break the link between misdeed and money. Nigerian investigators talk about how hard it is to probe grand corruption, in cases where the proceeds have been taken as banknotes, stashed in a safe house for months, booked onto a flight to Heathrow Airport as hold luggage, locked in a bank vault somewhere in London, then handed to an estate agent willing not to ask any questions. If the whole deal is done in cash, there is no electronic trail to connect the house bought in London to the crime from which it originates. But there are downsides here, too.

Firstly, it is intrinsically suspicious to possess vast amounts of cash, as Nigerian regional governor Diepreye Alamieyeseigha discovered, when arrested at Heathrow in 2005. Police officers raided his London home and found $1.5 million in various currencies, which they confiscated and returned to Nigeria. Secondly, money is vulnerable: if your house burns down, it's gone; if the airline sends your luggage to Barcelona, it's gone; if your courier gets greedy, it's gone. You'll be lucky to find an insurance company willing to honor a claim for a lost suitcase full of $100 bills.

And this is where corporate vehicles—companies, foundations, trusts, partnerships—come in. By owning a company, which in turn owns your assets, you are putting a gap between yourself and embarrassment. It's like picking up a dog turd with a plastic bag: it keeps your hands clean. Every study of grand corruption or tax avoidance shows how crucial shell companies are to the process of de-embarrassing assets, and this is not a new problem. As long ago as 1937, Treasury Secretary Henry Morgenthau complained to US president Franklin Roosevelt about the then tax haven of Newfoundland, which is now part of Canada, which was allowing Americans to hide behind its corporate structures. "The stockholders have resorted to all manner of devices to prevent the acquisition of information regarding their companies," he complained. However, as the example of Formations House and 29 Harley Street makes clear, the speed and cheapness of modern communications have made creating these companies ever easier, with devastating results for the law enforcement agencies trying to investigate them.

John Tobon, deputy special agent in charge of Homeland Security Investigations in Miami, Florida, was very open about it. A big guy, with hair parted at the side, when I went to see him in early 2017 he wore a turquoise and gold knuckleduster ring with the scales of justice on it, and a blue shirt with thin mauve stripes. Miami is a magnet for crooked money from all over the world, and he sits on the front line, whether that's fighting kleptocratic cash from China, the billions earned by the drugs mafias, or fortunes owned by

Americans in the many tax havens—the Bahamas, the Caymans, the British Virgin Islands, St. Kitts and Nevis—just over the blue horizon.

The internet has made his job much harder. A decade or two ago, if a crook wanted a Pacific shell company, they had to go to the Pacific to get it. Now, they can get it online from their living room. "Via the internet, any jurisdiction, even jurisdictions where record keeping is pretty good ... they're still vulnerable. The real challenge comes in the layering, in the nesting," he said. "You can have a corporation created in a very transparent jurisdiction that will then be nested in a more obscure jurisdiction and so on and so forth. That's really where the challenge is."

The creation of these long, nested chains of corporate structures across multiple jurisdictions is an extremely effective way of hiding both the origins of assets and their ownership. The more plastic bags you wrap around a dog turd, the harder it is for outsiders to realize what's inside. And if the last bag says Tiffany & Co. on it, perhaps no one will ever realize it's full of shit.

Tobon said he had to send requests under Mutual Legal Assistance Treaties (MLATs) to places like the Seychelles, rely on US diplomats to make sure they were followed through, and wait months for a response, all to investigate property owned right there in Florida. And increasingly that was in small-scale crimes, rather than just big fraud cases. "It's more of a retail market than a high-end market. So, twenty years ago, creating a corporate structure like this, you had to go to Harrods to buy it, now you can go to the corner store. We're seeing less sophisticated organizations, using more sophisticated methods."

And, if it were possible to abolish shell companies, what difference would that make? Could he imagine what his job would be like if he could easily find out who owned all the property he ended up investigating?

"It would probably cut the investigative time by half, which is huge," he said. "We would be able to concentrate our efforts on putting the pieces together, rather than trying to find the pieces. Right now, we spend most of our time trying to find the pieces. By the time we're ready to put the pieces together, all sorts of things happen. Sometimes, by the time we get the information, the statute of limitations has gone, you're done ... In that respect, it would do a world of good."

Thanks to investigators like Tobon and his team, we have a growing body of material showing how companies have been misused. The World Bank's Stolen Asset Recovery (StAR) initiative, the US Senate's Permanent Sub-committee on Investigations, Britain's Financial Conduct Authority, cases brought under both America's Foreign Corrupt Practices Act and the UK Bribery Act, as well as legal proceedings in Jersey, Switzerland, France and elsewhere—they all contain crucial details of the intricate scams committed over the decades. The origin of the source material gives the overwhelming impression that this is an Anglo-American problem, though that is at least as much a reflection of the two countries' relative willingness to prosecute (or, at least, discuss) cases of corruption and fraud as it is a sign of their open-ness to dirty money. There is also a trove of material from non-governmental organizations like Transparency International, the Tax Justice Network, Cor-ruption Watch, Sherpa and Global Witness, which have done more than most countries to expose how the wealthy have abused the world's financial architecture for their own private gain.

In January 2016, Global Witness published the results of an elaborate sting operation, in which its employee approached thirteen different law firms in New York, posing as an adviser to an African politician seeking to bring clearly suspect funds into the United States, and surreptitiously filmed the resulting conversations. Only one of the lawyers turned the approach down flat, while the others all suggested using anonymous companies or trusts to hide the origin of the assets. One of the lawyers was James Silkenat, who at the time was president of the American Bar Association, and he suggested the very kind of structure that Tobon of the Miami HSI was so concerned about. "Company A is owned by Company B, who is owned jointly by Com-pany C and D, and your party owns all of or the majority of the shares of C and D," Silkenat told the undercover investigator. His colleague Hugh Finnegan added: "Many foreign owners just don't want anybody to know who they are. So they set up limited liability companies and it's usually one or two other companies up the food chain, making it more difficult to identify."

Of course, neither lawyer—nor, indeed, any of the others who discussed the hypothetical African minister with Global Witness' investigator—committed a crime, and none of them followed through on their sugges-tions. The NGO's final report did conclude, however, that it was concerned about "the ease with which prospective clients can obtain ideas on how to move suspect funds into the US, and the need for reform of the legal system to make it more difficult to move suspect funds."

In a case brought in London against Frederick Chiluba, the former president of Zambia, the judge referred in his judgment to the way Chiluba's crime could not have taken place without the assistance of lawyers like these, people able to navigate the legal systems of Western countries. "This is classic blind eye dishonesty," Mr. Justice Peter Smith concluded. "[The lawyer] did not ask because he knew precisely what was going on, namely that there was a conspiracy to defraud and he participated in it willingly. The other possibility is that he did not ask because he did not want to know the answer. In my view it is not necessary to decide which of the two is the most likely scenario. I am quite satisfied, however, that no honest solicitor in his position would have done what he did."

The lawyer in question was later struck off by the Solicitors' Regulation Authority, but there is more going on here than just lawyers being dishonest—turning a blind eye, or otherwise. It was not a crooked London solicitor or a dishonest New York attorney that made it so easy to create companies; that was the work of government. The crucial attribute of corporate vehicles is that they are legally separate from their owners and their owners' liability for their debts is limited. What that means in practice is that, if you operate through a company, society as a whole is taking responsibility for your debts. It's a kind of insurance. If your business fails, only the assets of the limited liability company will be at risk, not those of its owner.

This is an exceptionally powerful tool, and one whose power is seldom appreciated. Imagine if it was as easy to register people as it is to register companies—you could go online, fill in a form, pay £13, and have proof of a person's identity within a couple of days at most—the opportunities for fraud would be virtually unlimited. Your "person" could claim benefits, enter business agreements, open bank accounts, and then you could kill them off when they got in trouble, leaving the whole mess behind you.

England and the Netherlands created the first recognizably modern companies in the seventeenth century, but even in these European outliers, only parliament could give permission for companies to be created, meaning that the number in existence remained small. "Corporations have neither bodies to be punished, nor souls to be condemned, they therefore do as they like," said Edward Thurlow, lord chancellor of Great Britain in the late eighteenth century. Elsewhere he is quoted, more colloquially, as saying: "Did you ever expect a corporation to have a conscience, when it has no soul to be damned, and no body to be kicked at?"

With this kind of distrust prevalent at the highest levels in Europe, it had to be in America that the real innovation happened. In 1811, New York legislated for the creation of limited liability companies, and thence the idea spread, at first slowly, and then—from the 1850s—more rapidly. In 1855, Britain followed suit, with spectacular results. In 1860, half of all securities traded in London were government bonds; by 1914, company shares made up more than 95 percent of the market. Limited liability is, in the words of the *Economist*, "the key to industrial capitalism." Companies are good; without them, our modern prosperity would have been impossible.

Every year, the World Bank publishes its influential *Doing Business* report, which ranks countries from 1st to 190th, across ten areas of business activity, then gives them an aggregate score. In 2017, the worst place in the world to do business was Somalia, which just slipped in behind Venezuela, Libya and Eritrea. A high ranking in the survey is crucial for countries seeking to attract foreign investment, and governments often tailor their policies deliberately so as to move up the table. One of the ten ranking areas is "starting a business": the easier it is to create a company, the better your score. "In many countries the bureaucratic obstacles and high costs imposed by inefficient company registries deter people with good business ideas from embarking on the path of formal entrepreneurship," the 2015 report explained.

According to the latest *Doing Business* report, New Zealand is both the easiest place in the world to do business, and the easiest place in the world to set up a company. And here is one of the consequences of that. In late 2009, Thai soldiers at Bangkok airport raided an Ilyushin IL-76 cargo plane, which was supposedly carrying equipment for oil exploration. What they found instead were thirty tons of weapons, including explosives, rocket launchers and missiles originating in North Korea and bound for Iran, in violation of a United Nations arms embargo. The plane had been leased by a New Zealand company called SP Trading, but when investigators tried to discover who was behind it, all they could find was Lu Zhang, a 28-year-old Chinese-born employee of an Auckland Burger King.

She said in court she had received NZ$20 for each company for which she agreed to be a director, and only realized she might have done something wrong when she saw the news reports about the seized weapons shipment. To this day, the real perpetrators of the arms-smuggling deal remain unknown, all thanks to the ease with which they could obtain an anonymous New Zealand corporation. And SP Trading was just part of a whole web of front companies obscuring money laundering, drug smuggling, procurement fraud, share ramping, and the Magnitsky affair—the theft of $230 million from the Russian treasury, some of which then passed through Nevis-controlled bank accounts. When seen from this perspective, it is hard to fathom why the World Bank's *Doing Business* team has not realized that making company formation as simple as possible isn't always an unqualified good. Rampant fraud, after all, makes doing business harder.

Doing Business rates the United States as a far trickier place to create a company than New Zealand. In fact, at 51st in the world, it is behind Egypt and Kazakhstan—neither of which is exactly renowned for its open and dynamic economy. However, that picture is misleading, because different US states have different systems, and some of them are deeply dodgy.

Karen Greenaway is supervisory special agent at the FBI's International Corruption Unit. During an hour-long chat at one of the Bureau's offices in Washington, during which she occasionally shifted the position of the pistol on her hip, she explained how embarrassing it could be when foreign counterparts ask her to obtain information on company ownership from Delaware, where you can form a company in an hour. If the person who bought the company is based outside the United States, then there simply isn't any information available for her to obtain. "If you think I'm going to go to a Delaware shell company and get you bank records and get you the contracts, that's not going to be there, because that's not what they're created for," she said. "I've got to go back and tell them, no, the bank account is not in the United States. The company that you're asking me about? Let me take you a picture of a storefront in Delaware."

Most company formation agents—the kind of people who would be sitting in the storefront in Delaware—are wary of talking to journalists. One man who is not, however, is Robert Harris. He lives in the small Nevada town of Fernley, forty minutes from Reno along Interstate 80, a featureless road packed with trucks and SUVs, and intermittently adorned with advertisements for lawyers, fast food and God. His bungalow is in a new development hidden from the road by a wall, where the streets are named after various golfing terms—Dog Leg Drive, Wedge Lane, Divot Drive—in honor of a nearby course.

When I went to see him, Harris turned out to be a friendly, funny and eccentric 70-year-old who has created some 3,000 companies over the last sixteen years, and who makes a living from the various administrative fees he can charge while doing so. He came to Reno as a young man aiming to make it big in the town's casinos. "But I'm not very good at that. No, not at all," he said, with a shrug and a smile. Instead, he spent the next three decades waiting tables, serving food and drinks to all the other people who came to Reno with the idea of making it big in the casinos. "But then I was too old to get a job. They wanted young girls, you know, pretty girls, so I went to an attorney friend of mine, and I learned the incorporation business."

He will sell you a Nevada company for just $249 and, for an extra $150, a "Nevada Nominee Officer," who ensures your name is kept off the paperwork. His top-of-the-range product is the "Deluxe Privacy Incorporation Pack," which provides an anonymous company together with its own bank account, for just $949. So, does he check that his clients won't abuse the tools he's selling?

"I don't investigate people. It's not a requirement. I couldn't afford to investigate a person before I incorporate. There's not a lot of profit in investigating people and I couldn't do that anyway. So, you know, you just take people's word for it," he told me. "It's more like going to the grocery store. They don't ask you your name and how much money you've got in the bank and all that stuff; you just buy your groceries, you know. It's the same thing if you want to incorporate: you pay for it, and you get it; that's it."

Our conversation was interrupted by a phone call. A woman called Nathalie, apparently using a speakerphone, wanted to know whether she could incorporate herself to improve her credit score. Harris told her he thought she could, though he didn't exactly push the issue, perhaps because I was there. "I don't really use the hard sell; it's more of a soft sell," he said, after she had rung off. "If they want to do it, fine. If they don't want to do it, fine. I'm not out to make a million dollars from this; I don't try to gouge anybody. I always keep my prices low and very direct. I treat people good and fairly. Christian ethics, that's what I use in business."

Harris has self-published several books of Christian doctrine, with a specific focus on the nature of the Rapture and its relationship to the Tribulation, and was far more interested in talking about them than the specifics of Nevadan company regulations. It was in creating a website for his ministry that he learned how to use the internet, and that's what allowed him to create his online incorporating service. He now sells his book *Get Ready! HERE I COME* alongside Nevada companies on www.nevadaincorporate .com.

Was he concerned that, if people use the companies he sells to commit fraud, that might violate his Christian mission?

"I don't worry about that, I don't have anything to do with that," he said. "I just give them their incorporation papers, that's it. If I knew somebody is a criminal organization that would be different. But people don't say, 'Hey, I belong to a criminal organization or the mafia or whatever.' They don't admit that."

It was thanks to people like Harris that, in an elegantly designed academic study published in 2014 under the title *Global Shell Games*, US incorporation agents were shown to be the laxest in the world when it came to providing companies to anyone who asked for them. The study's authors sent thousands of carefully prepared emails to agents in 181 jurisdictions, with subtly different wording to heighten the risk that the company could be used for fraud, or terrorism; then collated the responses, to see which jurisdictions had the best record for demanding identification. There was substantial variation between the different US states. Delaware came bottom, with a worse compliance rate than everywhere else in the world, then Montana, Alabama, Nevada and Wyoming. One agent replied to the academics' approach with the response: "We have many international clients with the same confidentiality concerns so I am happy to tell you that you have found the right service provider for your needs!"

The downsides of this approach were laid bare by the US Government Accountability Office (GAO) in 2006. It said US shell companies had facilitated crimes involving billions of dollars, which had proved all but impossible to investigate. "A Nevada-based corporation had received 3,774 suspicious wire transfers totaling $81 million over a period of approximately two years," the report noted. "However, the case was not prosecuted because ICE could not identify the beneficial owner of the corporation." In 2006, a US-registered corporation was behind the smuggling of a "toxic controlled substance" between two Eurasian countries. In another case, officials in Russia created companies in Pennsylvania and Delaware and used them to steal $15 million intended to help upgrade Russian nuclear infrastructure. Other examples involved tax evasion via Florida companies, as well as sanctions busting and more.

This is another example of money flowing across borders—in this case, state borders—and laws being unable to follow it. It is so easy to register companies in states that do not require you to disclose your identity that there is little point going to ones with higher standards. And there is no incentive for the more permissive states to clean up their act. Just like Jersey or Nevis, they have become hooked on the revenue that Moneyland brings. "A Delaware official said that 22 percent of the state's revenue comes from the company formation business. Also, Nevada and Oregon officials state that their offices were revenue-generating," said the GAO's report. It's the Moneyland ratchet again.

The consequences of this pose a clear threat to the nation's security. In 2017, the GAO concluded that the US government had no idea who owned fully one-third of the buildings leased by the General Services Administration for high-security purposes. Federal agents quoted in the report warned this left the agencies wide open to risks "such as espionage and unauthorized cyber and physical access."

It is not impossible for law enforcement to see through shell companies or to confiscate assets held via corporate vehicles, but it is expensive, laborious and time-consuming, even if you try to cut corners. Russian investigators, between 2004 and 2007, gained control of the large and profitable Yukos oil company despite its ownership being protected by a thicket of offshore companies. The complexity of the structure might well have prevented prosecutors or investigators in a Western country from forming a clear picture as to which individuals actually owned Yukos, but this did not particularly concern the Russian officials, who cut through the legal obstacles like bulldozers through a maze. That did allow Russia to take ownership of the company, but it ensnared the country in years of litigation in international courts and tribunals. In 2014, the Gibraltar company GML won $50 billion in compensation for the illegal appropriation of its assets. Although Russia overturned the ruling on appeal (another court ruled that the first tribunal lacked jurisdiction), GML has appealed the second ruling, and the case drags on—testament to the power of nested chains of shell companies to frustrate the will of governments, for good or ill.

For obvious reasons, the Russian approach is not one available to Western law enforcement agencies, whose actions are overseen and regulated by courts outside their control. That can be frustrating for investigators trying to probe people who have stolen their assets in one jurisdiction, and who are then exploiting the rules designed to protect the innocent in somewhere like the United States.

The FBI's Karen Greenaway said corrupt foreign officials were often little better than bank robbers. But while a bank robber could have his loot frozen while being investigated, kleptocrats can tap their stolen wealth to pay lawyers to keep it safe. "They walk through the door with droves of attorneys to defend this property right, and it puts us and it puts the country it's stolen from at an unfair disadvantage," she said. "Due process shouldn't mean that you get the best attorney money can buy with the money you've stolen. There's something wrong with that. If he really wants somebody to defend his property rights, what we say in court is that we'll give you an attorney. The fact that you don't like the attorney that we're going to give you, that should be immaterial."

What is most remarkable about this is that the companies that are protecting the stolen property and shielding it from Greenaway's investigators are entirely fictional, figments of lawyers' imaginations. You can wrap a paper chain of paper people around the world in an afternoon, but it will take investigators years of patient detective work to unpick it, and years more to prosecute.

If you want to de-embarrass your assets and enjoy them fully, a shell company on its own is not enough, however. A corporate vehicle is useful for wrapping around something, shielding it from legal cases, from investigation, from oversight, or just from public knowledge, but it's not dynamic; it won't allow you to move assets around in a way that will help you have fun. For that, you need a bank account. Once you have attached a bank account to your shell company, the possibilities for enjoying the use of your de-embarrassed assets expand in every direction, and you can start to go shopping.

Gulnara Karimova was an enthusiastic shopper. Karimova's father was president of Uzbekistan, an ex-Soviet dictatorship that forces children to pick cotton and sell it to the government, then resells it at a profit. She has had a number of personas over the years: ambassador to Spain and to the United Nations, Harvard student, fashion designer, philanthropist. Under the stage name Googoosha, she sang in auto-tuned English or Russian over mediocre pop beats, including in a duet with previously great French actor Gerard Depardieu, who often hires out what's left of his credibility to rich people from the ex-USSR. Reports from inside Uzbekistan described how she made her money by stealing successful businesses that caught her eye. "Most Uzbeks see Karimova as a greedy, power hungry individual," wrote American ambassador Jon Purnell in a 2005 cable later released by WikiLeaks. "She remains the single most hated person in the country. (Comment: We have no polling data to support that statement, but we stand by it.)"

Uzbekistan is not a place where journalists or investigators are able to work freely (or if they do, not for long), so most of the allegations against Karimova remained anecdotal until a series of prosecutions of foreign telecoms companies revealed the profits she had been making out of her government connections. Karimova used Takilant, a company in Gibraltar, to own bank accounts that channeled more than $114 million in bribes from VimpelCom, a Russian-owned, Bermuda-incorporated, Dutch-based telecoms company, from 2006 until 2012. The accounts were at banks in Latvia, Hong Kong, the Netherlands and New York, and the payments were disguised as consulting services, and came from companies in the British Virgin Islands. The bribes were so vast that they caused difficulties for VimpelCom, which didn't have the right amount of money spare in the right jurisdictions, and the subsequent investigation by US prosecutors resulted in thirty-eight pages of highly detailed indictment. Another investigation showed that a second telecoms giant, Teliasonera, paid her bribes in the same way to access the Uzbek market. Her takings may have exceeded $1 billion.

It's not known exactly what Karimova spent the money on, though she launched a new cosmetics line—Guli—in 2012, so some of it may have gone into that. The cases do reveal, however, how potent a Gibraltar shell company can be as a wealth-gathering weapon, once twinned with bank accounts around the world. Karimova is currently under house arrest in Uzbekistan, having been swept up in palace intrigue when her father became ill (he died in 2016). The criminal investigation against her has now spread to Switzerland, where prosecutors have frozen 800 million Swiss francs, and are investigating a private bank for allegedly laundering her money. The bank—Lombard Odier, which was founded in 1796—itself reported its suspicions about the money, although not until 2012, which is when the corruption investigations into her began.

But this sort of thing has not just been happening in tax havens or secrecy jurisdictions. In 1992, Citibank's private banking arm opened an account for Raúl Salinas, brother of the president of Mexico, waiving all checks on his financial background, employment record or assets. In an episode forensically dissected by investigators for the US Senate, Citi created shell companies in the Cayman Islands and elsewhere to own bank accounts in London and Switzerland because, as one employee explained, "this client is <u>extremely sensitive</u> about the use of his name and does not want it circulated within the bank." For that reason, Salinas was referred to internally as "Confidential Client Number 2," or "CC-2." By mid-1994, the accounts contained $67 million, and they earned Citibank more than $2 million in fees over four years. As Amy Elliott, Salinas' banker, explained in an email to a colleague: "this account is turning into an exciting profitable one for us all. Many thanks for making me look good."

Then things went wrong. On February 28, 1995, Mexican police officers arrested Salinas on suspicion of murder, causing a flurry of phone calls between bankers in London, Switzerland and New York, although the bankers' concerns were not what you might have imagined. "The private bank's initial reaction to the arrest was not to assist law enforcement, but to determine whether the Salinas accounts should be moved to Switzerland to make discovery of the assets and bank records more difficult," a later Senate investigation concluded, based on the bank's automatic tape recordings of the conversations. The bankers also scrambled to fill in the client file they were supposed to have written years earlier, to give backdated details about the source of his funds.

That November, Salinas' wife was arrested in Switzerland, and $132 million was frozen in various banks. A Swiss court later returned the money to Mexico and a Mexican court convicted Salinas of murder, in a case that became the biggest political scandal in the country. It was never clear-cut, however, with suspicions widespread that investigators had cut corners in their zeal to put Salinas in jail. He was acquitted on the murder charge at a retrial in 2005; Swiss prosecutors—despite years of work—never managed to bring a case for money laundering; and a Mexican court dismissed corruption charges in 2014. The point remains, though, that Citibank failed to conduct any of the checks that even its own internal standards required. So why didn't one of America's most important banks have any suspicions about the president's brother receiving such a vast amount of money? Because, in the words of Elliott, who managed his account, it wasn't really all that big a deal.

"Raul Salinas' account was not the largest, the most profitable, or most important account I managed," she wrote in a statement for the Senate's investigators. "In fact, it was one of the smallest accounts, and one of the least active. As large as the amounts seem to us in personal terms, they were not unusual in the context of the wealthy Mexican business people who are clients of the Private Bank."

That may have been the case, but a 2011 study into private banking by Britain's Financial Services Authority suggested a more disturbing—and more Moneyland—explanation for bankers' failure to do the checks they should do into the origin of their clients' funds. The FSA published the report fully a decade after a similar probe revealed deep shortcomings in how willing British banks had been to accept money from the Nigerian kleptocrat Sani Abacha, yet the banks were still making the same mistakes when it came to dealing with high-ranking foreigners (Politically Exposed Persons [PEPs], in the jargon of the industry). Fully three-quarters of the banks failed to adequately check whether the money in the accounts had been legitimately acquired; half of them failed to identify adverse information about their client; a third of them dismissed serious allegations made against their client without checking them properly.

"Some banks appeared unwilling to turn away, or exit, very profitable business relationships when there appeared to be an unacceptable risk of handling the proceeds of crime," the FSA concluded. In plain terms, if a client was rich enough, a bank would break the rules for her. In one (anonymized) example quoted in the report, a large bank held an account for a wealthy customer from an oil-rich highly corrupt country. Although the client was closely allied to the country's political elite, the bank had not identified him as a PEP, meaning it had not done the more stringent checks such a designation requires. When the FSA challenged the money laundering reporting officer about this lapse, the bank employee told them his team had been unable to find any incriminating information on the client. "The first result of a simple Google search of the customer's name linked the customer to serious and credible allegations of corruption," the report stated laconically, the author's incredulity leaking through the rather dry language.

In another bank, a member of the anti-money-laundering team approved a relationship with a politically prominent family, despite their being under international sanctions and credibly accused of the embezzlement of millions of dollars of government funds. "In my view, provided there is sufficient business to justify the risk then I am happy to recommend we proceed," the banker wrote. That is not how things are supposed to work.

What this all means is that, once again, if you're rich enough, the rules are negotiable. If you could afford the $8,000 fee to open an account at a bank in the Cayman Islands, then you didn't need to worry about paying US taxes. If you are the family of a wealthy foreign official, then private banks in London and New York alike have a history of bending the rules to make sure it is they who get your money, rather than one of their competitors. If everyone is applying the law, then there is money to be made in being the banker who doesn't, which is a strong incentive for no one to be too scrupulous. The Moneyland ratchet always leads to looser and laxer regulations for the rich. And the highly intelligent bankers, accountants and lawyers will keep hunting for tunnels for their clients to slip their money through.

Wealth-X, a consulting company that maps the movements of the super-rich as if they are wildebeest, calculates that in 2016 there were 226,450 people in the world with assets worth more than $30 million (it calls them ultra-high-net-worth people, or UHNWs), a 3.5 percent increase on the year before. Collectively, their wealth had increased over the previous twelve months by 1.5 percent to $27 trillion, which is roughly equivalent to the entire output of China and the United States added together. And the outlook for further increases is good: "SOLID GROWTH EXPECTED ACROSS THE ULTRA WEALTHY SECTOR," proclaims the company's *World Ultra Wealth Report 2017*. "The global ultra-wealthy population is forecast to rise to 299,000 people by 2021, an increase of 72,550 compared with 2016 levels. UHNW wealth is projected to rise to $35.7 trillion, which implies an additional $8.7 trillion of newly created wealth over the next five years." If this prediction comes true, the planet's UHNWs will have added the equivalent of the GDPs of Japan and Germany to their stock of wealth, in half a decade. Wealth-X sells its insights to the global class of lawyers, bankers and professionals that manages this wealth. The more wealth there is, the more they get paid. They have moved on from simply de-embarrassing assets, and now husband them, protect them, multiply them, and make them available to anyone who needs them anywhere in the world. The world has come a long way since that first elaborately organized eurobond drilled holes in the tanks of the great oil tanker of the world economy, and allowed tax dodgers and kleptocrats to make a fortune.

This is a lucrative business, the basis of much of the economies of Switzerland, London, Manhattan, the Cayman Islands, the British Virgin Islands, and many more places all over the world. The logical consequence of their effectiveness in preserving their clients' wealth is the creation of dynasties, which will ensure that a family's temporary advantage is never removed, but instead becomes entrenched, and that the inequality of this precise moment is maintained in perpetuity.

Brooke Harrington, an American academic, has written a book about this wealth management industry called *Capital without Borders*, having interviewed many of its practitioners, attended conferences, and studied their professional literature. It is a sober and careful work, which is perhaps why its warnings about the enablers of Moneyland are so startling. "Their work radically undermines the economic basis and legal authority of the modern tax state," she concludes. "Using trusts, offshore firms, and foundations, professionals can ensure that inequality endures and grows in a way that becomes difficult to reverse short of revolution."

We're going back to Ukraine now, to look at a specific example of what she means.

7

CANCER

On February 4, 2014, President Viktor Yanukovich visited Ukraine's Cancer Institute. The president, dressed in a white coat, smiled unctuously at the young patients, their heads chemotherapy-bald, shook hands with their parents and handed out white boxes of presents, while photographers and cameramen scurried around to get the best angles. The institute's director, Igor Shchepotin, pointed out various features of the facilities, which treat the most serious cases from all over the country, and the president promised some new equipment to improve treatment and diagnosis. It was supposedly, according to the news broadcasts, an entirely routine visit to mark World Cancer Day, but it was in reality a propaganda trip, an attempt to make this venal and self-interested kleptocrat appear to be a nice guy, someone who cared for the people he had been stealing from throughout his lengthy political career.

The doctors at least were not convinced. Their already busy working day had been disrupted to make way for the president's security detail, as well as for the camera crews and hangers-on. Guards were already in place at the institute by seven in the morning, checking anyone trying to get in, even the regulars. Inside the buildings, they looked above the tiles in the suspended ceilings, they sent round sniffer dogs, and took away the wastepaper baskets in case someone put a bomb in them. The institute consists of three smoke-gray six-story blocks on the edge of Kiev, surrounded by fences. The external walls of the blocks are tiled, with occasional scars where some tiles have fallen off and the bricks peep through. The Soviet workmen who built the blocks wrote the date—1968—into the walls of one of them with varicolored bricks and, since then, maintenance appears to have been erratic. It was quite a walk from the front gate to the block where consultant anesthetist Konstantin Sidorenko had his office, and he found the disruption caused by the president irritating.

"They wouldn't even let us drive onto the site," he told me. "In front of me was a car bringing food for the patients—milk, I think, and various other things—and they wouldn't let them enter either. The driver had to plead with the guards for, like, ten minutes. It wasn't that our work was paralyzed so much but that there were serious inconveniences for the patients, for the staff, for anyone trying to walk around the institute. And on top of that there were snipers everywhere. It was a whole day. I think people just hated him even more by the end of it."

At the time, Yanukovich was fighting for his career: his cabinet had resigned, tens of thousands of protesters were camped out behind smoldering barricades in central Kiev, and his political allies were deserting him. If he was worried, though, he showed no sign of it. "I would like to express gratitude to you for your attention," a beaming Shchepotin told the president. "All the treatment in the institute is conducted free of charge."

That was not true, and pretty much everyone watching—whether inside the institute, or on television—must have known it. Ukraine's constitution guaranteed free healthcare, but in reality patients paid for almost everything. Supposedly, the institute's budget was adequate for all of its needs, but doctors' salaries were tiny, and they were forced to ask patients to fund their own drugs, and even to contribute money toward the upkeep of equipment. One onlooker was Natalya Onipko, a slim blond woman who runs Zaporuka, a charity that helps children undergoing treatment at the institute. Patients from outside Kiev can stay with their families in a hostel she runs, giving them a measure of normality during their long stay in the capital. She talked to her guests every day, and she knew very well that payments were being demanded of them. She is normally a careful woman in what she says, but seeing the president beam while being told how everything in the institute was wonderful tipped her over the edge. "What a swine," she wrote on Facebook. "Everyone has been forced to take off their medical masks, although for these children any virus is a deadly threat. The lives of 50 children for one scumbag."

As it turned out, the allegation wasn't true (parents removed the masks so the children looked good on TV) but went viral anyway, with the country's biggest news sites reporting that the president had risked children's lives to advertise himself. It fit with the national image of Yanukovich as self-centered and amoral, and it helped doom any PR value the trip might have had. The president's authority eroded further and, just over a fortnight later, he fled to Russia, leaving Ukraine in the hands of his opponents. This left Shchepotin—the institute's director—in a bit of a spot. A blotchy-looking man with sandy hair, he was now in the unfortunate position of having lied to benefit an unpopular president shortly before a revolution.

It was in the days after the revolution that unmarked Russian troops occupied Crimea. Ukraine's military had been shown to be outgunned and outmaneuvered, and Ukrainian patriots were raising money to help redress the balance. Shchepotin declared that the institute's employees would be contributing part of their salary for the cause, an announcement that garnered considerable media attention. Many of the employees were already doing this, and many of them felt their boss was using their money to win favor from the new government. One such employee—a young surgeon called Andrei Semivolos—complained publicly via Facebook, the chosen medium of the revolutionaries.

Shchepotin retaliated by upbraiding Semivolos publicly, and bringing in the television cameras to show him doing it, via a Soviet-era practice called "the collective." The collective is technically an open meeting, at which anyone can say anything. However, since the attendance and agenda are controlled by the management, it is really a tool for humiliating and controlling subordinates. Semivolos, who has an athlete's build and pale skin, stood impassive while his colleagues told him he had defamed the institute and should be ashamed of himself. As punishment, Semivolos was forced to serve as duty surgeon for his colleagues, which would deprive him of the face-to-face meetings that could earn him donations from patients. Without such meetings, it would not be possible for him to support his family on his official salary of 2,300 hryvnias (then $200) a month, so this was essentially an attempt to force him to resign.

What followed was a battle that not only mirrored the revolution in the whole country—one side using television, the other side using social media; one side with power, the other without—but also revealed the way corruption works in healthcare, and quite how difficult it is to do anything about it. The Cancer Institute became, for a little while, a small version of Ukraine.

Cancer is Ukraine's second highest cause of death (after cardiovascular disease), thanks to high smoking rates, poor primary healthcare and thus late diagnosis, and the aftermath of the Chernobyl nuclear disaster. Doctors have worried for years about the country's failure to make progress in battling the condition, as well as to control epidemics of tuberculosis, HIV/AIDS, hepatitis and other conditions spread by poor living conditions, prostitution, injecting drug users and more. In 2008, after the previous anti-corruption revolution, the president asked his government to find out what was going wrong, and ministers asked the secret service, the SBU, to look into it. The SBU commissioned one of its agents to write up his findings on the state of healthcare in the country, and what he wrote was startling. He described a healthcare system devoted not to treating the needs of an ailing population, but instead to making money for a caste of privileged insiders.

The agent is, in his own words, "not a public person," but he agreed to speak to me if not identified by name. And so he spent hours telling me quite how far Ukraine had gone wrong in its failure to stop officials looting its healthcare system.

In Soviet times, he said, the government under-valued doctors, who were paid little. Ordinary citizens, however, were grateful to the medics who helped them get better, and brought them presents: candy, or alcohol. These weren't bribes so much as genuine gifts. They were given not in expectation of a reward, but as an expression of gratitude, but they became the norm. If you went to the doctor, even though healthcare was free, you took something along to give her. After 1991, when the Soviet Union collapsed, the situation changed, however. Doctors began to realize how much their Western colleagues were earning, and also began to appreciate the heft of their position. They literally had power of life and death over their patients; if a senior doctor decided the team would not treat you, you'd die.

"When we became a market economy, candy or brandy didn't cut it anymore," the agent said. "The doctors wanted money, actual banknotes, and people started paying them. The system we have now suits doctors very well. They don't want to change anything. If you're a senior doctor, you have a hospital. It might be bad, it might leak, but it's free, the state provides everything. The profits you earn, however, you don't have to share them with anyone; you don't even pay any taxes. You operate, earn two or three thousand dollars, stick them in your pocket, and off you go."

Ukrainian healthcare costs are socialized, in that the government pays for the facilities, the buildings and the infrastructure. The profits, however, are privatized, in that the doctors get to keep what they earn. It's great for the senior doctors, but it's terrible for the country.

"I don't think there's corruption in Ukraine, and I'll explain why," said the agent. "Corruption exists where you have a healthy state; and it takes up just 10, or maximum of 15, percent of the country. When it takes up 99 percent of the country, that's not corruption, that is the state. Do you understand the logic? It's total. It's total at all levels. Even an old granny selling sunflower seeds is part of this, because the policeman going past takes five or ten hryvnias from her. She gives, he takes, and this suits them both fine, because she knows she's got someone looking out for her."

The agent's story was long and complicated. He talked as darkness fell outside the window, and he kept talking as the bats looped in the night sky. The basic principle of what he was saying was that every reform that was imposed was exploited. If there were loopholes, these were identified and used for profit; if there were no loopholes, the law was amended by parliament until there were. When Ukraine brought in a new program for buying insulin, to make sure all of its diabetics received reliable treatment, healthcare bosses saw a gold mine. They inflated the number of diabetics on their lists, increased the budget for the amount of insulin they needed, and diverted the extra money into their own pockets.

Other diseases were harder to profit from. Tuberculosis requires specific chemicals delivered in specific quantities. But there was a way to make money here, too: the healthcare insiders cut the amount of chemical in each dose, by pretending the average patient weighed less than he did, and thus saved on the amount of chemicals they needed to buy. The consequence was that the drugs didn't work, which drove the growth of the multidrug-resistant TB strains that are now such a threat there. "It doesn't matter what the question is, the mafia has only one answer: the more, the better," said the agent. "It doesn't matter if it's a child, a granny, a grown man, who's sick. Who cares? The more, the better."

Different groups specialized in different aspects of the healthcare scam, but in general the pattern was the same. Health ministry officials allied with private sector companies to dominate a part of the budget, whether that was supplying medicine or equipment, repairing buildings, or controlling the passage of new legislation. Business was conducted via shell companies in Cyprus to hide the scams from oversight, and billions of dollars were sucked out of the country. Anti-corruption activists worked out that, in 2012, Ukraine's health ministry was overpaying for HIV and TB medications by 150–300 percent, compared to charities that bought the same drugs; and this was at a time when there wasn't enough money to provide anti-retrovirals to everyone who needed them. The same handful of distributors popped up again and again, hiding behind shell companies, and competing against themselves in a process that looked transparent but which was really a sham. The whole process was protected by senior officials, and everyone got a share.

Onipko, the blond woman who ruined the president's PR stunt with her well-timed Facebook post, told me navigating the thicket of rules and exceptions created to shield the fraudsters is a full-time job, since the rules are deliberately overcomplicated. The rules are so complicated, in fact, that it is all but impossible to abide by them, which is the point. Anyone in on the scam can ignore the rules, which is the basis of their profits, while the excessively complex regulations deter outsiders from getting involved, particularly since enforcement is a matter for the same dishonest officials who are making the profits. "I've been working with cancer for ten years now, almost ten years, and believe me, I have heard everything. But I want to tell you that, in ten years, none of my mums, the mums who live here, none of them has wanted to talk about it," she said, as we sat in the small office in the hostel she runs for the families of children with cancer. "All the parents want their children to be treated, and they're scared to speak out, to behave badly, because the doctor can always discharge their child."

The power imbalance is complete. Senior doctors can earn fortunes, while patients and their relatives can do nothing about it. While Onipko was talking, a group of six mothers, some of them with their children, were relaxing in the hostel's kitchen. Onipko asked them if they were prepared to speak to me, and they agreed, providing they were not identified in any way. At first they seemed reluctant to admit they had paid bribes, as if they were ashamed about breaking the law. But it wasn't reluctance that stopped them from speaking. It was amazement that anyone could be so naïve that they didn't know how the system works.

"Of course we could complain, but then they wouldn't treat us," one said, as she caressed the hairless head of her little boy. "You need to pay to get into a regional hospital, pay to get to the institute, pay to get an operation. If you complain, they'll send you back, they can say there's nothing they can do for you. Do you have children? Yes? Well, there you are, you wouldn't risk them, would you?"

The other mothers nodded in agreement, and thus began a brisk competition in relating the most egregious ways that doctors had asked them for bribes. One explained how a doctor had written the number "100" on a piece of paper, then pointed upward to make sure she'd understood he meant dollars, and not hryvnias. Another one explained how an anesthetist had done it with his fingers.

"Two fingers meant two hundred," she said, and the others laughed in disbelief. "Oh yes, sorry, thousand. Two fingers is two thousand. Three fingers: three thousand."

And so it went on around the table. And there was remarkably little resentment about it. The parents accepted it, aware that there was nothing they could do, that they should just make the best of it. Eventually Onipko chipped in.

"On the one hand, I understand that, yes, they're taking bribes, that it's awful. How can you take a bribe from a child with this diagnosis? But on the other hand, I think: 'OK, they're taking €100, but they need to live, too. They also have to go places and get things.' I think you understand what I'm talking about, it's the system. Everything is connected. I am more than convinced that every hospital in Ukraine works in the same way," she said. Later, after we left the kitchen, she was a little harsher in her assessment: "I try not to criticize the doctors in front of the parents, because they have to trust their doctors," she said. It was a good point. Criticizing the doctors for being corrupt was like criticizing the clouds for raining. That was just the way they were. It would be better to spend your time finding an umbrella.

Sidorenko, the consultant anesthetist in the Cancer Institute, denied that he personally was making a profit out of it, however. He took a small cubic box out of the pocket of his white coat and held it up. It contained an oxygen sensor, and he needs ten of them a year for the machines in his intensive care unit, at a total cost of 40,000 hryvnias. Without them, he would not know if his patients were breathing properly, so without them his patients could die. Over the previous two years, he had received literally no money for new sensors, nor for any other replacement parts for the highly specialized equipment he needs to keep his patients alive.

That meant he was forced to seek money himself. He sometimes found sponsors, and the doctors all chipped in, but that could never raise the sums he needed: the doctors simply didn't have high enough salaries. That meant his patients had to help. "We don't demand anything; we don't ask for money. But the patients tend to know what's going on, they know the system," he said. He walked round to a high cupboard, up against one wall in his office, covered in dark-tinted wood-effect Formica. He opened a door and took out a pile of envelopes so tall it required both hands to steady it. Some of them were half an inch thick, and all of them contained banknotes. This was the money he had collected, and which he would use to keep his department running. It was all off the books, unofficial. So much for Director Shchepotin's claim that the department provides everything for free.

What was particularly frustrating for Sidorenko was that he sat on the commission choosing which equipment the institute needed to buy. He said he had seen systematic overpayment, including for a respirator bought for €130,000 more than it was worth. He could see only one explanation for what was happening: while his patients were forced to pay for their own care, the institute's managers were syphoning off cash into their own pockets, via their crooked control of the procurement process.

The system's workings were laid out in a case brought by the US's Securities and Exchange Commission (SEC) against Teva Pharmaceutical, the largest manufacturer of generic drugs in the world. In December 2016 Teva, which is based in Israel, paid $519 million to settle parallel civil and criminal charges brought under the Foreign Corrupt Practices Act, after being accused of paying bribes in Russia, Ukraine and Mexico to win business from their state healthcare systems (and thereby making $214 million in illicit profits). According to the SEC, Teva paid a Ukrainian official—whom it does not name but who, at various times between 2002 and 2011, worked at the National Academy of Medical Sciences, advised the president, and chaired the group that decided the prices to be paid for medical products—a total of $200,000 and funded his holidays. "[The official] is helping us very much in advancing Copaxone and Insulins in the Ukrainian market. One of the ways of settling our account is funding his trip to Israel once a year," one internal Teva communication stated.

Teva listed the payments as sales/marketing expenses, and as consultancy fees, which were then paid for by the Ukrainian state by means of inflated invoices. That in turn left less money in the budget to pay doctors' salaries, or any of the other things needed to run a medical system. Those doctors were then forced to recoup their salaries and their maintenance costs at the bottom of the pyramid, from their patients. Meanwhile, at the tip of the pyramid, the management extracted the money—from Teva, or the dozens of other healthcare companies vying to sell their products in Ukraine—via their control of the procurement process. The pyramid is a way of levying tribute on the population, without the managers having to go to the trouble of handling the banknotes, or dealing with the patients; they just take their cut in a lump sum from the budget. Perhaps the cleverest aspect—from the point of view of the kleptocrats—is that, while the doctors have to raise the money in Ukraine and in hyrvnias, the managers get their cut paid in dollars offshore. The kleptocracy system automatically transports its payments to Moneyland.

"Probably you would be able to do things honestly and profitably in Ukraine, but the system is set up in a way to make it more difficult to do so. If you are establishing a business, you would have a problem with VAT refunds while your competitors get them. If you need land rights, it will take years when others get theirs in weeks. And if you need to protect your rights in the courts and don't pay, this is also an issue," said Oleg Marchenko, a Kiev lawyer whose clients regularly come to him with complaints of corruption. "Being honest is very expensive in Ukraine, that's what I want to say."

With so much hidden behind the shifting screens of offshore, it is difficult to know what is really going on. Marchenko said he knew of a big European pharmaceutical company that had broken ties with its Ukrainian distributors because it feared they were corrupt, taking up with a new Ukrainian partner instead. Marchenko was surprised to discover, however, that the new partner was owned by the same people as the old one, and the realignment had been entirely cosmetic, obscured by shell companies and designed to keep US prosecutors off the big company's track.

One Western investor was happy to discuss the situation providing he was not identified in any way, for fear of falling foul of British and American anti-bribery legislation. He described a situation that was in some ways more convenient than an honest jurisdiction—he appreciated, for example, being able to pay off a policeman instantly if he was caught speeding—but which was also unpredictable and annoying. You never knew if your payoff would be exceeded by that of a rival, so there was no certainty about any official decision. Also, even if you'd paid them off once, they kept coming back for more. "The police, well, you have to have a relationship with them. They ask for money and you have to give it to them or they arrest you. Or the fire service will come and close you down for failing inspection. The secret is to negotiate a low price," he said. "I would not be here, though, if it wasn't a mess. Because it's a mess, people like me, who put up with it, find we can make a decent living."

All of this—but across the whole country; and with names, numbers and details—was the essence of the SBU agent's report in 2008. His conclusions and findings were so controversial that he wrote two reports. One sanitized version was for public consumption. It was still damning, but it lacked data. The second version was solely for the eyes of the government, and it laid out the whole system from beginning to end, naming names and pointing fingers. The agent thought it would be devastating if published widely and so it proved. Someone in government leaked the report to a Soviet-era dissident called Semyon Gluzman, a doctor and president of the Ukrainian Psychiatric Association, and Gluzman leaked it to the press. "I'm happy to criticize the president, the prime minister, I'm happy to do a lot," Gluzman said. "But this, and I'll say it openly, this scared me. I understood that these were bandits without any political beliefs. Their only belief was in money."

Ukrainians were accustomed to bad behavior from their officials, but even the most hardened cynic was appalled by the idea that profits were being made so systematically from the most desperate members of society. Someone named in the report appears to have been appalled, too. On October 16, 2008, an assailant threw a grenade at the SBU agent as he got out of his Honda on Tatarska Street in central Kiev. Shrapnel shredded his car and scarred walls and cars all down the street. The SBU agent survived but needed extensive treatment in an Israeli hospital. "The pharmaceutical mafia ordered the hit," the agent said. "But the investigation was never finished. It was closed, someone paid for that, and so it never led to anything. To this day, with all my contacts and skills, I still don't know who was behind it. It would have been in the interests of any one of the clans that are still working the system."

Anger over healthcare corruption was one aspect of the rage that drove the protests against President Yanukovich. When he finally fled, and a caretaker government was appointed in his place, in February 2014, a leading revolutionary took over as health minister. Oleg Musy, a slim, tanned doctor with a grizzled beard, had led the protesters' medical corps during the months of demonstrations in central Kiev. He was determined to complete the stalled reforms that made so much money for the mafia clans, to fund healthcare properly, and to secure decent treatment for ordinary Ukrainians. It was an ambitious program, but perhaps he was the kind of outsider who might finally force through genuine change.

Finding a time when he could talk to me was difficult, since he worked long hours and rarely took a break, but occasionally he would agree to meet late in the evening at the health ministry, a detached block behind parliament in the center of the city. He would range in his answers over the whole spectrum of corruption in the country, always coming back to the point that a third or more of his ministry's money was being stolen, while ordinary citizens were having to make it up in the cash payments they made to doctors. "This was all very convenient for the previous administration, because it couldn't take money from the budget directly. It needed intermediaries, which the budget would give money to, and who would then pass it on," he explained, during one conversation in the summer of 2014. "There are many people who would like to revive these black, shadowy schemes that previously existed in the health ministry. But I am not allowing them to."

His reform plan was ambitious. He envisaged a health system with total transparency about its spending, in which the state would lose its monopoly over healthcare and be replaced by ordinary people, by non-governmental organizations and by doctors themselves. A system under which the state paid for everything—or, rather, the state supposedly paid for everything but in reality the money was stolen—would be replaced by an insurance system, similar to that in France, with multiple stakeholders and extensive oversight. He had also launched investigations into leading institutions, including the Cancer Institute, and identified millions of dollars in misspent funds, including on expensive equipment that was not being used but instead sat in a basement gathering dust. He had suspended Shchepotin, the institute's director, but was unable to sack him. Under Ukrainian employment law, you could not sack someone who was unwell and Shchepotin had checked into a hospital.

The trouble for Musy was that people did not stop needing hospitals just because he was trying to reform them. While he was attempting to change the way the healthcare system was being run, the system had to keep distributing medicines, and treating people, and maintaining equipment. His task was like trying to rebuild a plane while it was still flying and doing so with the constant opposition of other members of the crew. Within months of his appointment, members of parliament were agitating for his dismissal, and negative stories were appearing in the press. It became increasingly clear that he could not reform the healthcare system on his own, and that the rest of the ministry staff were so implicated in the previous system that either they were not prepared to work with him or he was not prepared to work with them.

By October, seven months into his stint in the ministry, he had failed to arrange for the purchase of medicines. Even allies inside government had turned against him. "It's a real problem," one reform-minded official told me over lunch that autumn. "Who do you want? A patriot but a disastrous manager, or an effective manager with questions hanging over him?"

The official was eating a filled croissant and watching a televised screening of that day's parliamentary session. "We took away Yanukovich and his guys but it's another matter replacing all their schemes. Everyone is ready to carry out reforms, to make everything open, except for things that affect themselves."

The prime minister suspended Musy that October, then appointed a new minister, and suddenly the former revolutionary had all the time in the world to talk to me. He scheduled a meeting in one of the buildings in central Kiev that had been a headquarters for the protesters, and which still had something of their unwashed smell hanging in the air, despite all the months that had passed. In the weeks since his ousting, the ministry had completed most of the purchases that he had refused to undertake. "All the old middlemen, and the old companies, won these tenders. This is what's called the war against corruption," he said with a weary smile. "I fought the old system for seven months. But as soon as I was removed, the old system took its place again. Fighting this system from inside government proved impossible, because there are so few people who really want to do anything about it."

With Musy gone, Shchepotin recovered from his mysterious ailment and returned to work at the Cancer Institute. He repeatedly refused to respond to any questions I sent him, and declined to discuss the allegations made against him by Musy and his own doctors. "I do not want to discuss the themes that you are proposing. They are for me a sign that you are not a serious person. You are interested in rumors, innuendo and the rest of it. This is the business of the yellow press, and I don't give interviews to the yellow press," he said, during our sole conversation, before putting the phone down on me. When I tried to interview him at his office in late 2014, he saw me in the distance and hurried off in the opposite direction.

Sergei Kaplin, however, had a little more luck. A member of Ukraine's parliament, he presented a television program called *People's Prosecutor*, in which he confronted officials accused of corruption and asked them to comment on the allegations. Accompanied by a camera crew, he asked Shchepotin whether it was true that he owned a house worth $2.5 million and a $50,000 watch. Shchepotin denied the allegations, but not before Kaplin noticed he owned a Vertu, a luxury telephone brand whose handsets are handmade in England and which include a concierge button, which can sort out anything you want ("as long as it's legal"), anywhere in the world, twenty-four hours a day. It was certainly an eye-catching possession for a doctor, if not itself proof of anything illegal. Perhaps it was the controversy created by this program that persuaded Musy's replacement in the health ministry to finally replace Shchepotin altogether. In February 2015, his contract as director was not extended, and the minister advertised for a new chief oncologist. It had taken a whole year for a revolutionary government to fire one doctor.

Shchepotin had a parting shot, too. According to Ukrainian officials, he arrived back at work four days after his contract ended and demanded to be allowed to operate, much to the distress of the family members of the patient involved. According to the story he told Russian media, however, the situation was very different. He said he was in the middle of an operation when Semivolos—the doctor who accused him of being unpatriotic in the immediate aftermath of the revolution—and others burst into the operating theater and forced him to leave, despite the risk to the patient's health. Whom to believe? The health ministry? Or a doctor? Or neither of them? As a finale, it made it all but impossible for outsiders to know what was happening. Was the battle for the Cancer Institute really against a corrupt director who had been preying on vulnerable patients, or had it all along been about an honest manager being conspired against by a group of corrupt doctors? The last media reports concerning Shchepotin describe him being offered a job near Moscow, while Semivolos has moved to a private facility in Kiev.

The media squabble over Shchepotin's final day at the Cancer Institute, and the doubts it raised over the motivation of all concerned, were appropriate, because the most corrosive aspect of corruption is the way that it undermines trust. When corruption is widespread, it becomes impossible to know whom to believe, since the money infects every aspect of state and society. Every newspaper article can be criticized as paid for, every politician can be called corrupt, every court decision can be called into question. Charities are set up by oligarchs to lobby for their interests, and those then provoke doubts about every other non-governmental organization. If even doctors are on the take, can you trust their diagnoses? Are they claiming a patient needs treatment only because that would be to their profit? If policemen are crooked, and courts are paid for, are criminals really criminals? Or are they honest people who interfered in criminals' business? Not knowing whom to believe, you retreat into trusting only those closest to you—your oldest friends, and your relatives—and that reinforces the divisions in society that corruption thrives on. It is impossible to build a thriving economy, or a healthy democracy, without a society whose members fundamentally trust each other. If you take that away, you are left with something far darker and more mercenary.

8

NASTY AS A RATTLESNAKE

Frederick Forsyth's 1974 thriller *The Dogs of War* is set in the fictional African republic of Zangaro, which is ruled by a paranoid megalomaniac named Jean Kimba, who has killed everyone in the country with an advanced education and terrorized the rest. The president is, in the words of one of Forsyth's characters, "mad as a hatter, and nasty as a rattlesnake." Zangaro is "corrupt, vicious, brutal. They have seas off the coast rich in fish, but they can't fish ... So the locals have protein deficiency. There aren't enough chickens and goats to go round."

The country is, unbeknownst to the president, home to a mountain containing $10 billion worth of platinum, which is why a crooked British industrialist decides to mount a coup against Kimba and install an equally nasty, but more pliable, puppet in his place. Zangaro is so chaotic that it takes a strike force of just a dozen mercenaries in three inflatable dinghies to seize the presidential palace, kill Kimba, scatter his ragtag army and take control. Along the way, the mercenary leader navigates the creaky but serviceable offshore world of the 1970s, hiding his money in Switzerland and structuring his companies via Luxembourg. *The Dogs of War* is a racy, enjoyable book, perhaps Forsyth's best, and provides a fascinating if fictional glimpse into the early days of Moneyland. But its portrayal of Africa feels awkward to modern sensibilities. Surely this crude parody of an African republic couldn't have borne any resemblance to reality?

Curiously enough, it did. Zangaro was a close copy of Equatorial Guinea, a small West African nation that became independent from Spain in 1968. Forsyth spent time reporting on the conflict in neighboring Biafra, and on the ground in Equatorial Guinea to discover political conditions. He spoke to arms dealers and mercenaries for advice on how to stage a coup. His book is such a perfect blueprint for knocking off a country that there is still speculation, more than four decades after its publication and despite his many denials, that he was part of a group that planned to implement the scheme laid out in the book, and he only wrote it up when the plot was foiled. At the time Forsyth was writing, Equatorial Guinea was ruled by Francisco Macias Nguema, who ran as a nationalist in the country's first (and last) free elections. In photographs he looks every inch the reserved statesman, tie sober with two thin stripes, a pen tucked into his breast pocket. In reality, he was a maniac every bit as bad as Forsyth's fictional Kimba.

The reason there was no fishing was because he'd banned boats, to stop his citizens from fleeing. That did not prevent a third of the population from seeking refuge abroad. He killed tens of thousands of his citizens, declared himself president for life shortly after taking power, banned religion, and promulgated the slogan "There is no God other than Macias Nguema."

He eventually turned on his own family, which provoked his nephew Teodoro Obiang to stage a coup, to sentence him to death 101 times, and to have him executed by a flown-in Moroccan firing squad in 1979. Obiang has ruled the country ever since, making him the world's longest-serving non-royal head of state. He won a new term in office in April 2016, with 94 percent of the 300,000 votes cast. No other candidate gained more than 5,000 votes. "Mismanagement of public funds, credible allegations of high-level corruption and other serious abuses, including torture, arbitrary detention, enforced disappearances, repression of civil society groups and opposition politicians, and unfair trials persist," noted Human Rights Watch in its review of 2017. Equatorial Guinea is one of the bottom ten countries on Freedom House's annual rating of the world, and is not even included in Transparency International's Corruptions Perception Index, because not enough information leaks out for an assessment to be possible.

On the eve of independence from Spain, Equatorial Guinea had been one of the most prosperous countries in Africa, with almost universal literacy, more hospital beds per capita than Spain itself, and healthy crops of both cocoa and coffee. Equatorial Guinea is in short an extreme but sadly not entirely atypical example of how—for so many ex-colonies—the sweetness of freedom can turn sour.

Every ex-colony is different, and those that have turned into impoverished dictatorships all have their own reasons for having done so. Inherent in this process, however, is the very nature of colonies. They were created and run to enrich the colonial power. No matter how honest the officials sent out to administer them, their job remained to extract value from the colony and to send it home. State export agencies, for example, set prices for agricultural products in colonies all across Africa. They were originally created—or were said to have been originally created anyway—to help farmers, but the agencies quickly became a way of squeezing money out of peasants by paying below-market rates for their crops, then reselling the crops abroad for the enrichment of foreigners. The flags flying over the capital cities changed during the 1950s and 1960s, but the decisions taken by those in government often remained remarkably consistent.

After independence, the new governments maintained the export agencies, nominally to raise capital for industrialization, but in reality just to continue the scams, with the surplus being diverted to cronies now, instead of the old Western masters. This is just one of multiple examples of how the new governments quickly learned the old tricks. "The new nations of Africa were born in a moment of hope. It is difficult to recapture the emotional tone of that moment. But the depth of it, the fullness of it, and the promise it offered left its mark on all who were in any way touched by the events of that era. It was called a new dawn, a new birth, a new reawakening," wrote Robert Bates in his 1981 book *Markets and States in Tropical Africa*. "The dreams of that period have given way to disillusion ... Public institutions no longer embody a collective vision, but instead reinforce a pattern of private advantage that may often be socially harmful."

This was not just an African problem. All across the world, countries born in the glorious dawn of nations that was the post–Second World War period went stupendously wrong. Often observers were loath to point it out, perhaps out of the same optimism or foolishness that led people like me to think 1990s Russia was merely suffering from a few growing pains; or perhaps out of fears that criticism would be construed as racist (which indeed it often was). In many cases, foreigners knew about the greed and misgovernance, but did not care about it, provided the individuals involved were reliable supporters of whichever side of the Cold War it was that they favored. Whatever the motivation, this reticence allowed rulers of many of the newly independent colonies to loot their people unhindered.

Sinnathamby Rajatnaram was not someone prepared to let this pass unremarked, however. As one of the group that led Singapore to independence in 1965, he was part of a government that—although authoritarian, and impatient of democracy—insisted on honesty from its civil servants, as well as from its ministers, and oversaw a remarkable economic success as a result. Rajatnaram trained as a lawyer, but, when he was stranded in London during the Second World War, he turned to journalism. He wrote pieces for George Orwell's Indian Section of the BBC and then, after the war, a column (whose name nodded to Orwell) called "I Write as I Please" that was extremely influential in the final days of Britain's presence in Southeast Asia. On November 14, 1968, he was three years into a twenty-five-year stint as Singapore's foreign minister, and made a speech in which he laid out his concerns about the way some fellow ex-colonies were being looted. He may have been thinking of the Philippines, since luxury-loving first lady Imelda Marcos was even then beginning to amass what would become her world-famous shoe collection. As Singapore's chief diplomat, he was careful, however, not to single out anyone in particular and to make clear he was talking about "everywhere and nowhere."

What he described was a gradual degradation in morals, in which the idealism of the first post-independence years had fallen away, and in which ministers and officials had lost the pride they had taken in an almost puritanical lifestyle. Now, he said, politicians were living in a degree of luxury that simply could not be squared with their official salaries, while their wives attended official functions in gowns and jewels that they should not have been able to afford.

Mathematics dictates, declared Rajatnaram, that if a crooked politician is to keep getting richer, he must steal ever more, which will anger his subjects. That means he must buy the support of more and more officials, which will require more money, which will necessitate more theft, and provoke yet more public anger. "He must win over all the instruments of state power—the army, the police, the entrepreneurs, and the bureaucracy. If he must loot then he must allow all his subordinates from the permanent secretary to the office boy to join in the game," he wrote. "In most developing countries, a few years of this kind of freebooting affluence led to economic anarchy, political instability, and the eventual replacement of democracy by civilian or military autocracies."

Rajatnaram rejected then prevalent academic theories that corruption could aid economic development by oiling the wheels of commerce, and ensuring businesses were able to operate with minimal interference. On the contrary, he said, there was nothing beneficial about corruption at all. "A society that is indulgent toward corruption and the successfully corrupt is not, as is often argued, a liberal sophisticated society inspired with a shrewd understanding of human nature," he said, according to the published transcript of his speech. "On the contrary, it is what one sociologist has aptly termed a 'kleptocracy'—a society of the corrupt, for the corrupt, by the corrupt."

The sociologist he referred to was Stanislav Andreski, a widely traveled Pole who founded the sociology department at the University of Reading and wrote *The African Predicament*, which was published a few months before Rajatnaram made his speech. The problem, he wrote, was not only in the extractive nature of the governments of colonies, but in the very structure of the countries, too. Since so many of these new states had been created by European powers with no concern for local political realities, no knowledge of local history, and no curiosity about whether their inhabitants had any sense of belonging to a shared entity, it is hardly surprising that many officials lacked the patriotism necessary to refrain from corruption. These officials felt ties not to their countries, but to their families or their ethnic kin, and they acted accordingly.

"What is regarded as dishonesty in countries well indoctrinated with political ideals, may appear as morally in order in a society where the bonds of kinship are strong and the concept of nationhood remains something very recent and artificial," Andreski wrote. He was one of the first thinkers to realize that corruption is organized as a pyramid, with rulers extracting large sums at the top, while state employees have to take bribes to feed themselves at the bottom. The bribes collected from citizens essentially replace the money the rulers stole, meaning the government has outsourced the collection of its illicit wealth to everyone employed by the government. Andreski did not condemn the low-level officials who participated in the pyramid, recognizing that they had no choice about how they operated in a system designed to force them to act corruptly, but he was clear that corruption is disastrous when it afflicts a whole country, and does nothing but harm to any prospect of equitable or healthy development.

"Graft distorts the whole economy. Important decisions are determined by ulterior motives regardless of consequences to the wider community," he wrote. "The essence of kleptocracy is that the functioning of the organs of authority is determined by the mechanisms of supply and demand rather than the laws and regulations; and a kleptocratic state constitutes a curiously generalised model of laissez-faire economics even if its economy is nominally socialist."

He said that the most accurate reflections of African political reality were often found in novels, rather than textbooks, partly because it was unfashionable to doubt the honesty of the newly independent governments, but mainly because it was hard to write critically about a kleptocratic country without being expelled. He did not single out any particular novelists ("lest this might get them into trouble") but it seems likely he was referring to Chinua Achebe, the Nigerian author whose 1958 masterpiece *Things Fall Apart* established him as one of the most vital writers in the world, let alone Africa. It was Achebe's second novel, *No Longer at Ease*, which appeared in 1960—the same year Nigeria gained its independence—that held the best insights into how hard it was proving for former colonies to build honest political cultures. It centers on a young man called Obi, who is sent to study in England on a scholarship paid for by his neighbors in the town of Umuofia.

When he returns to Nigeria, these neighbors expect him to enter government service and favor their interests, thus providing them with a return on the investment they made in his education. He has other ideas, however, and wants to act as a disinterested bureaucrat who makes all decisions entirely as the law demands. The novel details his—eventually disastrous—attempt to live as an honest man in a crooked system, as well as his observations on the officials, police officers and others whom he sees calmly taking bribes, and favoring the interests of their friends and relatives over that of the state. At one point he ponders, in his rather pompous manner, what would be required to get Nigeria onto the right track. "Where does one begin? With the masses? Educate the masses? Not a chance there. It would take centuries. A handful of men at the top. Or even one man with a vision—an enlightened dictator.

People are scared of the word nowadays. But what kind of democracy can exist side by side with so much corruption and ignorance?" It is a beautifully written case study of the dilemmas that corruption creates. In a dishonest system, it is not only futile to attempt to improve things by acting honestly, but almost certainly counterproductive: you will be punished for it, since you are threatening the business interests of your colleagues.

With independence, things in Nigeria became worse. Officials used their power over the census bureau, or the electoral register, to inflate the number of people supposedly existing. This gave them the power to claim more votes, or to demand more money, in a remarkable orgy of greed. The military staged a coup in 1966, supposedly to return honesty to government, but in reality the corruption accelerated. Any attempts to protest at what was happening would lead to prosecution or harassment, and Achebe himself ended up in exile in the United States after campaigning loudly against the Biafran War.

In 1983 (the year of yet another military coup), he published an essay called "The Trouble with Nigeria," in which he castigated the country's leaders—civilian and military—for their failure to set the example of honest government required to force their underlings to fall into line. Writing after a series of sharp rises in the price of oil earned billions of dollars for his homeland, Achebe lamented that this money, which should have been sufficient to improve the lives of all its inhabitants, had instead simply been stolen.

A moment he witnessed while driving from Nsukka to Ogidi with his wife and daughter became a metaphor for everything he was talking about. They had heard a siren and, along with the other cars on the road, pulled over to allow a police convoy to pass. The convoy consisted of a jeep, a car and a lorry. "From the side of the lorry a policeman was pissing on to the road and the halted traffic," he wrote. "You may not believe it, and I can't say I blame you. Although I clearly saw the fly of his trousers, his sprinkler and the jet of urine, I still would not have believed it if I had not had confirmation in the horrified reaction of other travelers around us."

***

Everywhere that researchers have looked, they see a correlation between corruption and misery. The greater the level of corruption, the more money is earned by the elite, which drives inequality and frays the bonds connecting societies together. In the dry language of economists, money invested in schools and healthcare and roads and safety has a higher multiplier effect—you get a better return for the economy from every dollar you spend—than taking it offshore and spending it on ostrich-leather shoes. Better-governed countries have a higher standard of living, better health, longer life expectancy, improved educational outcomes, and better-performing economies.

Both Rajatnaram and Andreski used the word corruption as well as kleptocracy, and it is clear they did not consider them to be interchangeable. Corruption was something Andreski knew from Poland, where it was called "the socialist handshake," to reflect the passing of banknotes from palm to palm during an unofficial business deal. Kleptocracy, however, was a new phenomenon distinguished by far greater volumes of theft. "Many of them have simply transferred big sums from the Treasury to their private accounts, but the practice of getting cuts on government contracts constitutes the chief fount of illegal gains. In Nigeria, the customary cut is 10 percent, and for this reason the expression 'ten-percenter' is often used to designate anybody active in politics," Andreski wrote.

That volume of money couldn't be hidden under a mattress, or concealed within the hand and passed over during a handshake. Processing these large sums would require banks willing to accept the money, and able to move it around, in a way unavailable to officials in Poland. Andreski was aware that he was witnessing something qualitatively different from previous forms of corruption. What he was seeing, although he did not realize it, was the first flicker of the impact of globalized finance on African society, and the opening of the Moneyland tunnel: steal–hide–spend. Modern communications were unleashing offshore on Nigeria, and Nigeria has never recovered from it.

"We have become so used to talking in millions and billions that we have ceased to have proper respect for the sheer size of such numbers. I sometimes startled my students by telling them it was not yet one million days since Christ was on earth," wrote Achebe. "Nigerians are corrupt because the system under which they live today makes corruption easy and profitable; they will cease to be corrupt when corruption is made difficult and inconvenient."

In the circumstances, it is unsurprising that—by the 1970s already—

development specialists were starting to become concerned about what was happening. Jack Blum, the American lawyer who went on to investigate corporate bribery for the Senate's Foreign Relations Committee and who told me there was no point going to Nevis, was hired as a consultant to draw up an anti-corruption convention for the United Nations. Blum is a clear-sighted observer whose analysis of corruption, kleptocracy and offshore-enabled greed (which we shall come back to shortly) has been of vital importance. He was out of his depth, however, in the political swamp that was the United Nations.

Sitting in a café in Annapolis in 2017, he described how he drew up a twenty-page draft back in 1975, and handed it in to the diplomats. "They took a look at it, and they started laughing, and they said we have to put this in UN language," Blum remembered with a tone of amusement that he presumably did not feel at the time. "There was the Arab bloc, which wanted to have Zionism as corruption; the African bloc, which wanted to have racism as corruption; the Soviet bloc, which wanted to have capitalism as corruption. As you can imagine, this draft convention got nowhere. By the time they finished fiddling with the language, instead of twenty pages, it was ninety-something pages and utterly worthless. It was referred to for years around the UN as the disaster of 1976."

The key problem lay in defining what exactly corruption meant, since for many politicians it isn't a concept with a specific meaning so much as an insult to throw at your enemies. This fluid and non-specific understanding of the word corruption gives us the curious situation where Transparency International can label Somalia the most corrupt country in the world, while Italian mafia expert Roberto Saviano can label Britain the most corrupt country in the world. The first assessment is based on where the bribes are paid, and the second assessment is based on where those bribes are laundered. Both TI and Saviano have a point, since both actions are undeniably corrupt. However, the fact that the term corruption covers such divergent actions as paying a ransom to persuade pirates to release a seized ship, as well as the subsequent use of that money to buy a flat in Knightsbridge, is a sign that the term is so broad as to be almost meaningless.

Trying to analyze what has gone wrong with so many of the world's poorest countries, while relying on a word as imprecise as "corruption," is extremely frustrating. Imagine oncologists at Kiev's Cancer Institute, for example, trying to discuss their trade, but lacking the specific terms—lymphoma, melanoma, carcinoma, leukemia, and so on—that they use to single out specific conditions, and instead having to make do with just the word "cancer." Alternatively, imagine the guests at an English dinner party trying to have a thorough discussion of the weather, if the only term they had to describe the various ways that water can fall from the sky was "precipitation." In both cases, it would clearly be all but impossible to attempt any kind of precise analysis of the nature of the phenomena involved. That specific and detailed vocabulary is lacking for the problems of corruption, which is one reason they remain so poorly understood.

Another reason for our failure to adequately engage with their mechanics is that Westerners often do not realize how rare it is now, or how unique it is in a historical perspective, for anyone to live in an honest and prosperous democracy. Much Western political thought envisages the liberal democracies of the "developed" countries as the natural end point of a historical process, and refers to other societies as "developing," as if they are trains on a track that will eventually deliver them to the terminal station where we now live. The political theorist Francis Fukuyama—who has given up on the idea that history has come to an end—argues in his 2011 book *The Origins of Political Order* that this is a damagingly wrong way of looking at the world. The liberal capitalism of Western Europe, the United States and the other Western countries is not only extremely unusual, but also just one of multiple kinds of government. Corruption, he writes, often emerges where a Western-style state and economic structure have been imposed through ignorance or arrogance onto a society with totally different traditions.

"The failure of Westerners to understand the nature of customary property rights and their embeddedness in kinship groups lies in some measure at the root of many of Africa's current dysfunctions," he wrote. "Europeans deliberately empowered a class of rapacious African Big Men, who could tyrannize their fellow tribesmen in a totally non-traditional way as a consequence of the Europeans' desire to create a system of modern property rights. They thus contributed to the growth of neopatrimonial government after independence."

In essence what this meant was that the ex-colonies gained a dual form of government: kinship-based structures on the one hand, and a European-style state structure on the other. The post-independence rulers were able to use whichever form of government benefited them at any particular time, whether to enrich themselves or to punish their enemies, and to switch back and forth between them as often as they wanted.

For many Westerners, or at least any Westerner with an email account, the most prevalent manifestation of this kind of corruption was perhaps the advanced-fee fraud. This kind of fraud—in which you are asked to give a little money up front, on expectation of a large payoff that never materializes, as in the Las Vegas scam that linked back to 29 Harley Street—has been around for centuries. But it really took off with the arrival of faxes and then email.

The masters of the scam have long been Nigerians, who refer to it as a 419, after the relevant article of the criminal code that it violates. In case there is anyone in the world who hasn't been approached by a 419 fraudster, what happens is you receive an email purporting to be from someone with access to vast amounts of embezzled money, who wants you to help them extract it from Nigeria (or Russia, or Brazil, or wherever; my email spam folder currently contains an offer to send me money purporting to be from a general in Iraq, and another from the FBI). Perhaps the ur-example of the genre claimed to be from Maryam Abacha, the widow of Nigeria's former president Sani Abacha: "I have deposited the sum of $15 million dollars with a security firm abroad whose name is withheld for now until we open communication. I shall be grateful if you could receive this fund into your account for safekeeping," and so on. Enterprising Nigerians sent out millions of these emails and, if any of the recipients fell for the ruse, would ask for small payments before the payoff could be delivered, thus earning them an income before they vanished. There are legends in Lagos of frauds so elaborate that whole office complexes and armies of extras were kitted out, to gull Westerners who flew in and handed over large sums before realizing there never had been any money in the first place. The 419 kingpins made fortunes, while many younger Nigerians earned a decent living from their jobs communicating with the potential victims.

Of course, the scams worked because Nigeria had the image of being—in the words of one writer—"a reservoir of corruption." It is easier to believe that a Nigerian might have access to that kind of cash than, say, a bureaucrat from Scandinavia. But there is also a second reason that the scams were believable, and this one has achieved much less recognition or examination. For the frauds to work, the victim had to accept that it would be quite routine for a Nigerian to trust a Westerner with their crooked cash. Nigerian corruption was widely discussed; Western enabling was not. The unavoidable conclusion of the success of the 419 scams was that everyone who knew about Nigerian corruption also knew—if only subconsciously—about the Western enabling of that corruption: that the stolen money always ended up in Switzerland, London or somewhere similar. And that meant there has long been a widespread, if unrecognized and unexamined, acceptance that Nigerians—or any modern kleptocrats—are not alone in looting their homelands. They have had the enthusiastic collaboration of Western professionals (and officials: bribes paid abroad were tax-deductible in many Western countries until the early years of this millennium).

This is where straightforward corruption takes wings. Modern kleptocracy is not just a question of stealing anything that's not nailed down. It also consists of magicking those assets into the liminal offshore world where laws are negotiable, and the police cannot follow. For the kleptocrat, putting the money you steal into Moneyland means you don't need to worry about ever giving it back.

The economist Robert Klitgaard worked as an economic adviser in Equatorial Guinea for two and half years in the 1980s. Klitgaard is a charming and relaxed guide in his 1990 memoir *Tropical Gangsters*, as often describing his quest for surf on remote bits of the coast or his jam sessions with local musicians as his attempts to impose Washington-style rigor on the local accountants. He describes a country both wrecked and traumatized by Macias' unhinged rule ("Africanists who calibrate such things rate Macias as worse than Uganda's Idi Amin, worse than the Central African Republic's Emperor Bokassa"). The reports he saw indicated that the average person in Equatorial Guinea had seen their income decline more over the previous twenty years than anywhere else in the world.

Some bureaucrats were genuinely trying to create a stable and prosperous country, but the politicians were not. They were venal to an extreme, taking advantage of any proposed reform or improvement to earn money for themselves. When the World Bank sought to restore the cocoa industry, ministers "nationalized" all the best farms; when foreign donors tried to establish a program to supply eggs to an undernourished population, politicians took so many of the chickens that the farm had to shut down.

A repeated theme of Klitgaard's recollections is the contempt shown by the various international development experts and diplomats toward government ministers. A World Bank/IMF official called Gabriela explained her negotiating tactics: "You can't give them an inch or they will sneak away from you. You have to treat them like little children. You must be very strict with them." A Spanish diplomat was even blunter: "These people are just barely out of the jungle, just barely out of the trees." And the American ambassador was essentially resigned to nothing ever improving: "[I]t's like going back hundreds of years. When you talk to them, they may not understand you, or me."

In reality, Equatorial Guinea's rulers appear to have understood far more than they were letting on; they were just playing by different rules. Even before Klitgaard was living in the country, oil prospectors had discovered their first offshore oilfield, and were scouring the seabed for further signs that the abundance of oil in the waters of Nigeria to the north were repeated here, too. By the mid-1990s, significant production was beginning and the money poured in. President Obiang amassed a personal fortune of $600 million, according to *Forbes* magazine, which placed him eighth on a 2006 list of the world's richest kings, queens and dictators, and made him $100 million richer than the British Queen. That isn't bad for a man supposedly unable to grasp the US ambassador's concepts.

His son Teodorin made a fortune of his own, some $110 million of which he shipped to the United States. He was associated with dozens of accounts at Riggs Bank in Washington DC from 1997 onward, which received millions of dollars in deposits. According to a later Senate investigation, he used the money to indulge his passion for buying extremely expensive real estate, cars and luxury goods, as well as for partying and showing his girlfriends a good time. A US Department of Justice memo explained how Teodorin imposed a "revolutionary tax" on timber and other industries, and demanded the money be paid directly to him in cash or to a shell company he controlled.

He employed American lawyers, bankers, real estate agents and escrow agents to move his money around. And if any of his professional advisers questioned the provenance of his money, he had no trouble finding a replacement.

His lawyer Michael Berger created shell companies to allow Teodorin to conceal his identity when buying a Maserati ($137,000), a Ferrari ($332,000), another Ferrari ($280,000), a Lamborghini ($288,000), and another Lamborghini ($330,000), and making out a check to cash for $3.3 million. At one point, Teodorin saw someone running down the street in a pair of "jumping stilts," decided he wanted some, and had Berger create a Paypal account for him in the name of a shell company so he could buy them online. Berger was paid for his services, but also appears to have enjoyed the fringe benefits of the Teodorin account. "Thank you very much for inviting me to the Kandy Halloween party @ The Playboy Mansion and getting me the VIP treatment. I had an awesome time. I met many beautiful women, and I have the photos, email addresses and phone numbers to prove it," Berger wrote in one particularly cringeworthy email to his client.

The point is that Westerners have been not only passive observers of corruption in developing countries, but active enablers of it. It was little more than a decade since development experts had been sneering that the Obiang family was "barely out of the trees," yet here was Teodorin navigating the offshore labyrinth with consummate ease, something he could not have done without the help he received from the likes of Berger. It is lawyers and accountants who guard the tunnel into Moneyland, and they can unlock its doors, and usher anyone able to pay the entrance fee past its gilded threshold.

In many cases, they have been acting in the full knowledge that the money they are handling has been stolen. In the 1990s, Citibank held accounts for kleptocrats from Nigeria, Gabon and elsewhere at its private banking unit (again, we have the Senate's tireless investigations subcommittee to thank for these revelations). The bank's 1997 client profile for Ibrahim and Mohammed Abacha, two sons of the then president of Nigeria (and of the woman who gained enduring fame in the most legendary of all the 419 scams), quite openly stated: "wealth comes from father who accumulated wealth as head of state of major oil producing country." The 1996 file on Omar Bongo, president of Gabon from 1967 to 2009, was even more straightforward: "Source of Wealth: self-made as a result of position. Country is an oil producer." When regulators asked for further information on the source of the millions of dollars that had been flowing through Bongo's accounts, one bank employee wrote: "neither Bill nor I ever asked our client where this money came from. My guess, as well as Bill's, is that the French government/French oil companies (Elf) made 'donations' to him." One bank employee said he was reluctant to ask Bongo where his money came from "for reasons of etiquette and protocol," but other employees made a calculation that the president was receiving around 8.5 percent of Gabon's budget each year for his personal use—something they were apparently absolutely fine with. The Bongo family had accounts with Citibank in Bahrain, Jersey, London, Luxembourg, New York, Paris and Switzerland, sometimes managed in the name of a Bahamian shell company. And the private bank referred to the account, perhaps unsurprisingly, as an "extremely profitable relationship" for Citi.

These Western professionals magic so much money offshore that it is impossible to put a reliable figure on it. In 2000, Oxfam published a groundbreaking report saying that $50 billion was being embezzled each year from the world's poorest countries—a sum then roughly equivalent to the entire aid budget of rich countries sending cash the other way. While Teodorin Obiang was spending incredible sums on fast cars, fast women and flash property, the population of his country was stuck in persistent poverty, with the eleventh-highest HIV rate in the world, as well as high rates of dengue fever, malaria and malnutrition.

It may look obvious that Obiang has broken the law here, but actually that is a more complicated subject than it initially seems. If someone has not been prosecuted, or even investigated, in his home country, then is he a criminal? That is a metaphysical or perhaps a philosophical question, far removed from the practicalities required in a court of law. Certainly it is not grounds for treating someone as guilty. Western legal systems are predicated on the core assumption that individuals are innocent until proven guilty, which causes a problem. If someone can take control of a country's legal system, can use that control to make a fortune, can smuggle that fortune to somewhere where highly paid lawyers are skilled at enforcing the rights of defendants to a fair trial, and can control what evidence might emerge at that trial through his domination of the original country, then how can that person ever be prosecuted? We begin to see what a well-defended place Moneyland is.

In 1999, the IMF's African department produced a fascinating paper called "Institutionalized Corruption and the Kleptocratic State," which analyzed this very problem. It described this modern form of offshore-enabled corruption not as something alien to a political system and preying on it (like a mafia family in New York, say) but the very heart of the system itself: "the natural result of efficient predatory behavior in a lawless world." The authors of the report addressed Andreski's idea of a pyramid of corruption, and described it as being an extremely efficient way of extracting rents from a population. If you can persuade all state employees to work for you (by under-paying them, and thus forcing them to take bribes), then you effectively outsource your own bribe demands and take them hostage at the same time; anyone who speaks out is as guilty as you are, because they're on the take, too. It is not a question of the government running everything, but of the government obliging state employees to levy unofficial taxes on everything, then stashing it somewhere inaccessible. They're offshore bandits.

"The confusion surrounding the term corruption stems from modern societies that have come to take political legitimacy for granted and liberally transpose the term to societies based on wholly different objectives and structures," the paper concludes. "When analyzed in the light of rent-seeking dictatorship, 'corruption' is systemic rather than coincidental."

And increasingly, the system is escaping its borders. Why shouldn't it? After all, its papers are all in order.

9

THE MAN WHO SELLS PASSPORTS

Deep inside the Savoy Hotel in central London is a large room with white and gold walls. Perhaps when the Savoy was built in the nineteenth century, as Britain's first luxury hotel, this room was for dancing, or dining. But now it is for conferences, which is why, in November 2016, it was filled with long ranks of tables at which were sat hundreds of men and women, mostly forty-somethings, mostly white, but with a scattering of Asian and Caribbean faces among them. They were lawyers and other professionals, people who specialized in very wealthy clients, and they had convened to discuss one very specific aspect of their trade.

Just a few moments before, they had been milling around in the corridors and the stairwell outside the conference room, exchanging business cards, making new connections. But now they were silent, facing the stage, upon which a slim, straight-backed man was pacing. Every male member of the audience wore a suit, but the speaker was casually dressed in a navy blazer and brown chinos, with a snow-white shirt open at the neck and a brown and blue handkerchief in his breast pocket. His hair was silvery, its curls held back from his forehead with a product that made them glisten slightly. His name was Christian Kalin, and he was there to tell the audience that they, and their clients, should be terrified.

Their problem, he said, was transparency. The world was turning into the kind of place where wealthy people had to provide details of their wealth to the tax authorities, and borders were becoming as permeable to law enforcement as they had long been to capital. This would be a world where the tunnel into Moneyland was open to everyone, not just the wealthy: a worrying thought. Once bureaucrats had the details of their assets, he posited, who else might be listening in? Criminals, terrorists, corrupt officials? The possibilities were horrific.

"There will be an increase in kidnap and ransom around the world, more identity theft, more hacking of IT systems. Personal security will be a hot topic from Venezuela to England, from South Africa to Vietnam, and from Italy to Mexico," he said, in his clipped Swiss-German accent. The hall was silent, his audience rapt. "I wonder if that's really the world we want. Very unfortunately, I think we do not have a choice. So, wealthy individuals and families, they will have an increasing need to protect themselves."

Judging by the opening of his speech alone, Kalin could have been an arms dealer, the commander of a mercenary army, or someone who builds panic rooms inside the houses of the very rich. How else to explain the silence in which these ranks of well-paid people were listening to him? But Kalin doesn't sell muscle, or armor, or blast-proof doors. He sells something far more valuable: citizenship.

Kalin is the chairman of Henley & Partners, which calls itself—with good reason—the "Global Leader in Residence and Citizenship Planning." Having stunned his audience into fearful silence, he calmed their nerves with a list of the jurisdictions prepared to sell passports to their clients (he prefers the more delicate phrase "citizenship by investment," but the principle is the same). He started with Malta, which had, he said, raised more than €2 billion from its program so far. From there we were off to Cyprus, Montenegro, South America (where a nation was apparently planning to launch a new scheme, although he would not specify which one) and the Caribbean. After each section of his speech he stopped and sang the words "stay tuned," in a curious high-pitched refrain. The first time he said it there were a few titters in the hall; the second time, he raised a full-blown giggle. The final time, the audience was expecting it. They laughed out loud and began to clap.

I had come here for the Global Residence and Citizenship Conference, something Henley has been organizing every year for a decade. Speakers included a top BBC journalist, a former British cabinet minister, and the philosopher Alain de Botton, as well as lawyers, academics, accountants, five Caribbean prime ministers, the president of Malta, at least two ambassadors, and representatives from another half-dozen countries, all looking to persuade rich people to invest in them rather than their peers. Henley likes to call its clients—the people who buy the passports—"global citizens." It bestows a Global Citizen prize once a year, awarded by a panel featuring, among others, the queen of Jordan. In 2015, the medal went to Harald Hoppner, the founder of an organization that rescues migrants left in unseaworthy ships in the Mediterranean. A year later, it went to Dr. Imtiaz Sooliman, a South African philanthropist.

The tone was high-minded, if a little smug, but that is how the attendees appeared to like it. Once Kalin had finished, any remaining concerns about the threat of transparency had fallen away. It was all going to be OK: their clients had plenty of options and they were going to have plenty more. From now on, no rich person need be trapped behind national borders.

"It is very worrying and very unnerving not having the ability to plan one's own future when Great Powers are at war," Dmitry Afanasiev, a leading Russian lawyer who was attending the conference, told me. "And that is the single fundamental risk that our clients are struggling with in their personal and private lives." He said the sanctions imposed on Russia and Russians after the annexation of Crimea had caused great concern to his clients, many of whom had realized that they needed to avoid falling hostage to Vladimir Putin's foreign policy. The way Afanasiev told it, an extra passport was a form of insurance for his clients, since they could never be sure what the Kremlin would do next. It is simply sensible to have a second passport in your safe, so you always have the option of dropping everything, hopping on a plane and getting out. Your money is offshore already and, once you have a new passport, you are effectively offshore yourself, beyond the reach of your home country's law enforcement. "There's a fear of selective prosecution, there's a fear that if you disclose your offshore assets, they come after you, or after your wife, or after your adult children," Afanasiev said. "People are put in an impossibly difficult position where they have to choose between the safety of their families, or breaking the law. And people deal with that stress mostly by leaving."

Henley plays on that concern all the time, and regularly sends out mischievous press releases claiming that it has seen an upsurge in demand for second passports as a result of particular news headlines. Shortly after the 2016 US presidential election, it insisted that "fear over Trump pushes wealthy Americans to look for alternative citizenships." After Britain voted to leave the EU, Henley's in-house magazine warned of the "Argentinasation" of British citizenship, suggesting that perhaps it was time for Brits to look into getting travel documents from Malta or Cyprus so as to maintain their EU rights.

In the Savoy Hotel, the giant conference room led through to an upstairs exhibition center, with a stand for each of the countries selling visas and passports. EU countries touted luxury property developments—"for exceptional seafront living, exclusivity, rarity, and security of investment, ONE is the most sought after address in Cyprus"—and the excellence of their legal systems, in brochures scattered with photos of yachts, restaurants, and smiling middle-aged couples holding hands on beaches, and handed out by attractive young women.

Many of the stands advertised not citizenship, but residency. Wealthy countries, led by Canada, America and Britain, have sold special visas to rich people since the 1980s. The crowds, however, thronged around the stalls advertising passports; their advertising material was just so much more attractive. The Caribbean island of St. Lucia, for example, touted its recently launched passport program—"citizenship has its rewards"—in a booklet that promised blue seas, green hills and fresh fruit delivered to your yacht. I wished I had a yacht.

The different passports cost different amounts of money, and came with different advantages. Henley helpfully published a Citizenship Index, listing how many countries a passport could get you into without a visa: Germany was best; Afghanistan was worst. All of this would be explained to you by a helpful Henley broker, of whom there were dozens in attendance.

After a few hours, the conference became overwhelming. Citizenship is something most people consider intrinsic to who they are, something they are born with, or at least something they inherit from their ancestors. Selling passports and visas as if they're first-class plane tickets feels a bit like selling membership of your family. But that's just the emotion talking. Once you examine the question dispassionately, you realize this is simply another manifestation of offshore. In the same way that countries use their sovereignty to undercut each other on tax rates, they use their sovereignty to undercut each other when attracting wealthy citizens. This is the twenty-first century, after all.

Where there are loopholes, there is Moneyland, and there are professionals making sure that the world's richest people have access to privileges and possibilities denied to everyone else. In some ways, the citizenships and residencies being touted at Henley's conference act like a Moneyland passport, but the passport-for-sale industry did not begin like this. In fact, it did not begin as an industry at all.

It began in 1984, as a three-quarters-crooked wrinkle in a new piece of legislation in the then newly independent Federation of St. Kitts and Nevis. It was here, in St. Kitts' ramshackle capital of Basseterre, that the wheels that ended with Kalin selling passports to the richest people in the world were set in motion. The story of how that happened is a strange one, and proved tricky to research. I think you'll like it.

The islands of St. Kitts and Nevis have a combined population of a little over 50,000 people and, when drawn on a map, resemble a fish swimming to the northwest, away from a tennis ball. Nevis, which we have already visited in this book, is the ball, and the smaller of the two islands. The fish is St. Kitts, home to most of the population as well as the capital, Basseterre. With just 13,000 inhabitants, Basseterre is small, which means walking between the various government buildings is extremely easy. Finding someone willing to talk in any of those government buildings is rather more difficult.

My attempt to uncover the history of the genesis of the world's passport-selling industry began in St. Kitts' Citizenship by Investment Unit, the government body that actually does the trade. No one there was prepared to talk to me, so I tried the governor-general's office, where no one would talk to me either. Next came the prime minister's office, which directed me to the national security ministry, where the receptionist directed me to the cabinet secretary, who put the phone down on me three times before telling me to speak to Valencia Grant in the press office, who had already failed to reply to three emails. I finally got through to her on the phone, at which point Grant refused to talk to me: "I will tell you very clearly, that people are reluctant to talk to journalists. There has been a lot of work, an awful lot of work to improve this program, and they won't want that derailed by gutter journalists." (Considering the kind of dirt that has stuck to this program over the years, being called a gutter journalist was a little galling.)

By now it was clear that, if I wanted to discover anything, I was going to have to do so by myself, and that meant I needed to get into the archives. I found the chief archivist, Victoria O'Flaherty, surrounded by piles of papers and books in an astoundingly messy office. Another dozen or so large boxes full of documents waited outside in the corridor, alongside a large green gas canister. If that looked like chaos, however, it was nothing to what she unveiled when she pulled open the great green fireproof door of the archive proper.

The windowless room beyond was filled with the heavy vanilla smell of old books. It contained ranks of gray steel modular shelving systems, piled with spiral-backed documents, fawn folders with pages spilling out of them, box files, leather tomes, and more. On the floor between the shelves and the door were more boxes full of paper, and a filing cabinet, with long shallow drawers full of cassettes. O'Flaherty was—in marked distinction to anyone else I met who worked for the government—remarkably helpful, but the assistance she could provide was limited by a degree of chronic disorganization the likes of which I have never before seen, and which clearly long predated her time in the role. She explained that there were no transcripts of the parliamentary sessions at which the passport-by-investment law was adopted. The filing cabinet contained recordings of them that I could listen to if I wanted, although I would have to find my own audio equipment, since the archive did not possess any. I went to find a stereo, at which point it transpired that there weren't, in fact, any tapes; they had gone missing, if they ever existed in the first place. There is, in short, no record of parliament's discussion, or any way of knowing precisely why this little country pioneered the passport-for-sale business.

O'Flaherty pointed me toward a nearby auto spare parts shop, whose proprietor—an 84-year-old gentleman called Richard Caines—had been in government when St. Kitts and Nevis achieved independence. That meant he had been part of the contemporary cabinet discussions. She said he had kept his papers from that time, despite her entreaties that he add them to her archive. Perhaps he would let me look at them.

In the back room of Caines' shop were yet more modular shelving units, here piled with tires and light bulbs and other car-related paraphernalia. A battered gray filing cabinet, with each of its three drawers labeled "confidential," contained his old government documents, which he waved me toward with an instruction not to make too much of a mess. The papers were in no particular order, and wrapped up in yellow and pink cardboard folders, each tied with a ribbon. Once I had sorted through them it became clear that the collection was not complete. Caines' minutes of the cabinet meetings had a large gap for the crucial period—1983–84—when the new law was being discussed. The only reference to it came from a meeting on November 16, 1983, when the ministers agreed that a passport should cost each potential investor $50,000 plus a "substantial fee."

"We had persons wanting to come here to do business and we felt that we had to find a way to encourage them," said Caines when I asked him what he could recall. Pressed on how many passports they sold, he said: "I won't be able to remember the number. It certainly wouldn't have been a lot, but it made several differences. One, you were getting an income you would not otherwise have gotten, no question about that. The other part of it is that they were doing some sort of business in order to obtain that level of acceptance in our country. A win/win situation."

But who were these businessmen who bought the passports? What business were they in? Who profited from attracting them? Caines had answers to none of these questions. He did, however, insist that there would be a full set of the cabinet and parliamentary minutes, if not the actual transcripts, somewhere in the government archives. So that took me back to Victoria O'Flaherty, who rang the government's legal department. She listened for a while, asked a few questions, then put the phone down. The department had the documents, but I couldn't get to them.

"No, they are not confidential. It is just that they are in a room that is full of papers, and the corridor to that room is also full of papers. You literally can't get to them," she said, with a rueful smile. She did, however, reveal that she might have a lead for me. We went back through the fireproof door and she carried out two large folders, containing the government's official newspaper collection from 1983 and 1984. I might not be able to find the ministers' and MPs' own words, but I could at least see the reports of them, as described by the journalists of the time.

In the early 1980s, the key political rivalry in St. Kitts and Nevis was between the Labour Party and the People's Action Movement (PAM). Policy differences between the two parties have not tended to be significant, and there is rarely much difference in how they govern, but the personality clashes between their respective leadership groups are profound. Each party had its own newspaper and each newspaper had a diametrically opposed view of almost every major issue. By reading them both, however, it is possible to gain some understanding of the reasons why St. Kitts had decided to put its citizenship up for sale. PAM was in government at independence in 1983, so it pushed the legislative agenda that defined how the new country would address the world, explaining it all through its newspaper *The Democrat*, much of which is full of assaults on its Labour rivals, and party chairman Fitzroy Bryant. For example: "in the kingdom of the blind (that is, Labour) the one-eyed man is king (that is, Bryant) ... Bryant is also exceedingly smug and conceited. Just what he has to be conceited about is hard to tell."

Bryant and his colleagues fired back in the columns of *The Labour Spokesman*, which repeatedly cast its PAM rivals as seeking to sell St. Kitts to foreigners, and to undermine the country's newly acquired independence for their own personal gain. As such, the opposition party focused much of its fire on PAM's citizenship law, and specifically on section 3(5), the clause allowing the government to sell passports. "The Cabinet can peddle St. Kitts-Nevis passports all over the world as they wish—to criminals, drug-pushers, murderers, thieves, traitors, provided they have a few dollars," the paper announced on its front page of February 22, 1984, the day the motion was debated and then approved by parliament.

Three days later, Bryant penned an editorial headlined "For Sale—St Kitts with every man, woman & child in it," which claimed the passport policy was simply the latest in a series of corrupt privatization deals seeking to deny Kittitians their birthright. "Ministers of government are going to make millions of dollars out of their offices to assist international gangsters, on the run from the law of their own countries ... Some PAM trumps living in St. Kitts, New York and elsewhere are going to make millions of dollars out of hawking St. Kitts citizenship and St. Kitts passports in the underworld market."

The same day, *The Democrat* published its own report on the passing of the law, and used it to deny that PAM was depriving any Kittitian of anything, before adding reverse accusations of corruption against its Labour rivals. "The situation is incredible when one realizes that the same Labour Party ... had already printed and hidden masses and masses of Passports for foreigners," it claimed, with pictures on the opposite page of what it insisted were fake passports prepared for sale by the opposition.

All in all, the newspapers cast rather more heat than light, but they did suggest that—on both sides of the political divide—there was the firm belief that corrupt politicians would sell passports to foreign criminals, thus helping them evade the law of their home countries. Despite this worrying prospect, the program went largely unnoticed outside the island, apart from a brief flurry of interest when St. Kitts citizenship was marketed to the Hong Kong Chinese, many of whom were concerned about British plans to return the colony to Beijing's rule in 1997. In this, St. Kitts was not alone. Several small countries adopted its passport-selling idea, including nearby Dominica, Tonga and a couple of others, with an eye on the Hong Kong market. The *South China Morning Post* reported in 1991 that a private company was selling St. Kitts and Nevis passports for $50,500 for an individual, or $96,500 for a family of five, with the documents delivered in just sixty days. "The St. Kitts and Nevis government is ready to consider anybody as long as they have sufficient means, are healthy and law abiding," the businessman involved was quoted as saying.

Despite an advertisement in Hong Kong newspapers pointing out that there was no need to visit St. Kitts to get one's travel documents, the program does not seem to have attracted many takers. "There have been embarrassingly few applications," PAM prime minister Kennedy Simmonds told the same paper a year later. One lawyer who sold a passport was Dwyer Astaphan, a veteran Kittitian media personality. I met him in late 2016 for a chat at a bar at Friars Bay, a beach popular with the locals and largely overlooked by tourists.

Wearing a short-sleeved shirt adorned with lizards batiqued onto a blue background, he looked every inch the Caribbean politician he once was. Back in the 1980s, he sold a passport to an Italian, who wished to keep his trade with the Soviet Union secret from the tax authorities. "He wanted to have a different address, a different jurisdiction," Astaphan told me. "It was just tax avoidance, which is perfectly acceptable. Evasion is not a good thing, but you can always reduce your tax bill without being illegal or unethical."

He said the real brains behind the passport-for-sale project was William "Billy" Herbert, one of the founders of the PAM, whose career proves the wisdom of concerns that corrupt politicians might profit from the sale of passports. But to understand quite how he did that, we need to go back in time a little, and to see how the Brits (mis)managed the divestment of their empire.

It was relatively easy to make many of Britain's Caribbean colonies independent, since they were large, well populated and geographically coherent (say, Guyana or Jamaica). It was harder for the dozens of smaller islands, some of which (like Nevis) had only a small population and would clearly struggle as independent countries. At first, Britain tried to link all of the Caribbean territories into a single unit, but that fell apart thanks to disagreements between the larger islands, which argued over who would host the capital city. Then it tried to link smaller islands together with larger ones to create more viable units. But there were some islands that didn't fit easily into this pattern, above all Anguilla, which was adjacent to the Dutch/French island of Sint Maarten/St. Martin, but annoyingly distant from anywhere British. With a population of only 15,000 or so, it couldn't really be independent on its own, which is why officials in London decided to add it to St. Kitts and Nevis in an ugly three-headed federation, despite there being some sixty miles of water between them.

Back then the island of St. Kitts was ruled by the Labour Party, which was allied to the sugar workers' trade union, and which in turn dominated the federation, by dint of having more people than the other two islands put together. In the early 1960s, Billy Herbert returned from London where he had obtained a PhD in law and offered his services to the Labour government, which turned him away. Together with some friends, he formed the PAM as a new party and they contested their first election in 1966, winning 35 percent of the vote to Labour's 44 percent, but only two seats to Labour's seven. This meant Labour formed the government, despite having won no seats or (according to some reports) not even any votes in Nevis or Anguilla. For Anguillans, this looked very much like they would now be a colony of St. Kitts, which was not something they wanted anything to do with.

They rebelled, rounded up the government's police officers, put them in a boat to St. Kitts and declared independence. The Labour government overreacted, arresting the PAM leaders and putting them on trial (they were acquitted, but this partly explains the bad blood between the two parties). Britain sent in troops and police officers to restore order. They arrived expecting trouble, but were greeted with such enthusiasm that the whole episode turned into something of a farce. (In 1969, the *Daily Express* published a picture by the veteran cartoonist Giles showing a line of male police officers in helmets and uniforms, paddling on a palm tree–shaded beach with local beauties. One of the officers is looking inland where a Navy helicopter is unloading a cargo of women with handbags and overcoats. "When I volunteered for special duties in Anguilla they didn't say anything about sending out wives," he is shown remarking crossly to a colleague.)

It may have been a joke in Britain, but it was serious for the locals; Anguilla and St. Kitts were never reconciled. The existence of two separate jurisdictions with mostly the same legal system is one of those loopholes that Moneyland loves; and it is one that Billy Herbert made a career out of. With his friends and colleagues in government in Basseterre, he enjoyed a dual career as the St. Kitts and Nevis ambassador to the United Nations and as an Anguillan offshore lawyer and banker. That gave him diplomatic immunity, plenty of opportunities to make use of it, and plenty of clients to sell passports to. "He had a reputation," Dwyer Astaphan said sardonically. "He was a person of interest to Scotland Yard."

Don Mitchell is a veteran Anguillan lawyer who knew Herbert well, having worked alongside him for decades. In the 1970s and 1980s, he said, Anguilla had a strange and perhaps unique status as a free port, created by the fact that it had revoked many of the St. Kitts laws without bothering to replace them with anything else. This meant that, while much of the rest of the world had capital controls stopping the free movement of cash between jurisdictions, Anguilla had total freedom. "The banks in Anguilla prospered because of the number of Britons, Americans, Swiss people, not to mention innumerable West Indian businessmen, who flew into Anguilla with suitcases full of currency to deposit," he remembered. "There were no laws, none of the modern thinking that you might be bringing to the table about money laundering or the financing of terrorism. It was a simple banking transaction, privately conducted between a customer and a banker."

He and Herbert had run two of only a half-dozen legal practices on the island, but he said they had been naïve, rather than crooked, and had accepted this cash without really considering where it was coming from. "In those days, cheating the tax collector was almost a civic duty; it was never considered to be a real crime," Mitchell said. "You'd sign whatever they put in front of you, and only much later would you find out that they'd been stealing it, or that it was unlawfully acquired money by all sorts of fraudulent mechanisms." Herbert was at the dirty end of that, Mitchell explained.

One of his clients was Kenneth Rijock. Rijock had served in the US Army in Vietnam. In the late 1970s he got into laundering money for drug smugglers, just when the cocaine boom meant there was plenty of money to launder. It's a story he told in his 2012 memoir *The Laundry Man*, but he changed Herbert's name in the book, meaning no one had previously made the connection between the birth of the passport industry and this remarkable Kittitian lawyer. Rijock is an open-faced man with a big grin and a large handshake. I met him in 2017 in a Starbucks in Key Biscayne, Florida, to talk about his time with Billy Herbert.

Herbert's primary weapon, Rijock explained, was Anguilla's Confidential Relationships Ordinance, a law that made it a crime to even ask who owned a company, making it impossible for foreign law enforcement to glimpse behind the secrecy the British territory's companies afforded. That was a useful law for Rijock's clients, and a very lucrative law for Herbert's legal practice.

"He became pretty much a beacon for anybody that wanted to do anything with dirty money," Rijock said. "I'd first got to go down there with a reference, what we call the secret handshake, because lawyers don't tell other lawyers that they're doing criminal activity without a reference. So, with the legal handshake I go down there and form a bunch of corporations, and then he takes me across the street to the Caribbean Commercial Bank where he's a 10 percent shareholder. He says, you know, open up some corporate accounts, start moving money. That's what I started doing. I started making Learjet trips down there with clients and moving millions of dollars."

Once Herbert had secured the money in his bank, which he owned jointly with the head of the Anguillan government, Rijock used elaborate means to get the money back to North America, sending it to Panama, then to Taiwan, then to the City of London, then to Miami or Canada, where his drug smuggler clients would buy up shopping malls and apartment blocks with money that looked legitimate. "He was extremely successful, very agitated, very focused," Rijock said. "He was bulletproof. He was UN ambassador, he was their version of Henry Kissinger, he couldn't be touched."

And that's where the passports came in. Drug smugglers were worried they could be hunted by the police, so they wanted new identities and new documents. Rijock represented a French cocaine smuggler called Georges, who worked with Colombia's infamous Medellín cartel. Georges returned from Panama with an envelope full of photographs of members of the cartel. "He said, 'Give them St. Kitts economic passports, and give me one, too,'" Rijock remembered. "It wasn't too long after, when I'd already started processing it, and I'd already got the money in escrow, that his whole gang got busted, and Georges fled to China ... There were blanks, people were selling blanks."

Billy Herbert eventually overreached himself. According to the FBI, Herbert helped launder money via Anguillan shell companies for a gang of Boston marijuana smugglers, who then used the proceeds to buy weapons for the IRA to use in its campaign against the United Kingdom. That was going too far. A little dope could be tolerated, but gunrunning crossed the line. A combined UK–US police operation busted Herbert's Anguilla office in 1986 (this same operation eventually jailed Rijock, too), and the Boston smugglers were arrested a few months later.

Herbert resigned as ambassador within days, but was never charged with any crimes, thanks to his diplomatic immunity. He did, however, disappear seven years later after going on a routine Sunday boat trip with his family. Simmonds, who went out on the boat with Herbert many times, insisted this was a simple accident caused by Herbert's complete indifference to safety equipment. Despite that, however, there has been an enduring conspiracy theory that his boat was booby-trapped as retribution for him leading police to the IRA. (An alternative conspiracy theory suggests that he was buried under a swimming pool and his boat sunk as a diversion; another, that he isn't dead at all but faked the accident and moved to Belize, a remarkably dirty Caribbean tax haven that got going around this time.)

"They were supposed to come back to this beach here," said Astaphan, looking out at the steeply shelving sands of Friars Bay, where gentle waves lapped each other in a steady procession.

It was a lovely day, with a light breeze, the kind of steady warmth that attracts people to the Caribbean. A pair of Carib beers sat on the table in front of us, next to a couple of empty bottles. The weather on the day that Herbert disappeared was very different, however, both hazy and windy, with lots of whitecaps on the water; the kind of conditions that severely complicate any search-and-rescue efforts. "They never returned. Father's Day 1994. Scotland Yard came and did an investigation," Astaphan said. The report from the British police revealed little, except that no one wanted to talk to the Scotland Yard officers: a habit that appears to be ingrained in Kittitian public life, perhaps for good reason. Five months after Herbert's disappearance, the island's chief of police was shot dead while on his way to meet his British counterparts.

The association of the likes of Herbert with the St. Kitts passport program helped prevent it from ever emerging from the shadows of the criminal underworld and gaining respectability in the 1980s and 1990s. It may have raised a little money for the government, but no one is sure how much, and it doesn't appear to have been a significant contributor to state finances. Prime Minister Timothy Harris (of a government that includes PAM, although he is from a splinter Labour group) said in 2015 that the government had no idea how many passports it had sold before 2005. Any attempt to find out would be "an onerous task," he said, which I can well believe given the state of the government's archives.

The passport program probably would have remained nothing but a sordid and barely remembered law on the books of a corrupt and generally overlooked country, had it not been for the price of sugar. In 2005, the European Union finally submitted to appeals brought against it by Brazil, Thailand and Australia, which said it was artificially supporting the price of sugar for its own farmers and thus depressing the world market. This, they said, ran counter to trade deals that the Europeans had signed up to. Brussels agreed to reduce its subsidies, which was bad news for many European farmers.

It was even worse news for a group of twenty or so small countries, mostly ex-colonies with links to Britain and France, which had long enjoyed privileged access to the European market. St. Kitts–produced sugar would no longer share in Europe's subsidy regime. The country's most important industry collapsed instantly, and it badly needed to raise some revenue from somewhere else.

At that time there were only three countries that sold passports: Austria, Dominica and St. Kitts and Nevis. Austria's program has always been small, expensive and bespoke, while Dominica, like St. Kitts, had a reputation for selling cheap passports to anyone who wanted them, for the benefit of a few insiders.

Christian Kalin, of Henley & Partners, was looking for something different. He wanted a model that could be scaled up, which could turn a passport into a prestigious commodity, a financial instrument that would appeal to Moneylanders rather than criminals. As the St. Kitts government stared at the imminent prospect of national bankruptcy, he spotted an opportunity. "In St. Kitts at that time, you had . . . a very cumbersome process. It took sometimes three months, and sometimes two years, unpredictable, no proper controls. It was very slack," he told me over tea in a swish west London hotel, while a violinist played tunes by Frankie Valli and the Four Seasons. "We said you need to reform the structure, create a central unit to operate this properly, take it out of the hands of government ministers. And, I have to say, to the credit of the then PM, he saw the point, and the choice was relatively simple."

At the time, people looking to buy a St. Kitts passport could either buy government bonds or invest in a property development. Kalin suggested a third option: give money to the government, which it would put in a transparently managed Sugar Industry Diversification Foundation (SIDF), which would act like a national trust fund. The government would get some money, the investor would feel virtuous, the world community would be satisfied that the money was not being embezzled, and the investor would gain access to a whole new travel document. To satisfy other countries' security concerns, he proposed bringing in private sector companies to do background checks on all the applicants.

"Before 2007, there was basically no due diligence; they just checked Interpol, and that's it," Kalin told me. "For a program to attract serious applicants, the program has to be serious. It's that simple. And the more serious the program, the more successful." The government consented to all of Henley's proposals, and the program took off like a rocket, with sales more or less doubling every year for the best part of a decade.

In 2005, St. Kitts sold 6 passports; in 2006, it sold 19; in 2007, it sold 75; in 2008, it sold 202; in 2009, it sold 229; in 2010, it sold 664; in 2011, it sold 1,098; in 2012, it sold 1,758; in 2013, it sold 2,014. Sales began to flatten out at that level, with 2,329 sold in 2014, and 2,296 in 2015. (These numbers do not include dependents who received passports, alongside the primary applicant, so the real number will be significantly higher.) From half a dozen passports a year before Kalin and Henley got involved, the program was shifting more than 2,000 a year a decade later.

Henley had created something entirely new, and Kalin's intervention was as visionary in its way as the invention of the eurobond in the City of London had been fifty years earlier: he made a passport into something that could be sold off the shelf. The success of the St. Kitts and Nevis Economic Citizenship Program (ECP) changed the way the world works, and it made Henley's name and fortune, thanks to the $20,000 it earned each time someone became a Kittitian.

"The strong ECP inflows in St. Kitts and Nevis have supported economic recovery, improved key macroeconomic balances and boosted bank liquidity," wrote three IMF analysts in a 2015 paper devoted to analyzing the effect of this new iteration of Moneyland. "The fiscal balance has substantially improved to a surplus of about 12 percent of GDP in 2013, notwithstanding an increase in total spending of about two percent of GDP."

This money has built a whole hillside of houses, as well as several hotels and a golf course, in a tourist enclave southeast of Basseterre (across the fish's waist, if you're still picturing St. Kitts as shaped like a fish). And it is helping to fund a whole new settlement at the base of the fish's tail, called Christophe Harbor, which is creating a luxury tourism venue in a previously unpopulated part of the island. The development takes up 1,000 hectares, which is around 6 percent of St. Kitts' total surface area. I was shown around by a sales executive for the project. He had perfect American-white teeth and honey gold skin, and he drove a large black SUV. Not too long ago, the journey would have been an ordeal, but now, thanks to a brand-new road running down the spine of the island, it was easy.

The vegetation of St. Kitts is either astonishingly green where there is water, or scrubby where there is not. And this was a scrubby part, the road winding through a landscape that could almost have been Sicilian. Then the road dipped and revealed the resort, which is truly spectacular. There was once a large circular salt pond at this end of the island, but the developers cut through the narrow belt of land separating it from the ocean, dredged it out, and constructed a superyacht marina. The harbor was not yet finished when I visited, but there was already a yacht moored on the concrete slips, a yacht so large it took me a while to notice it had a helicopter parked above its stern. *Vanish* (its rather inappropriate name) is sixty-six meters long, can accommodate twelve guests and seventeen crew, and can motor from London to Cape Town without filling up with gas. It has two helipads and was launched by a Dutch shipyard in 2016.

"That's a real boat, bro," the sales executive exclaimed. "I do know who owns it, but I won't tell you. You would know some of their connections. But just like most of the rich people in the world, you wouldn't have actually heard of them. The richest people in the world are not actually celebrities; they are financial people who are involved in huge corporations or family businesses. They're super-unassuming and that's what we have specialized in."

Berths in the yacht harbor sell for $1.8–2.8 million, depending on the size. The mud dredged out of the lake has become spits and peninsulas, on which restful-to-the-eye villas sit in the pleasant sunshine. The most expensive building plot is on the market for $8 million, although the average is just a little over a million (building the house itself will cost you another million or three). We drove down into the village, admiring a few of the more delightful properties, and then stopped at the club, where palm trees towered over a thatched-roof bar and an infinity pool overlooked a white beach and the great blue ocean. There are six beaches in the development; a Park Hyatt Hotel was almost finished; a golf course was planned; and there was a laid-back beachfront bar artfully faced in rusty corrugated panels that had once clad the island's sugar-processing factory. That was a nice touch.

Because of the way the St. Kitts Citizenship by Investment program is structured, an investment in real estate of more than $400,000 qualifies you for a passport. Many of the plots have sold to people seeking passports, but not all of them. Christophe Harbor's developer, a highly experienced American called Buddy Darby, has a good name among US clients. Many of them are more attracted by the pleasant nature of the project, and the ease of getting to St. Kitts from the United States, than by any desire for a passport. But beyond the US, the passport is a key attraction. "Russia, they need it; people in the Middle East, they need it," my guide tells me. "We had four from the Asian market: one Japan, one Taiwan, two Chinese. Look, that house is a bit more like it, that's 1,100 square feet." He smiled and waved to a security guard sitting in a glass box looking out onto the road. "This is what people like, gated community, very nice."

On leaving I picked up a brochure for the development. I had seen barely a third of its total surface area, but the scale of the ambition was still stunning. This is the kind of transformational project that perhaps the original architects of the passport-for-sale idea, had they been honest, might have hoped it could achieve. In 1984, when the law was passed, St. Kitts and Nevis was an impoverished country, dependent on sugar, and struggling to compete with the more efficient industries of Brazil and elsewhere. Now, the brochure showed tourists surfing, sailing yachts racing, motor yachts gleaming, slim blond women walking barefoot on white sand, people sitting in the evening sun drinking cocktails and chatting happily.

There is a troubling aspect to the brochure, however, which becomes obvious if you look at it for a little while: there are only two black people in the whole thing. One of them is a male concierge in uniform, and the second is a waitress carrying a tray of drinks. And that ties in with what I saw while being driven around. The only locals in Christophe Harbor are servants: security guards, builders, drivers. The money building the project may be contributing to St. Kitts and supporting the government's budget, but it is doing so by bringing in foreigners with no involvement in the traditional life of the island, no connection to their supposed fellow citizens.

As it happens, this is exactly what the opponents of the passport-for-sale program warned about in 1984. "The obvious intention of the Simmonds government is to sell off the entire Salt Pond peninsula to foreigners," Bryant warned in a column in the Labour Party newspaper back in February 1984, three days after the law passed. "The possibility that the new owners will then build a separate, white State at the peninsula, which native Kittitians will only be able to enter as servants or taxi drivers, is of no concern to the government."

So who were the people who bought these passports, thus helping St. Kitts overcome the problems of a collapsed sugar industry, but also building this foreign-owned enclave on a formerly homogenous island? "The number of investment passports are distributed over 127 countries across all continents, with the Asian and European continents being the most popular," Prime Minister Harris said in 2015. One country had provided 2,272 of the 10,777 primary applicants, he said, but he was not prepared to say which country it was, or to reveal any further information. Other islands with similar passport-for-sale programs have been more transparent. Antigua and Barbuda has published the nationality of all of its applicants. Dominica has committed to publishing its applicants' names (although since the list is found only in the official gazette, which is available only from the government stationers, and even then the list is incomplete, the commitment to transparency is partial). St. Kitts has provided nothing like that level of detail but, judging by what it has released, its program has more or less the same client base as its two Caribbean neighbors: equal parts Chinese, Middle Easterners and residents of the former Soviet Union, with a final quarter made up of everyone else.

Roger Ver, whose success in the world of cryptocurrencies has earned him the nickname "Bitcoin Jesus," was happy to sit down and chat with me about his decision to swap his American passport for a Kittitian one. He has made a fortune out of his website bitcoin.com, and reckons he's 10 to 15 percent more productive now he doesn't have to fill in a US tax return. But he's not exactly a typical applicant, partly because he doesn't believe in passports any-way ("It's a big giant rock in space. Like, if you happen to be born on one part of the rock, you can't go to another part of the rock? That seems kind of crazy to me") but mainly because he's not from China, the Middle East or the former USSR.

More typical is Kamal Shehada, whom I met at a new development be-ing built in Dominica, but who only found time to talk to me in the casino of the Marriott hotel in St. Kitts, while he watched Barcelona play football and drank rum cocktails. He is a civil engineer from Palestine, and his lack of an alternative passport has plagued him all his life. He was born in Gaza, shortly after his parents fled Jerusalem following the declaration of the state of Israel in May 1948. His three older brothers were born in Jerusalem, but are unable to go back there.

When he was a boy, his family moved to Libya, where he grew up and went to university. But then a friend was deemed disloyal by Colonel Muammar Gaddafi, who had taken power in a coup against the king in September 1969, and Shehada had to flee. He ended up in the UK, where he studied for a master's degree, becoming an expert in space frame, the lightweight construction technique used in the roofs of many modern buildings. Dubai was building a new airport, and asked him to help.

"I had a sister there, so I went for three days, and it's now thirty-eight years," he said. "But after thirty-eight years, they can still cancel my residency at any moment. My son, he was born there, but when he reached twenty-one they canceled his visa. He's now of age, he's grown-up, so he has to make a new visa."

Thanks to their newly purchased passports, all these irritations have been done away with. His elder daughter now has a Dominican passport, while the other kids have ones from St. Kitts, giving them advantages the average Palestinian can only dream of: they can travel throughout most of the British Commonwealth and the European Union without trouble. "Having a Palestinian passport, I cannot enter any of the Arab countries even," he said. "Unfairness is everywhere, all over the world. Ninety-nine percent of Palestinians cannot afford a passport ... But I don't feel bad, the fact that I have the money and I bought a passport means I can come and work here and earn more money and use it for these people. I have twenty-five students in Gaza that I sponsor."

That's the power of Moneyland; it allows its wealthy citizens to slough off the ingrained injustices their fellow citizens have to carry around with them, and enjoy a life of freedom and ease. There are now millions of wealthy people from poor countries who can duck out of the messy and slow process of improving the world's unfair visa system, and instead buy their way to instant mobility. It is hardly surprising that other countries have sought to get into this lucrative business. Dominica joined back in 1992, and more recently so have Antigua and Barbuda, St. Lucia and Grenada. In Europe, the Austrian scheme remains small-scale and secretive, but both Malta and Cyprus have launched larger schemes that have brought in hundreds of millions of euros from Russians, Middle Easterners and others. There are so many rich people looking to buy passports that it remains a seller's market. In fact, that's where St. Kitts went wrong. They got greedy.

Kalin declined to discuss why Henley stopped working with St. Kitts, which it did after seven years, but sources on the island said politicians began coveting the money in the SIDF, and dismantling the safeguards built up around it.

In May 2014, the US government's Financial Crimes Enforcement Network (FinCEN) warned that St. Kitts passports were being used to facilitate financial crime, and that Iranian nationals were receiving the passports despite the government in Basseterre insisting that they were not eligible. "As a result of these lax controls, illicit actors, including individuals intending to use the secondary citizenship to evade sanctions, can obtain passports with relative ease," FinCEN stated. In March that year, the US Treasury had sanctioned an Iranian who had obtained St. Kitts citizenship. Another Iranian, Alizera Moghadam, turned up in Canada in later 2013, with a Kittitian passport, leading Canada to cancel visa-free travel for St. Kitts nationals, severely harming the prestige of the program, as well as the interests of ordinary Kittitians.

And the scandals have kept coming. Jho Low, a Malaysian being pursued by the US government for $540 million supposedly defrauded from the 1MDB sovereign wealth fund, has a St. Kitts passport. A St. Kitts passport holder defrauded McGill University Health Center out of $22.5 million in what Canadian police call the country's biggest ever case of corruption (he died before being brought to trial). In 2016, the St. Kitts government had to revoke the passports of a US lawyer and his wife who had paid for their citizenship with funds misappropriated from clients. That same year, the *New York Times* reported that an online scam in Pakistan, which earned hundreds of millions of dollars, was run by a man who had obtained St. Kitts citizenship.

The repeated scandals helped bring down the government of St. Kitts, which is why Harris became prime minister in 2015 and revealed the little information that we have about the identity of the purchasers of St. Kitts passports. His government relaunched the program, with new partners to replace the departed Henley, and new rules in place. But by that stage, St. Kitts was far from the only player on the pitch. Henley now works with Antigua and Malta, as well as a number of the other countries. Passports have become a commodity. In fact, buying a passport is almost a bit boring these days. There is a far more interesting product on the market.

10

"DIPLOMATIC IMMUNITY!"

Christina Estrada is a retired supermodel and, on February 21, 2012, she turned fifty. Her husband, Saudi billionaire Walid al-Juffali, lured her to Abu Dhabi with the promise of a small, intimate party. In reality he had something far bigger planned. He flew in 200 friends on private jets from London, Geneva, Jeddah and Beirut, put them up at a luxury hotel resort on the edge of the Empty Quarter, treated them to an Arabian Nights–themed dinner, and provided multiple activities including quad biking, camel riding and archery over three days.

The birthday party was written up in *Hello!*, the soft-focus British celeb weekly. The magazine's photos show Estrada posing in flowing robes amid the dunes, the billowing waves of the sand echoing the curves of her body, visible through translucent fabric, her feet bare. On the next page, she is shown with a falcon on her wrist, her long legs encased in denim and calf-length boots, her rich dark hair tousled backward. The falconer, a local man in a white robe and embroidered waistcoat, looks on, ready to step in, although she appears to be perfectly relaxed.

The female guests are slim, glossy and expensively dressed, while their menfolk are chunky, sleek and tanned. Al-Juffali himself features in only two pictures, wearing a cravat and a cream dinner jacket with jewel-edged lapels, while his wife cuts into a cake the size of a bathtub.

The magazine's journalist covering the event was British socialite Tamara Beckwith ("I have known Christina for about 15 years and I count her and Walid as very good friends ... as a wedding present, they threw me and Giorgio a magnificent masked ball in Venice, where they own a fifteenth-century palazzo"), so it wasn't exactly hard-hitting journalism. But her article still offers a fascinating and rather sweet glimpse into the married life of the mega-wealthy. "It was incredible that my husband would do this for me," Estrada told Beckwith. "I was singing and dancing for three nights, I had so much energy and was so happy." Apparently she had known her husband was planning something since Christmas, but he didn't reveal any of the details: "he felt it was a big birthday—that life has given us many changes and many chapters so it needed to be celebrated."

In the interview, Estrada explained that she normally lived in Surrey (in a £100 million house whose grounds adjoin the Queen's Windsor Great Park), but in the school holidays they'd take their daughter to Gstaad, or to Venice, or Jeddah, so it was nice to have a chance to see all her friends in one place. "He is like most men in that he doesn't tell me all day, every day how great I am or how good I look," she said of her husband. "But he is absolutely generous to a fault, often bringing me home something he thinks I would like. I think, like many couples, we have a compatibility. So although we support each other, we also have our independence."

The interview and the photos ran in the magazine a month after the party, on March 23, by which point al-Juffali had already married someone else. His marriage to the Lebanese model Loujain Adada took place two days after the party, and his new wife was precisely half the age of his old one. The party planning suddenly doesn't seem so romantic, when you realize he had been secretly wooing another woman the whole time.

Al-Juffali and his new bride celebrated their union that November in Venice. For the ceremony, Adada wore a Karl Lagerfeld–designed white dress, said to have cost $300,000. He wore a simple dark suit with a dark tie. Four bridesmaids supported the dress's train as they processed down the aisle, while the guests snapped pictures on their phones.

At the reception, he wore a military-style uniform, complete with medals clamped all the way down to his stomach, like a South American dictator in the fourth decade of his reign. She was slim and elegant in a Rococo-inspired satin and floral appliqué gown featuring a crystal-strewn fuchsia ruffled-train skirt and a pearl embroidery bodice. A vast feathery headdress finished off the ensemble, and she looked spectacularly beautiful. The bride's necklace alone, according to media estimates, cost $3 million.

Al-Juffali could afford it. His wealth was, according to a later court judgment, immeasurable: "in common with men of his wealth and background, he crosses and re-crosses the world, largely by private jet, staying in properties in various countries owned by, or on his behalf, through elaborate financial structures." His family ran extensive infrastructure projects in Saudi Arabia, and his father had made its fortune by securing partnership deals with Western companies, such as Electrolux, Mercedes, IBM, Siemens and others. Walid took over as chairman of the family firm, E. A. Juffali & Bros, in 1994. Besides the £100 million mansion near Windsor, he also owned a converted church in Knightsbridge, a country retreat in Devon, and property in Saudi Arabia, Switzerland and elsewhere. In a 2005 charity auction he spent almost half a million pounds on two photographs: one of a nude Tamara Mellon; the other of a nude Kate Moss.

As a Muslim from Saudi Arabia, al-Juffali could take up to four wives, but Estrada was not prepared to tolerate that. In August 2013 she demanded a divorce, but they were reconciled after he promised he would get rid of the new girl. She never officially served the divorce papers, which was a mistake.

In December 2013, he flew across the Atlantic to St. Lucia, where he spent two days talking to members of the government. Four months later, St. Lucia appointed him as its ambassador to the International Maritime Organization (IMO), a London-headquartered United Nations body that is responsible for the safety and security of global shipping. The IMO is an important organization, but is not one that St. Lucia, which has a population of 180,000 or so and which became independent from the UK in 1979, had ever taken particularly seriously. Previously, its ambassador in London did this job on top of his usual official duties, and it was not apparently very onerous. Al-Juffali's visa only allowed him to spend 180 days a year in London and he had no maritime expertise of any kind, but neither of those points was deemed an impediment to his new position.

In August 2014, St. Lucia informed Britain's Foreign Office that al-Juffali was its new IMO ambassador and he was duly included in the London Diplomatic List, an official compilation of all the diplomats in the UK. That appears to have been what he was waiting for. The next month, he pronounced the *talaq*, the formulation by which a Muslim man can divorce a woman by repeating the words "I divorce you" thrice, and a month later he informed Estrada that he had done so. He was just in time: in November, the Lebanese model he had promised he would rid himself of, but whom he had instead moved to London and established in a £41 million property on Walton Street, gave birth to their first child, a daughter.

In December, Estrada's lawyers approached him with the first salvos of what looked like being an extremely expensive battle over the division of their family assets. He replied with something entirely unexpected: he was an ambassador, the British law could not touch him, she would get what she was given. He had bought an asset even more valuable than a passport or a visa: safety from the law. He had found a tunnel into the most secure part of Moneyland yet.

"I'm struggling to think of any more cowardly abuse of the mighty institution that is diplomatic immunity," wrote Mark Stephens, a renowned British solicitor and former president of the Commonwealth Lawyers Association, a few months later. "Is the international community really prepared to accept the prospect of wealthy fraudsters and crooks—perhaps the next Bernie Madoff, criminals like drugs kingpin El Chapo or even sponsors of terrorism—skirting around legitimate justice systems simply because they had a diplomatic passport from an impoverished nation?"

It is all very well to lay out the problem like that, but much harder to think of anything that can be done about it. The immunity of diplomats from prosecution is at the foundation of international order. It is what allows ambassadors and their colleagues to be confident they can work freely without being targeted by their host governments. This is not always a good thing, as demonstrated by the 1989 cop/buddy movie *Lethal Weapon 2*. In the film, an apartheid-era South African diplomat laughs at Danny Glover when he busts him in a huge smuggling racket. "Diplomatic immunity," the South African states, holding up his identity papers. In the film, Glover unilaterally "revokes" the South African's diplomatic status by shooting him in the head, but in real life he would have had to let him go. A country can expel another country's representatives, but it cannot otherwise touch them, not least because that would leave its own diplomats vulnerable to retaliatory proceedings elsewhere. The basic principle that al-Juffali was exploiting was that St. Lucia can appoint anyone it likes; that is its sovereign right. And Britain has to respect that; that is its treaty obligation.

Estrada's lawyers asked St. Lucia to consider waiving their ambassador's diplomatic immunity, which is something friendly countries tend to do for each other if their diplomats commit non-political offenses: car accidents; assaults. In November 2015, however, St. Lucia's prime minister, Kenny Anthony, declined to do so. "The Government of St. Lucia has expressed the view to the lawyers of the former wife that this is a civil matter in which it does not desire to get involved," the official statement said. It noted also that it was happy with the work that al-Juffali was doing as ambassador, and that he was going to establish a medical research industry on the island. August and September had, apparently, been packed with meetings with nurses and doctors, and a global diabetes research center would be launched in early 2016. "The government of St. Lucia assures the public that all necessary due diligence was done prior to the appointment of Dr. Juffali and is satisfied that he is eminently suited to perform his diplomatic duties."

The next month, the British government sent the same request, which was rather more serious for the island. It was one thing for St. Lucia to ignore an appeal from a rich woman's lawyers, but quite another to ignore a letter from London. St. Lucia is a Commonwealth country; the British Queen continues to be its head of state and her likeness adorns its currency; St. Lucia has benefited from millions of dollars in British aid in recent years. That didn't matter, however. In a New Year's speech to the nation, Anthony was clear that his mind was made up. "It was not an easy decision to make, given the pressures involved, but we must always seek to do what we believe is right even if we are alone," he intoned. "I am confident, too, that the motives of those who sought to compromise, tarnish and impugn the reputation of this Government and our country will be exposed wherever they may be."

In January 2016, the court hearings began in London over whether al-Juffali's diplomatic status should allow him to avoid paying his wife a divorce settlement. Estrada had four barristers on her team, two of them with the elite Queen's Counsel status. Al-Juffali had retained Mishcon de Reya, the divorce specialists, who had brought in three barristers, two of them also Queen's Counsels. The court sat for five days, hearing arguments on the nature of diplomatic immunity, as well as on the nature of their relationship, including the revelations, firstly, that al-Juffali had never been to a single IMO meeting, and secondly that he was dying of cancer. In the court ruling, al-Juffali is referred to as H (for husband), and Estrada as W (for wife).

"It is clear that since his appointment H has not undertaken **any** duties of **any** kind in the pursuit of functions of office," Justice Hayden remarked in his judgment (the use of bold text is his own). "H has not, in any real sense, taken up his appointment, nor has he discharged any responsibilities in connection with it. It is an entirely artificial construct ... my conclusion seems to fit comfortably with the classic definition of 'sham.' "

Estrada attracted a lot of media attention while in court (*Daily Mail*: "Is this the most glamorous divorcee ever?"), and the judge's decision to uphold her case against al-Juffali gained even more (*Sun*: "Sheikhdown!"). But Justice Hayden's decision to perform the judicial equivalent of Danny Glover's fifty-yard head shot in *Lethal Weapon 2* and unilaterally revoke al-Juffali's diplomatic status panicked the British government. The Foreign Office inserted itself into the appeals process as an "intervener," with another Queen's Counsel and two more barristers besides. The appeal hearing followed in little more than a month, with the government imploring the judges to overturn their colleague's decision. The basic problem was that, if a British court could declare a foreign diplomat's status to be a sham, a foreign court could do the same to a Brit. "The conduct of foreign relations ... could be seriously hampered if the acceptance of accreditation of diplomats and Permanent Representatives was not regarded as conclusive," the government's lawyers argued.

Britain's position was that, although it might be true that al-Juffali's diplomatic status was a sham, and it might be true that Estrada would suffer an injustice as a result, the country's international role required that the sham and the injustice be maintained. And, in her judgment, the appeal court judge agreed: if St. Lucia said al-Juffali was a diplomat, then that's what he was. Sovereignty had been restored.

But al-Juffali couldn't relax just yet. Lady Justice King had a joker to play, which would trump what might otherwise have been a winning hand. A little quirk in the law deemed that a diplomat was only entitled to complete immunity if he arrived in his post after taking it up. If a diplomat was already a permanent resident of the state where he fulfilled his functions before he began fulfilling them, then the immunity only extended to acts undertaken during the exercise of his official functions. It was a technicality, but an eminently useful one. Attempting to stop his ex-wife from getting a fair divorce settlement was clearly not part of al-Juffali's role as ambassador to the International Maritime Organization, and it was clear that—although he had not lived permanently in the UK—all three of his marital homes had been in or around London. The court decided that the fact that he kept his children in Britain meant he had been resident there before 2014, so he lacked immunity. Therefore Estrada could make a claim on his assets, as British law says every wife should be able to. Justice was done, by a whisker.

(Incidentally, there has been no news of St. Lucia's supposed diabetes research center since May 2016. It appears to have died with the appeal.)

It was at this point, when he lost his appeal, that we first hear from al-Juffali himself. His lawyers released a statement in which he said he was sorry that his ex-wife was trying to "tarnish his reputation." He stated that he was paying Estrada a £70,000 a month allowance, as well as their daughter's school fees, and the costs of their ten-bedroom house in Surrey. He had also bought her a $12 million property in Beverly Hills and spent another $3 million adapting it to her satisfaction.

But that was not enough for Estrada. In the discussions over her divorce settlement, she revealed her financial demands on her ex-husband. They included, among other things, an annual allowance of £116,000 for handbags, £46,000 for expenses incurred attending the Wimbledon tennis tournament and Ascot horse races, and £1 million for clothes (including £83,000 for cocktail dresses). Her half-term break in Paris each October would cost £247,000 a year, and four bottles of face cream would add another £9,400. "I am Christina Estrada. I was a top international model. I have lived this life. This is what I am accustomed to," she said.

Ultimately she was awarded £75 million in cash and assets, one of the biggest divorce settlements in British history. Although al-Juffali died in July 2016, complicating her efforts to get hold of it, justice was eventually done.

Or up to a point. Al-Juffali may have tripped at the last hurdle in his bid to gain the ultimate untouchable Moneyland status, but, in doing so, he showed clearly where that last hurdle was to anyone running behind him in the race. His error was to obtain ambassadorial status when he was already present in England. If a billionaire wishes to move to London now, or to New York, or Miami, or any other major Western city, all he needs to do is find a cash-hungry country willing to appoint him as a diplomat before he arrives. If he takes that one simple precaution, he is trouble-free: no one will ever be able to touch him. It's not just divorce he could get away with: he'd be free from prosecution, for any crime.

This scandal was one of many factors that helped doom St. Lucia's prime minister Kenny Anthony, who lost the election to opposition leader Allen Chastanet in June 2016. A few months later I drank tea with Chastanet at the Coal Pit, a pleasant little restaurant on the edge of the water in Castries, the St. Lucian capital, and asked him if his government would consider running the same kind of scheme.

"I can say to you: that stops," he promised, as the mosquitoes whined around us. "We give diplomatic passports, but only for honorary consuls or diplomats who are going to be doing their proper work. The guy didn't attend any meetings, he had nothing to do with the Maritime Organization, so I would like to think that whatever person that we choose, he can withstand scrutiny."

That's good news, of course, but there are almost 200 countries in the world, many of them even more cash-strapped than St. Lucia, and many of them no doubt happy to issue diplomatic papers to someone who can pay them a few million pounds. In fact, they're already doing it. Kazakh oligarch Mukhtar Ablyazov's wife was reported in 2013 to have been living in Italy with a Central African Republic diplomatic passport; former Nigerian oil minister Diezani Alison-Madueke possessed Dominican diplomatic credentials at her arrest in London in October 2015; Chinese billionaire Xiao Jianhua had a diplomatic passport from Antigua and Barbuda when he was abducted in Hong Kong in January 2017.

If there is one thing we know about Moneyland, it is that it keeps mutating, it keeps expanding, and the wealthy keep finding new tunnels down into it. This trade in diplomatic immunity is just the beginning of a business that will have extraordinary consequences for how the world is run and how the world is policed. The diplomatic passport industry, when it really gets going, will make the St. Kitts government's sale of ordinary passports look positively quaint. And that is a worrying thought. If governments are unable to tackle the world's wealthiest people when they commit crimes, then that task will be left to journalists and activists. Moneyland's gatekeepers have thought of this, and taken action accordingly.

11

UN-WRITE-ABOUT-ABLE

In 2014, after Vladimir Putin annexed Crimea and undermined Kiev's control of eastern Ukraine, Western powers began sanctioning officials and businessmen from the two countries. Anyone deemed to have undermined Ukraine's territorial integrity, or to have abused their power to steal the state's assets, had their bank accounts and property frozen in the United States, the European Union, Australia, Japan and their smaller allies.

Many of the individuals and companies on the sanctions lists were well known. Chechnya's thuggish ruler Ramzan Kadyrov, for example, was tangentially inconvenienced by the fact that his thoroughbred horses were barred from prestigious Western competitions, and their winnings frozen. Other individuals had obscured their assets in Moneyland, owning them via shell companies or anonymous bank accounts, making the tracing process very hard. But there is one trick available to the persistent investigator: oligarchs have children. Actual people leave a trace, particularly if they are wealthy and young and like to use social media. Find the children, and you find the money.

One evening in 2014 I found a pair of (grown-up) children whose social media habits allowed me to follow their father's money backward in just this way. The pictures and words these children were putting online gave me insights into their father's assets, his physical location, and the financial tricks he was using. It was an extraordinary case study into how one crook is able to abuse the structures provided in Moneyland to get away with what might almost be called Grand Theft Nation.

Over the course of the next two years, I traveled widely to check every aspect of the story, to make sure I had it completely airtight. I visited the city where his primary asset is based and tracked down two of the shareholders who had lost their stakes in the company to him. I then found the company documents that confirmed the ex-shareholders' stories and spoke to company officials to make sure I had not misinterpreted them. Then I visited two of the jurisdictions that hosted the shell companies that obscured his ownership of the stolen asset, and—thanks to a fortuitous leak—obtained company documents showing how he had responded to his addition to the Western sanctions list by burying his property deeper into Moneyland. I badgered his lawyer, both at her office and her home, until she confirmed their provenance.

The man in question refused to talk to me, but the evidence was utterly convincing: he had stolen a highly profitable company, stashed it offshore, and got away with it, thanks to willing conspirators in Western law firms, accommodating business partners and the lax legal systems of various tax havens.

He had sent his children to live in a Western country shortly after the collapse of the Soviet Union, so they had gained an excellent education in schools the likes of which their compatriots could never have enjoyed. When the children came of age, their father used them as cutouts on his corporate holdings, registering them as the nominal shareholders, even though they were 18-year-olds with no relevant business experience. The older child seemed to lack interest in the family firm, and instead pursued a career as a socialite, hiring a succession of famous Americans to follow them around. Sadly, despite what must have been a substantial outlay on this project, fame did not follow, perhaps because of a lack of talent. Judging by a handful of interviews given to small-circulation celebrity-focused YouTube channels, the child lacked charisma of even the most basic kind.

The second child's career may have been more to their father's liking, since this one came to head a number of companies through which the family empire diversified into commercial real estate, entertainment, finance and transport across Europe and into the Middle East. In partnership with a famous European investor (you might not recognize the investor's name, but you'd know the companies), this second child was expanding the family business empire at great speed, as attested to by boasts on social media about the pace of sales and the speed of construction.

The reason I was so excited by this story was that it encapsulated the Moneyland pathway—steal–hide–spend—in one remarkable whole. It started with an oligarch stealing a fortune; then that fortune being obscured via complicated corporate structures in various jurisdictions; then that fortune being spent in the West as if it were legally acquired, including on celebrities sufficiently famous to grab the attention of the average reader. It was the quintessential example of how legal tricks and stratagems are available only to those rich enough to afford them, right down to the purchasing of residency in the European country in which the children grew up.

When the father was added to one of the Western sanctions lists (there were several updates to the lists in the months and years after the revolution), his assets were supposed to be frozen, yet that did not happen. His obscuring devices were so successful that law enforcement agencies didn't notice that he owned this rapidly expanding business empire, and therefore didn't know it existed. This was one of those moments when an article could make a real difference. Telling stories like this is what makes being a journalist so exciting, and I was delighted when I found a publication happy to publish it.

And then, just days before it was due to be printed and two years of work would pay off, came a highly unwelcome email: "the editor considers the piece, even with legal changes along the lines the lawyer is suggesting, too high a legal risk to publish at the moment." The words "at the moment" were unnecessary. That email meant the story was dead.

I was free, of course, to take it to other publications, and I approached a succession of editors with whom I had previously worked and who I knew would trust the quality of my work. Sadly, however, trying to interest a new editor in a story that has been killed by a lawyer is like trying to interest someone in a dog that has killed its owner. I received a series of polite and sympathetic refusals, until finally I gave up. The story really was dead; the oligarch had got away with it. He and his family had almost no connection to the United Kingdom, yet the simple fear of being sued by them in the British courts led the publication (quite a prestigious one) to jettison a story that revealed how offshore finance and all the Moneyland paraphernalia were neutering Western attempts to impose sanctions on those responsible for undermining Ukraine. It was the kind of infuriating irony that Joseph Heller might have identified if *Catch-22* had been written about today's globalized economy, rather than the US Army in the Second World War: the nature of Moneyland prevents the exposure of the nature of Moneyland.

This is why I have had to tell the story above in such general terms, and leave out any specifics, such as the gender of the children and the location of the stolen company. If I have done it right, it should be impossible for anyone reading this to identify the corrupt oligarch involved, even if they are experts in the area. For this I apologize. I appreciate that it is not polite to tell others that you know a secret and then refuse to say what it is, but I do not wish to be sued into bankruptcy. And this is one aspect of Moneyland's defense mechanism that gets very little attention, partly because we thought it was solved: libel tourism.

Britain became so notorious for allowing rich foreigners with almost no ties to the country to sue foreign journalists for articles that had not even been published in the UK that Parliament changed the laws around defamation in 2013. Before that, billionaires like Russian Boris Berezovsky (who sued *Forbes* magazine in 1997 in a British court, even though only 2,000 copies of its 785,000 worldwide distribution had been sold in the UK) and Saudi citizen Maan al-Sanea had used the UK to settle defamation cases despite having only a minimal connection to the country. In one particularly extreme case, a Tunisian businessman sued the Arabic-language television station Al Arabiya and won: the court accepted jurisdiction because the channel is available on satellite packages in the UK, despite clear evidence that almost no one in Britain watched it.

Under the 2013 reform, claimants were obliged to prove they had suffered harm from the publication, and to show a connection to the UK, before they could win damages. But the reform failed to address a significant problem with the whole structure of defamation law, which is that a Moneylander will always have more money to throw at a speculative case than a publication will have to defend it. This is not a case of publications being censored by overzealous courts, but of publications censoring themselves in a legal process of second-guesswork. It is not that they are scared of losing in court; the risk is of their being bankrupted before they get there. It is impossible to know how many stories—like the one I described above—have failed to appear because of worries over a potential legal action, but I know several other journalists with experiences equivalent to mine. In fact, it's not even the only time it's happened to me.

Shortly after the Ukrainian revolution, a television production company asked me to work on a film about corruption, which would expose the way the country's elite had benefited, while ordinary people had suffered. The film we made focused on a woman called Nina Astaforova-Yatsenko and her daughter Nonna, who suffered from a rare form of hemophilia. Hemophiliacs lack a crucial chemical in their blood, which means it does not clot in the way it is supposed to. This makes them highly vulnerable to nosebleeds, cuts and bruises, as well as liable to bleeding into their joints or their brain, with long-term consequences for their health. It is a nasty genetic condition that was once almost invariably fatal. Happily, it is now easy to control with injections of clotting factor, and it is no longer a major concern for anyone who lives in a developed country with an efficient health system. Sadly, Ukraine is not such a country.

Nonna, when we filmed her, was a 7-year-old girl with a mischievous bounce to her, and a passion for appearing on camera. Nina was the kind of mother anyone would dream of having, and was managing to keep her daughter alive in the most terrible of circumstances while maintaining a sense of humor. Thanks to the corruption that has sucked the money out of Ukraine's hospitals, the clotting factor Nonna needed (and which was her constitutionally guaranteed right) was simply not available, forcing Nina to turn to the black market and to friends.

"We love Ukraine, but somehow, Ukraine doesn't love us," she told us, while stroking Nonna's dark hair off her forehead.

In the film, interviews with Nina and footage of Nonna on a swing were interspersed with the story of a court case that took place in London concerning a bank account belonging to a Ukrainian businessman and ex-government minister called Mykola Zlochevsky. The idea behind the film was to show the complexity of mending a country after it has been comprehensively looted. The Zlochevsky subplot was comparatively minor, and at no point did we suggest he was guilty, but it served as a counterpoint to the emotional weight of seeing a mother trying to keep her daughter alive. Court proceedings drag on, justice is slow, lawyers make money, and ordinary people continue to suffer.

The film had some heavyweight supporters—TED, Sundance, Vice—and was due to be screened for the first time in May 2016, on the eve of an anti-corruption summit hosted by the British government. The screening was to be at the Frontline Club, a private members' institution popular with journalists, on a Monday evening. We released a trailer a few days before, to drum up a little interest. We were pretty excited, to be honest. It was a strong film, making some good points, and hitting at just the right time for the maximum attention and impact. We called it *Bloody Money*.

Then came a letter from Peters & Peters, a London law firm, to Vaughan Smith, who runs the Frontline Club. It was headed "pre-action protocol for defamation—letter of claim" and, even by the standards of letters sent to journalists by the lawyers of wealthy men keen to avoid embarrassment, it was hard-hitting. The lawyers admitted that they had not actually seen the film, but insisted that "it appears to contain false and defamatory allegations about our clients, including that they are criminals guilty of money laundering on a massive scale and that they have acquired their assets at the expense of the lives of others." It warned Smith and the club that, should they go ahead with the screening, then Zlochevsky would have no choice but to pursue it for damages.

"We and specialist defamation counsel have advised our clients that, should you show the film, they will be entitled to bring High Court proceedings against you for libel for an award of substantial damages and an injunction preventing further publication," the letter concluded.

The film was nothing like what the lawyers thought it was, and the word "bloody" in the title was intended as a reference to Nonna's hemophilia, rather than—as the lawyer's letter assumed—an allegation that there was blood on their client's hands. But the letter seriously perturbed Smith, and for good reason. Although Zlochevsky had no reputation in the UK to defend, and his claim should have been inadmissible under the revised 2013 law on defamation, it would still prove expensive to fight. The Frontline Club is a charity and, although it is committed to free speech as part of its mission, it cannot afford to get into protracted legal battles with multimillionaires. The club would have won, but that victory would have been worse than Pyrrhic; long before legal vindication arrived, the club would have run out of money and been forced to shut down. The screening was canceled and, as it turned out, the letter terrified pretty much everyone else, too: the film has never been shown. The story that Nina and Nonna spent so long telling us has never been revealed. Instead, that Monday of the canceled premiere, I had to sit through the real-life anxiety dream of telling a room full of people about a film I wasn't allowed to show them.

But if that was disappointing for me, imagine how Professor Karen Dawisha must have felt in March 2014 when she received a letter from Cambridge University Press (CUP), the publisher of her previous seven books, about her latest manuscript. She had written an academically rigorous and fascinating investigation into the links between Vladimir Putin and organized crime. The manuscript reached back even beyond the earliest days of Putin's time in the St. Petersburg city administration, and connected him forensically to the mafia clans that divided up Russia in the immediate post-communist years. It was particularly important since many of the insiders mentioned in the book were—at precisely that time—being included on those same sanctions lists as the oligarch I mentioned at the beginning of this chapter.

Nevertheless, CUP decided not to publish the book. "The decision has nothing to do with the quality of your research or your scholarly credibility," the company's executive publisher John Haslam wrote to her (according to copies of the letters that she provided to the *Economist*). "It's simply a question of our risk tolerance in light of our limited resources."

Haslam explained that the nature of English libel law obliged the writer and publisher to prove the truth of what they were saying, which would be extremely difficult, adding that this was one reason why English courts are so favored by the world's rich. He pointed out—in almost exactly the same words as I was told in legal comments about my article about the oligarch— that since Putin and his associates had never been convicted of a crime, it was impossible to say whether the allegations were true or not. This is one of the most frustrating aspects of trying to research and write about the activities that underpin Moneyland. The reason that Putin has not been convicted for any of the crimes that Dawisha describes is that the Russian legal system is corrupt and politically controlled, not that Putin is honest. Russian courts would no more convict Putin of committing a crime than the Chicago mob would have condemned Al Capone. But nonetheless, many of these people cannot be written about until they have been convicted, at which point they will have fallen from political grace and will no longer be in a position to commit the crimes.

"We believe the risk is high that those implicated in the premise of the book—that Putin has a close circle of criminal oligarchs at his disposal and has spent his career cultivating this circle—would be motivated to sue and could afford to do so," wrote Haslam, before unloading the really dispiriting legal payload. "Even if the Press was ultimately successful in defending such a lawsuit, the disruption and expense would be more than we could afford, given our charitable and academic mission."

Dawisha, who is American, sought and found a US publisher instead, and her book, entitled *Putin's Kleptocracy: Who Owns Russia?*, was published by Simon & Schuster in September 2014, to justifiably excellent reviews. But her response to CUP deserves quoting, since it is full of concern about how wealthy foreigners are able to abuse the British legal system to stifle debate about the origins of their fortunes. She laid out how Russian insiders (in common with other wealthy foreigners) were investing heavily in British real estate, settling their legal disputes in British courts, sending their children to study in British schools, and yet British people were barred from knowing where their money came from. "The real issue is the rather disturbing conclusion that no matter what was done, the book would not have been publishable because of its subject matter," she wrote. "We can only hope that British libel laws will indeed be 'modernized' and thoroughly tested so many authors can once again turn to CUP with the knowledge that it is indeed devoted to publishing 'all manner of books' and not just those that won't awaken the ire of corrupt Russian oligarchs out to make a further mockery of British institutions."

The nature of this threat prevents it from being public knowledge. Naturally, we are unable to read things that people are not allowed to publish, and often people only become aware of the problem when they themselves get caught up in it. Robert Barrington, executive director of the British chapter of Transparency International (TI-UK), is one such example. Under his direction, TI-UK has become significantly more outspoken and has published groundbreaking reports into the penetration of dirty money into British property, British visas and more. It was one of these reports that provoked a firm letter in early 2015.

"I was sitting here at my desk one day; a courier arrives with this letter and, you know, it felt like I'd been kicked in the stomach by a horse, like the whole edifice was going to come crashing down. Even if we'd won, we couldn't have afforded it," he told me. Could he tell me the name of the wealthy person the lawyers were working for? "I think, under the terms of our settlement I'm not allowed to. So that gives you a sense of what a chilling effect it has on a group like TI."

Transparency International has chapters all over the world, and he said even his overseas colleagues are not safe from the reach of British libel complaints. One chapter wanted to launch a report in London, since they felt it would have international resonance and wanted to attract media attention. That plan was scrapped after an oligarch's law firm somehow found out about it, and they decided to move the launch to Geneva. "But then we were informed by this very aggressive law firm, including if we put it on our website, that they were going to sue us," he said. "It is a real problem, actually. These people are bullies, and they're using London law firms to bully for them. They want to protect their reputations that they have built up over a number of years, putting a positive gloss on people who are doing very bad things."

This remains largely a British problem. American publications are protected by the free speech provisions of the US Constitution, which prevents these speculative libel cases from being brought in the first place. Indeed, in 2008, the state of New York passed a law making foreign defamation judgments unenforceable on US soil, if the jurisdiction in question lacks free speech protection equivalent to the First Amendment. That was a direct response to Khalid Bin Mahfouz, a Saudi businessman who sued or threatened to sue thirty-six times in British courts when journalists accused him of funding terrorists, notably against the American author Rachel Ehrenfeld (some twenty-three copies of her 2003 book *Funding Evil* had been sold in the UK, so a British court accepted jurisdiction). The law was welcomed at the time, but it does not give the protection you might hope for against the preemptive self-censorship caused by the fear of having to defend against a case. An editor from one major American publication, which has a worldwide presence and a significant readership in the UK, told me that it essentially followed British libel law to avoid expensive unpleasantness.

And US publications are also aware of the expense involved in defending a defamation case, even if it's thrown out at the first opportunity. When I tried to take the story about the oligarch and his free-spending children to a

US publication, its lawyers came back with the same response I'd heard in the UK. "The salient issue is: will an oligarch spend lots of money to go after you and Oliver if he or she feels insulted? Our experience tells us the answer is yes," the lawyer wrote in his advice to the editor. "As can be inferred from the article, the oligarch is quite resourceful, and one of the ways of retaliation could be hindering your future activities in geographic regions where the oligarch has his influence." The editor, having been keen, reluctantly sent me and my story on our way.

This isn't just worrying because you, the reader, don't get to find out what's going on in the world—though that would be concerning enough. It's also a problem because media reports are an enduring source for criminal investigations. Police officers around the world rely on journalists to alert them to suspicious behavior and, when journalists are silenced, that denies law enforcement agencies the information they need. And that leads to another unfortunate feedback loop: journalists struggle to make accusations of wrongdoing against wealthy litigious people if those people haven't been convicted of a crime, while police officers don't know anything wrong is happening, because journalists can't write about it, so those people don't get convicted of a crime. Private investigatory agencies also rely on the media for information when asked to check someone's background—for example, if that person has applied for a passport in a place like Malta—so this system of soft censorship hampers their work as well.

There is a whole industry in the UK of PR agencies, law firms and consultancies that maintains this loop, by creating reputations for wealthy foreigners so as to give them the protective force field that the British courts can provide. One employee of this industry agreed to meet me in 2016 at a central London pub, which was thronged with City workers having boozy lunches after long mornings at their screens, and to lay out the secrets of his business so long as I kept lining up the pints. The employee asked not to be identified in any way, or to have any of his clients and ex-clients mentioned, which was entirely understandable when he started describing the people he had worked for.

There is, he said, an established pathway for rich foreigners to take when they wish to launder their reputations in the UK. They start by buying property, somewhere large and impressive where they can host expansive dinners for important people, and they hire a PR agency. The PR agency puts them in touch with biddable members of Parliament, either MPs or lords, or often both, who are prepared to put their names to the billionaire's charitable foundation. The foundation then launches itself at a fashionable London event space—a gallery is ideal—and promises to do something uncontroversial: educate children; promote cultural understanding; support sports among people with little access to facilities. An alternative is to fund an all-party parliamentary group linked to their home country, which brings with it the possibility of taking politicians to a foreign capital, away from the prurient eyes of the British tabloid press, where they can be treated to the goodies their hard work has earned.

That's not enough, though. The billionaire needs to establish a connection of some kind, particularly if he's still in business in his home country. If he owns a gas company, then the PR advisers will push hard on energy security, boost him as an independent supplier of the vital resources that the West needs. If he has interests in agriculture, that's an easy one: food security is crucial to any country, and providing enduring sources of cheap, good-quality food is vital. There's always a connection that can be made, and once that has been done, he can host conferences to which he can invite famous ex-politicians. Perhaps a minor royal will agree to head some appropriately named organization. There are a lot of minor royals out there, and many of them are surprisingly short of cash.

Ideally, the billionaire wants to get his name on an institution, or become so closely associated with one that it may as well be. What institution that is depends on the billionaire's personal tastes: football clubs are popular, and good fun places to entertain influential friends. Endowing a university is also a favorite: Oxford, Cambridge and the London colleges are all aware that they have less cash than their American rivals, and have been consistently happy to ignore warnings about the origins of a donor's money if the check is large enough. This kind of upscale philanthropy then opens the door to parties full of the real A-listers: senior members of the royal family, cabinet ministers. Perhaps the billionaire can invite some of these people to stay on his superyacht? Hospitality is given, and that creates useful webs of obligation that begin to really embed the billionaire into his adopted home.

"There are two aims. The first is to make him too famous to kill. He's probably from somewhere pretty ropy, right? Somewhere violent, perhaps the government will come after him. It's happened. But if he's a famous philanthropist"—here he made air quotes around the word "philanthropist" (he was on to his third pint)—"then it adds an air of protection around him, a shield. There aren't many dictators who want to knock off someone who hangs out with the British government, right? That's aim one, to make him unkillable. The second one is to make him un-write-about-able. You try writing about one of my clients, seriously, we'd take you to the fucking cleaners."

So what happens when someone ignores the fear of being sued and presses ahead with publication regardless? The fund manager turned campaigner Bill Browder has shown us, and it isn't reassuring.

Browder is a wealthy US-born British citizen who moved to Russia in the mid-1990s, convinced that it was the best place in the world to make his fortune. So it proved. For anyone who knew him in Moscow in the early 2000s, he was an energetic fund manager famous for three things: always having time for journalists; accusing Russian companies of entrenched corruption; and defending the record of President Putin. The justification for the first two aspects of his approach was straightforward and rather elegant: if the companies cleaned up their corruption, then they would become more valuable, and his fund's shares would rise in price, thus making a profit. He made time for journalists because he wanted his allegations to be spread as broadly as possible. It was a little harder to understand why he was always so keen to defend Putin, particularly after Putin began jailing political enemies in rigged judicial proceedings. It may be that Browder just took a little longer than most to realize that Putin was not as devoted to the rule of law as he claimed to be. ("I naively thought that Putin was acting in the national interest and was genuinely trying to clean up Russia," is the way Browder explained it in his 2015 memoir, *Red Notice*.)

Then, in 2005, Browder was barred from entering Russia. That did not stop his fund from making a large profit on the liberalization of trading in Gazprom shares (which had previously been restricted), but it was a clear sign that trouble was on its way, so he pulled his money out. A group of corrupt police officers then took over the (now empty) companies through which he had traded, faked the accounts and claimed back the huge $230 million tax bill he had paid, keeping the proceeds. Browder could have ignored this, since the money was stolen from the Russian budget rather than from him, but he isn't the kind of person who ignores things. He asked his law firm to investigate, and they assigned an auditor called Sergei Magnitsky to the task.

Magnitsky forensically uncovered the full details of the fraud. Then police officers arrested him, held him in detention, and denied him medical attention until he died, on November 16, 2009. It was a grotesque example of police officers abusing their powers, and Browder has put the quest for justice at the heart of the second half of his life. He has campaigned ceaselessly for the culprits to be barred from traveling to the West (and succeeded; there are "Magnitsky laws" in both Canada and the United States, which do precisely this), and kept the crime at the forefront of public consciousness with all the publicity skills he previously employed in the service of his investment fund.

Among his efforts has been a series of films released onto the internet explaining the nature of the crimes that were committed. And the films accused, among others, Pavel Karpov, an investigating officer at the Moscow police at the time of the crime, and subsequently part of the Interior Ministry's investigative committee. According to the films, Karpov was a key figure in the conspiracy that defrauded the Russian budget, then harassed Magnitsky until he died.

In 2012, Karpov hired a PR agency and started legal proceedings against Browder in London through the legal firm Olswang, claiming substantial damages. Browder's response was typically combative. Via his lawyers, he told Olswang that he welcomed "the opportunity to engage with your client in relation to his role in these matters and the source of the funds which he uses to support his extravagant lifestyle (and expensive legal representation)." And so the case proceeded to the High Court, where it was heard over two days in July 2013, with both sides represented by two barristers, each team including a Queen's Counsel.

It would have been an expensive experience for a wealthy businessman, not to mention for an ordinary Russian policeman, and the source of Karpov's funds was investigated by the court, which declared itself satisfied that a friend had agreed to lend him the money for the case. The court did not, however, uphold Karpov's complaint, ruling that he had no connection to the United Kingdom and thus that the judge had no jurisdiction. It was a landmark case in the battle against libel tourism, and is often now cited by media lawyers.

The follow-up to it is less well remarked, however. Far from being a sign that British courts will prevent speculative libel cases from being used to bully people trying to investigate corruption into silence, it is a confirmation of the very concerns that CUP showed in relation to Karen Dawisha's book, or the Frontline Club showed in relation to my film about Ukraine. Karpov, having failed in his court case against Browder, was then ordered to pay the former fund manager's costs—some £850,000, of which only a fraction had been placed in an escrow account. Karpov simply vanished, leaving the bill unpaid, and Browder £660,000 out of pocket.

The British legal system has tried to wrestle the money out of Karpov: a judge ordered him to be jailed for three months in September 2016, and a warrant was issued for his arrest in May 2017. But this won't worry the Russian as long as he stays at home. Russian institutions have consistently defended Magnitsky's tormentors, rather than pursue those who committed the crime he revealed. A Russian court convicted Browder in his absence and, in 2013, Magnitsky himself was found guilty of tax evasion, despite being dead and thus—by all normal standards of justice—outside earthly jurisdiction. In short, there is no prospect of Browder wringing justice out of Russia, or getting his money back. On the contrary, he faces near ceaseless legal assaults.

"If I hadn't built a sizable personal wealth before this happened, I would never have been able to defend myself against any of this stuff," Browder told me in the conference room of his offices in central London in 2017. "When we got the cost order against him, he disappeared and there's nothing we can do. There's an arrest warrant in the UK for him, for contempt of court, but it's not international. And it's not a very demanding arrest warrant; it's just that the court doesn't want people to be in contempt."

This was only one front in the global legal assault that Karpov and other Russian officials have fought against Browder, who somehow—despite it all—remains as ebullient a man as he was back in 2003, when all he had to complain about was mismanagement at Gazprom.

"If you look at it more broadly, all of the strengths of our system, the adversarial legal system, the democracy system, the freedom of speech system, they try to abuse in every way possible. Wherever there are openings in liberal democracies, they'll try to abuse those openings," he said. Money crosses borders, laws do not, and Moneyland protects its own.

Few campaigners, and few media outlets, could be like Browder and cover a loss of £660,000, on top of the ongoing costs of multiple legal procedures in other jurisdictions. So they choose to be cautious about what they publish, even if they are sure of the truth of their statements. This means that a letter from a London libel specialist remains a useful tool for anyone looking to shut down discussion of the origin of their funds, whether or not there is any British connection. The industry described to me in the London pub does its job very well indeed.

12

DARK MATTER

There are a lot of estimates of how much cash disappears down the tunnel into Moneyland every year. The International Monetary Fund estimates that between two and five cents out of every dollar earned worldwide is illegal, which could come to as much as $2.6 trillion annually. The analysts from Global Financial Integrity, meanwhile, estimated that the world's total illicit financial flows in 2013 came to $1.1 trillion, and that total was growing rapidly. These numbers are just guesses, though, really, as can be seen by the number of zeros at the end of them ($1.1 trillion, written out in full, is $1,100,000,000,000), and even then they don't capture the full extent of the situation.

Because the money in Moneyland isn't just drug money, or stolen money, or bribes; if it was, the problem would be much easier to solve. All of that "bad evil" money is washing around with "bad naughty" money, which has dodged taxes, or regulations, and been stashed offshore to avoid detection. There's also money that has flowed out of economies like Russia, China or Venezuela that isn't the fruit of a misdeed of any kind, but is instead owned by people who fear that the government might take it away from them if they kept it at home. And this "flight capital" adds a whole new dimension to the amount of cash we're talking about. According to one estimate, some $2.5 trillion fled China in the decade to 2017, despite the increasingly onerous capital controls erected by the government.

Often this flight capital is hidden, visible only in what are called the "errors & omissions" (E&O) in government figures, the entry that statisticians add to the columns of numbers to make them add up. Analysts from Deutsche Bank made the discovery when they looked at British investment figures and realized that the E&O number was consistently positive over time. If this was a genuinely random statistical artifact, then E&O should have been negative as often as it was positive. The fact that it wasn't, however, suggested there was something suspicious going on.

Published in 2015, the report—entitled "Dark Matter," because no one can resist astronomy metaphors when confronted by a problem this big—looked at Britain, New Zealand and Sweden, and picked up huge movements of money that had avoided official detection. In the British case, some £133 billion had entered the economy since the mid-1970s, without anyone noticing, with £96 billion of that in the last decade. (The rate is accelerating, with current inflows totaling around a billion pounds a *month*.) Russian money appeared to make up around half of this total, with the rest sourced from elsewhere in the world, although even this was a guess, since the analysts were relying on discrepancies that could be masked by the far higher legal flows of capital. Sweden, meanwhile, has the opposite problem, and has leaked 1.5 trillion Swedish krona (around $180 billion) since the late 1980s, when the country abandoned capital controls and wealthy Swedes tried to reduce their exposure to their homeland's high taxes. ("This means that Sweden's national statisticians underestimate Swedish foreign wealth by 100 percent," the report said.)

If it is so hard to find accurate figures for the flows of money into and out of advanced economies, then it will be harder still to estimate global totals, since that would require relying on figures produced by less-well-resourced statistics agencies, as well as somehow circumventing the reticence of tax havens, which don't like to reveal the inner workings of their financial systems even to their own statisticians. Lawyers seeking to find stolen money in Moneyland, to confiscate it, and to return it to its true owners are like fishermen trying to catch eels in a dark tank, without knowing how many eels there are to be caught, or if they are fishing in the right tank in the first place.

There have been some successes in the global battle against the most egregious Moneylanders. Switzerland returned $800 million to Nigeria, which had been stolen by Sani Abacha and his family; and $600 million to the Philippines, after the collapse of the Marcos regime. But even here the silver lining has a cloud. In 2014, the European statelet of Liechtenstein followed the Swiss lead and returned $227 million that had been stolen by Abacha's son (almost two decades after the former president's death, and only after the

Nigerians promised that the Abacha family would be immune from prosecution if they dropped a swath of European lawsuits that were holding up the repatriation). A year later, Nigeria had failed to account for the money, leading to concerns that it had been stolen once more, and stashed straight back in the offshore labyrinth from which it had been extracted.

The United States' case against the rulers of Equatorial Guinea was almost as tortuous as the European cases against the ex-rulers of Nigeria. The Department of Justice pursued civil cases against assets belonging to the Obiangs, who had accumulated—among other things—a large collection of pop souvenirs. This gave rise to the court case *United States* v. *One White Crystal-Covered "Bad" Tour Glove and Other Michael Jackson Memorabilia.* The property the government was seeking to confiscate also included the jacket worn by the King of Pop in the "Thriller" video, several life-size statues from the Neverland Ranch, a Gulfstream jet, a mansion in Malibu, and various supercars, all to a total value of $70 million. A judge threw out the Department of Justice's first case, saying its lawyers had failed to prove Teodoro Obiang had broken the law, but allowed them to return with a new attempt (this time it was called *United States* v. *One Michael Jackson Signed Thriller Jacket and Other Michael Jackson Memorabilia*), which eventually forced the Obiang family to settle the case for $30 million. They got to keep the Gulfstream, and appear to have successfully smuggled the glove out of the country.

It was a victory, but only a partial one. Obiang was not convicted, despite the extraordinary discrepancy between his annual salary of less than $100,000 and his luxurious lifestyle, largely because the US lawyers lacked cooperation from officials in his home country. And, having confiscated the money, the US officials had to think of something to do with it, since they could hardly return it to the government they had just seized it from. Eventually, the Department of Justice decided to give most of the money to a charitable foundation to be used for the benefit of the people of Equatorial Guinea. That was in 2014. There have been no updates on how exactly it plans to do this.

It appeared to be basing its plan on a scheme launched in Kazakhstan after Swiss courts froze $84 million from bank accounts controlled by President Nursultan Nazarbayev. After about a decade of haggling, the countries involved agreed to hand the money over to a charitable foundation, which would use the money for the benefit of ordinary citizens of Kazakhstan. It funded vaccinations, education, social services, scholarships and more, in what proved to be a remarkably successful program, but one that would perhaps be hard to replicate. Part of the reason is that Kazakhstan isn't that much of a dictatorship or too enormously corrupt by the standards of the former Soviet Union, so it is possible to pay money to individuals and organizations that aren't controlled by the government. And the other part of the reason is that $84 million (plus the $12 million of accumulated interest) isn't that much money, and can be spent without too much trouble on worthy causes, in such a large country. Asset recovery cases related to Uzbekistan and Nigeria have generated much more money, and the countries are far more crooked, so there are many more difficulties in finding worthy recipients.

Howard Sharp is a British lawyer who previously served as solicitor-general in Jersey, which has belatedly woken up to the need to combat corruption, and has become surprisingly good at it. He successfully prosecuted a top-level Kenyan corruption case in February 2016, in which crooked officials had used a Jersey company—Windward Trading Limited—to stash bribes extorted from local companies. Having secured the forfeiture of the assets, Sharp attempted to extradite the suspects, including Kenyan ex–energy minister Chrysanthus Okemo. And there he ran into trouble, including from populist politicians accusing him of essentially trying to re-impose British rule on its former colony.

"Some of the times I've been in the court in Kenya, in the magistrate's court of the extradition proceedings, they would, somebody would, hire gangs of youths to appear in court and threaten me with violence. And I'd be called a white colonialist and all this," he told me. Officials in Kenya appeared to think the money was right where it should be—in the West. They had no intention of losing control of it in the Kenyan budget, where someone else might get hold of it, and didn't want him to succeed in his asset recovery case. He said he had seen similar obstruction from Nigerian and Brazilian officials. "It's a repeated pattern you get with these corruption cases. Normally, the victim country doesn't want the money back, will try anything to stop you successfully prosecuting whoever's responsible, and will generally be quite difficult about everything."

All in all it is hard to find money that has slipped into Moneyland, difficult to confiscate it, and extremely onerous to return it to its original owners. This is probably why countries like Switzerland, Britain and the United States have such a terrible record at doing so, despite the examples listed above (and other countries are even worse). World Bank figures suggest that the wealthiest countries returned only $423.5 million in the six years to 2012. Even if the smallest estimate for the amount of money stolen and stashed in Moneyland is correct—that is, $20 billion a year—that means less than a half a cent for every stolen dollar was recovered and returned to its original owners. If the amount of money stolen was as high as Global Financial Integrity estimated, then the return rate is less than a cent for every $1,000 stolen.

Karen Greenaway is supervisory special agent at the FBI's International Corruption Unit. In 2016 she described to me an early case she had worked on where a foreign official was stealing money from his country's treasury in pretty much the crudest way imaginable. "There was no way in hell that I was going to ever get the evidence out of the country where the guy who was writing checks to himself was. And in fact the guy had the evidence blown up. Literally," she said. "It was a paper crime. When the paper got blown up, that was me pretty much done." She laughed.

As with almost all the troubling aspects of Moneyland, this near impossibility of retrieving assets once they have vanished offshore is driven by the basic rule that money can travel where it wishes, while law enforcement stops at a country's borders.

"It's an outgrowth of this whole financial system that allows you to transfer money with a touch of a button," Greenaway said. "The start of the crime is the bribe paid, or the start of the crime is the fraud in the country committed by the government official through procurement of something, or whatever. So part of the challenge of doing these cases right at the outset is somehow we have to have access to the evidence, and either have it through a cooperative partner or have it through some other methodology of getting it."

The solution involves greater international cooperation, to try to allow information about suspicious money transfers to flow to law enforcement agencies as quickly and easily as the money moves. And this is why, shortly after the Ukrainian revolution unseated Viktor Yanukovich, politicians from dozens of Western countries convened in London to brainstorm how they could more efficiently find the money the ex-insiders had stolen and return it as quickly as possible, for the good of ordinary Ukrainians.

Dozens of countries sent representatives to the summit, from the United States and the United Kingdom down to the tiniest tax havens: Bermuda, Monaco, the Isle of Man. It is a mark of the seriousness of the summit that, although it was held in the UK, it was co-hosted by the United States. The world's two leading financial powers were getting together to cajole the rest of the world into cleaning up.

"We now know that, worldwide, the cross-border flow of proceeds from criminal activity, including corruption, has been estimated to be as great as $1.6 trillion per year," said the US attorney general, Eric Holder, adding a fresh entry to the list of guesses on the volume of dirty money sloshing around the world. "Corruption often serves as a gateway crime, paving the way for money laundering, transnational organized crime, and in some cases even terrorism. It's no exaggeration to say that it undermines the fundamental promise of democracy and legitimate self-rule. It siphons precious resources away from those in need. It imperils development, security, stability, and faith in financial markets. And it profoundly weakens that which is the basis of the desired modern society—the rule of law."

The summit lasted two days, with attendees swapping business cards and generally agreeing with each other that things would be different this time; that the asset recovery process had taken far too long in the past. On the final afternoon, they received a welcome boost from Britain's then attorney general, Dominic Grieve, QC, who made a dramatic announcement: the UK had already joined the fight. A transfer had been flagged as suspicious, and British authorities had frozen the accounts involved and initiated a money-laundering investigation.

"This week the UK's Serious Fraud Office (SFO) announced that it is investigating allegations of corruption linked to the Yanukovich regime and has obtained a court order to restrain assets valued at approximately $23 million," Grieve told the assembled delegates. "There will be no effective deterrent for corruption while levels of detection of illicit financial flows and recovery of misappropriated assets remain small."

If the frozen $23 million was indeed linked to corruption in Ukraine, it would still be only a fraction of what Yanukovich and his associates had been accused of embezzling. The new authorities estimated the country's loss over the previous three years at $100 billion (again, that's a lot of zeros). But the case was intended to send a message—about the West's determination to make sure Ukraine could regain what had been stolen, and that its looters be punished. This pleasingly specific number, $23 million, dominated headlines from the summit, where it was held up as concrete proof that the rulers of the West were finally helping the rest of the world fight corruption.

"The message is clear," Home Secretary Theresa May said. "We are making it harder than ever for corrupt regimes or individuals around the world to move, hide and profit from the proceeds of their crime."

The UK government trumpeted the freezing of the $23 million for two reasons. First, it was meant to be the initial installment of the many billions that would eventually help to rebuild Ukraine. If that sum could be confiscated and returned, perhaps so too could the hundreds of millions stashed in London, Latvia, Luxembourg, Liechtenstein and elsewhere. Second, the successful prosecution of a regime insider would send a message to the world's kleptocrats: your money isn't safe in London anymore. As it turned out, the message it sent was precisely the opposite one.

The $23 million was held in bank accounts at BNP Paribas belonging to two companies, which were in turn controlled by a Ukrainian politician named Mykola Zlochevsky. A large man with a shaved head, Zlochevsky wears boxy suits, dislikes fastening the top button of his shirt, and has been a fixture of Ukraine's public life for two decades. In 2013, according to the Ukrainian news weekly *Focus*, which almost certainly understated his fortune, he was Ukraine's 86th richest man, worth $146 million.

In 2010, after Yanukovich won election as president, Zlochevsky became natural resources minister. That position gave him oversight of all energy companies operating in Ukraine, including the country's largest independent gas company, Burisma. The potential for a conflict of interests should have been clear, because Zlochevsky himself controlled Burisma. But there was no public outcry about this, because almost no one in Ukraine knew about it. Zlochevsky owned his businesses via Cyprus, a favored haven for assets unobtrusively controlled by high-ranking officials in the Yanukovich administration.

This is the case that would have featured in the film that was squashed after Peters & Peters bullied the Frontline Club with threats of defamation proceedings. In that letter, Zlochevsky's lawyers insisted that he had never benefited personally from the decisions that he took while in office. "Mr. Zlochevsky has followed the letter and spirit of the law in his role as civil servant and has, at all times, held himself to the highest moral and ethical standards in his business dealings and public functions," the letter said. "Our clients have fallen victim to an entrenched and a cynical program of smear campaigns and misinformation." It continued: "Mr. Zlochevsky's wealth is not a result of corruption or criminal conduct. He made his wealth before entering office."

It is true that Zlochevsky was a wealthy man before 2010, but then his public life did not begin in 2010. Burisma's website makes clear that the periods when it has performed best have consistently coincided with the high points in its owner's political career. During a previous Yanukovich government, in 2003–5, Zlochevsky chaired the State Committee for Natural Resources, and companies under his control won licenses to explore for oil. Then Yanukovich fell from grace, and the new government tried to strip Zlochevsky's companies of their oil exploration rights—and he had to sue the government in order to keep them. Yanukovich won the presidency in 2010, Zlochevsky became a minister, and the good times returned: Burisma gained nine production licenses and its annual production rose sevenfold. After the revolution, Zlochevsky left the administration.

According to a court judgment from January 2015, the $23 million in the account that had been frozen in London was the proceeds of the sale of an oil storage facility, which Zlochevsky had owned via a shell company in the British Virgin Islands. The money arrived in London from Latvia, a minimally regulated Eastern European country where banks are famously welcoming toward money from the former Soviet Union.

On April 14, 2014, Zlochevsky's accounts were frozen at a special court hearing in London requested by the Serious Fraud Office. As described in the later court judgment, the SFO argued that "there were reasonable grounds to believe that the defendant had engaged in criminal conduct in Ukraine and the funds in the BNP account were believed to be the proceeds of such criminal conduct." The SFO investigator Richard Gould claimed in the April 2014 court hearing that Zlochevsky's dual position in Ukraine as both a politician and a businessman gave "rise to a clear inference of a willful and dishonest exploitation of a direct conflict of interest by a man holding an important public office such as to amount to an abuse of the public's trust in him."

The SFO further argued that "the complicated pattern of offshore holding companies established when he was still a serving minister was effectively to conceal his beneficial ownership of Burisma," which it deemed inherently suspicious.

By May 20, 2014, Gould had obtained 6,170 electronic documents from BNP Paribas related to Zlochevsky's money, and assembled a special team to examine them. Now he needed evidence from Ukraine, so he wrote to the head of the international department of the general prosecutors' office, Vitaly Kasko, in Kiev.

A lean man with a sharp chin and a luxuriant head of black hair, Kasko had been invited into the prosecutor's office after the revolution, and was made responsible for negotiations with all the Western countries that had promised to help at the London summit. He was hopeful that his colleagues would see the importance of regaining the $23 million and thus do all they could to help the SFO. He told me in 2016 that he translated the British request, sent it to his boss, and awaited results. "The investigation began but, no matter how much we pushed the investigators, it was not effective," Kasko said. Even when Zlochevsky's lawyers announced they would contest the freezing of the $23 million in a London court, the Ukrainian prosecutors still failed to send the SFO the evidence it needed to maintain the freezing order. "First the British wrote to me, then the Americans, with questions about what was happening with the investigation," Kasko remembered.

There had been many cynics who doubted that the London summit would usher in a new age of international cooperation, but most of them had imagined that any foot-dragging would have come from tax havens like the British Virgin Islands, not from the country that stood to benefit from the case moving ahead. It was bizarre that it was Ukraine that was delaying this case, and that it was US and British diplomats who were begging Ukraine to investigate, but that's how dysfunctional Ukraine had become. Eventually, six months after Gould first wrote to him, Kasko went to his boss in the prosecutor's office to demand action.

"I said I wanted this to be investigated properly, that the Brits be told about it, and they get what they wanted," recalled Kasko. "He said, 'If you want, get on with it.'" That was enough for Kasko, who formed a team and forced investigators to work evenings and weekends until they had assembled a dossier of evidence that Kasko felt supported the SFO's argument "that the defendant's assets were the product of criminal wrongdoing when he held public office." They sent it to the SFO, and in December 2014 announced officially that Zlochevsky was suspected of a criminal offense in Ukraine.

It was only thanks to Kasko that the SFO had received any useful documents from Ukraine at all. "I asked the Brits, 'What else do we need to do?'" Kasko remembered. "And they said: 'That's fine, that's more than enough to defend the freezing order in court.'"

Their confidence was misplaced. In January 2015, Mr. Justice Nicholas Blake, sitting in the Old Bailey, rejected the SFO's argument. "The case remains a matter of conjecture and suspicion," he wrote in his judgment. To confiscate assets, prosecutors have to prove that the frozen money related to a specific crime. This, he ruled, the SFO had failed to do. It was a humiliating reverse for British law enforcement, and for Gould, the lead investigator, who then moved to another agency. (Gould told me in July 2015 that he was "personally disappointed," but declined to comment further.) The judge unfroze the $23 million and handed it back to Zlochevsky.

The British government had made a big announcement of the original decision to seize the funds, but did not publicize this reversal. It is not hard to understand why. This was an embarrassing setback in a case that was supposed to herald a new age. When I contacted the SFO in May 2015, a spokeswoman told me: "We are disappointed we were not provided with the evidence by authorities in the Ukraine necessary to keep this restraint order in place," but declined to comment further because she said the investigation was ongoing. I contacted Dominic Grieve, who had made the dramatic announcement of the asset freezing. He is still an MP, but no longer in the government, and he told me he remembered nothing about it.

Zlochevsky's lawyers at Peters & Peters told me that the judge had "ruled unequivocally that there were not reasonable grounds to allege that our client had benefited from any criminal conduct." Burisma's lawyers have since repeatedly referred to the ruling as evidence of their client's vindication, which calls into question the decision of the UK government to use this particular case as an example of its determination to recover assets and return them to Ukraine, when it had been unable to prove that there were sufficient grounds to keep the $23 million frozen.

When Kasko read the judge's ruling, he had questions, but of a rather different nature. At the hearing, the tycoon's lawyers had not just attacked the case against their client, but also produced evidence of his innocence— evidence that came from the unlikeliest of sources. Justice Blake's twenty-one-page judgment made reference half a dozen times to a letter, dated December 2, 2014, signed by someone in the Ukrainian prosecutor's office, which stated baldly that Zlochevsky was not suspected of any crimes at all.

Kasko felt this was peculiar. Everyone in a senior position at the prosecutor's office must have known he was leading a frenzied investigation into Zlochevsky at that precise time, so how could anyone have signed off a letter saying that no investigation was going on? The letter appeared to be crucial to the judge's ruling, which stated that Zlochevsky "was never named as a suspect for embezzlement or indeed any other offense, let alone one related to the exercise of improper influence in the grant of exploration and production licenses."

As Kasko saw it, his colleagues had failed to help him when he begged them to investigate Zlochevsky. But when it came to writing a letter to help the tycoon, he believed they had happily done so. According to Kasko, there were really only three possible reasons for why a senior Ukrainian prosecutor would have written a letter for Zlochevsky rather than assisting Kasko. He was either incompetent, corrupt or both. Peters & Peters did not respond to specific questions I put to them about the letter ("the allegations implied by your questions . . . are untrue and entirely without foundation") but, whatever the explanation for it, the case highlighted a crucial flaw in countries' efforts to cooperate across borders. Even in the rare cases when the UK does freeze a foreign official's property, it is dependent for evidence from colleagues abroad who usually have fewer resources, less training and a decades-long tradition of institutionalized corruption. That means that any misconduct or incompetence by the Ukrainian prosecutors can undermine a case in the UK as surely as if the same actions were committed by the SFO.

After the scandal, Ukraine brought in David Sakvarelidze, an ethnic

Georgian, as first deputy general prosecutor to clean up the law enforcement system. Progress was slow, however. In fact, it was so slow that the US ambassador to Ukraine, Geoffrey Pyatt, decided to force the pace in a decidedly non-diplomatic manner. In September 2015, speaking in the southern Ukrainian city of Odessa, Pyatt stated that prosecutors "were asked by the UK to send documents supporting the seizure" of the $23 million, but "instead sent letters to Zlochevsky's attorneys attesting there was no case against him." "Those responsible for subverting the case by authorizing those letters should—at a minimum—be summarily terminated," he said.

The allegation was part of a long and damning speech, in which he laid out just how little Ukraine had reformed its law enforcement bodies. Ukraine's national finances were almost entirely dependent on the International Monetary Fund, where the dominant voice belongs to the United States. Pyatt was not just any ambassador, therefore, but the local representative of the government's paymaster. He was putting Ukraine on notice—sort out the prosecutor's office, because America is getting annoyed. But it didn't work. Rival prosecutors opened criminal cases against two of Kasko's investigators, and their allies in other institutions. "Sadly, the protection racket we uncovered ... turned out to be just the tip of the iceberg," Sakvarelidze wrote on Facebook in October 2015.

By then, almost two years had passed since the revolution and many Ukrainians had become disillusioned. The credibility of the United States was not helped by the news that, since May 2014, Vice President Joe Biden's son Hunter had been on the board of directors of Burisma, Zlochevsky's company. The White House insisted the position was a private matter for Hunter Biden, and unrelated to his father's job, but that is not how anyone I spoke to in Ukraine interpreted it. Hunter Biden is an undistinguished corporate lawyer with no previous Ukraine experience. Why then would a Ukrainian tycoon hire him?

Hunter Biden failed to reply to questions I sent him, but he told the *Wall Street Journal* in December 2015 that he had joined Burisma "to strengthen corporate governance and transparency at a company working to advance energy security." That was not an explanation that many people found reassuring. The *Washington Post* was particularly damning: "The appointment of the vice president's son to a Ukrainian oil board looks nepotistic at best, nefarious at worst," it wrote, shortly after Hunter Biden's appointment. "You have to wonder how big the salary has to be to put US soft power at risk like this. Pretty big, we'd imagine."

In September 2016, a court in Kiev canceled the arrest warrant against Zlochevsky, ruling that prosecutors had failed to make any progress in their investigation. That same month, the Latvian media reported that Ukraine had not helped a police investigation into money laundering, so 50 million frozen euros had passed into the Latvian state budget instead of being returned to Ukraine.

Zlochevsky was not the only former Ukrainian official to have assets frozen abroad. As part of Western assistance to the new Ukrainian government, European countries blocked the assets of Yanukovich and a couple of dozen others. The asset freeze was intended to give Ukrainian prosecutors time to investigate and prosecute, and thus prevent the individuals involved from burying assets in their favorite tax havens. The totals involved—around $300 million or so in cash and property—could buy a lot of medicine and build a lot of roads.

Britain's SFO, in evidence it submitted to a parliamentary committee in 2017, said the obstacles put in its path by offshore jurisdictions were a key cause of the failure of cases against wealthy Moneylanders. "Top tier defendants are highly sophisticated and operate internationally. They are likely to be acutely aware of those jurisdictions with an environment that is favorable to them, and from which it is very difficult (and in some cases impossible) to either trace, benefit or recover assets," the SFO said. "Such defendants are also likely to be astute in their use of financial products and other devices which they use to disguise their economic benefit from any crime."

The spirit of cooperation of the London summit has long since dissipated, and insider after insider has fallen off the sanctions list imposed by the European Union. Ukrainian prosecutors—held back by incompetence, or corruption, or both—have failed to advance criminal cases against the leading figures of the old regimes, while the insiders' British and French lawyers have fought hard to have their assets released, with remarkable success. As each wealthy Moneylander drops off the sanctions list, they regain control of their assets, and the Ukrainian people lose the chance to even make the case for regaining control of the money.

In fact, the insiders may end up the richer, judging by promises by their lawyers to seek damages for the inconvenience they have suffered. "The imposition of these sanctions has caused our client significant distress and reputational damage and has had a devastating effect on his business interests. Our client welcomes today's decision and intends to aggressively pursue damages for the harm these sanctions have caused," the law firm Gherson said after its client, the Ukrainian businessman Yuri Ivanyushchenko, was removed from the sanctions list in early 2017.

It was a dispiriting time to be a Ukrainian revolutionary, but Kasko had long gone by then. He resigned in February 2016, accusing the prosecutor's office of being a "hotbed of corruption." Sakvarelidze was sacked a month later and changed with a "gross violation of the rules of prosecutorial ethics." The whole reforming team came and went, without jailing anyone or recovering a single oligarch's foreign fortunes. Kasko told me he had resigned because he saw no point in waiting around impotently while his superiors undermined his cases. "I didn't want to stay there like the Queen of England and watch," he said. "The biggest problem in the prosecutor's office is corruption. Sakvarelidze and I went in to fight against it, and they threw us out."

This was not the first time that the world's leading powers had got together determined to help the post-revolutionary regime of a state looted by its rulers, only to find it far harder than they anticipated. After the Arab uprisings that began in 2010, a forum on asset recovery was convened to allow the new governments to share experience. It met in 2012, then again in 2013, 2014 and 2015. At that point, the attendees appear to have had the same realization as those trying to help Ukraine, and the forum quietly lapsed. The effort had begun well, in 2012, when the British government helped a Libyan team reclaim ownership of a £10 million house that belonged to the son of Muammar Gaddafi. "Libya's recovery of the mansion may be just one step in Libya's fight against impunity, but a first step is how every journey begins," wrote Mark Vlasic, a professor at Georgetown University who previously headed the secretariat at the World Bank's StAR initiative. In fact, this first step turned out to be how the journey ended; further cases have not materialized.

Asset recovery is hard. Moneyland does not give up its riches easily, the money piles up faster than you can count it, and it keeps moving around the world, sliding across frontiers; one, two, three, a million steps ahead of the people supposed to monitor it. Justice keeps bumping into national borders and, when that happens, it's not just thieves who escape unpunished.

13

"NUCLEAR DEATH IS KNOCKING YOUR DOOR"

In the small hours of November 3, 2006, an ambulance crew attended a house on Osier Crescent, a secluded residential street in the Muswell Hill district of north London. The ambulance's log shows that it moved fast, receiving the call at 1:49 a.m., and arriving at Osier Crescent just seven minutes later. The speed does not appear to have been a sign of urgency, however. It may well have simply been a quiet night, since the callout was routine.

"Patient thinks he has food poisoning. Two hours after eating yesterday evening he began vomiting, and today he has diarrhea," Julia Cole of the ambulance crew noted in her record of the attendance (I have expanded abbreviations throughout this chapter, to make the medical notes comprehensible). "Not wanting to go to hospital. Just wanted some advice from us." The patient's name was Edwin Carter, he was forty-three years old, and his wife was with him. A final note on the callout record perhaps reflects Mrs. Carter's concerns: "to ring 999 if worried," although the rest of the sentence is illegible.

They rang 999 again the next afternoon, bringing a new ambulance crew to 140 Osier Crescent. These paramedics clearly felt Mr. Carter's symptoms had been going on for too long; they drove him the five miles to Barnet Hospital, where a doctor took a look at him and made a preliminary diagnosis: gastroenteritis and dehydration. At the bottom of the scribbled page are the few details the doctor solicited about Carter's life: "past medical history: NIL. Self-employed writer, lives with wife and son." The doctors were sufficiently concerned about Carter's dehydration to admit him to hospital, but clearly didn't expect him to be there long. He was Category C; in the hospital's private ranking of the seriousness of their patients' condition, they had assigned him to the lowest level.

Should the doctors have been more worried about Mr. Carter? There were certainly signs that he wasn't all that he seemed. Why, if he lived permanently in Muswell Hill, did he tell the ambulance crew that his family doctor was "in Russia," for example? And why, as Cole had asked him when that first ambulance attended his house, if he had such a quintessentially English name, did he sound so very Russian? But these were tiny details only picked up later. Any doctor will tell you that the guiding mantra for dealing with newly arrived patients is that common things are common. If you see hoofprints, think horses, not zebras; if you see an otherwise healthy man vomiting and suffering from diarrhea, think gastroenteritis, not assassination ordered at the highest levels of a foreign government.

The next morning, Carter was started on ciprofloxacin, an antibiotic that would combat any nasty bugs that were upsetting his stomach. That was what is called an empirical decision. The doctors did not yet know what was causing the problem, but they were making an informed guess that he had some kind of food poisoning, and were treating him accordingly. They recognized, however, that the situation was slightly anomalous: Mr. and Mrs. Carter had both eaten the same food, yet only he had been so seriously affected. She was perfectly healthy. That meant the upset was more likely to be caused by a virus than bacteria, so antibiotics would be powerless. But still, better to be safe.

November 5 was a Sunday, a day when British hospitals are understaffed, so Carter wasn't seen again for forty-eight hours. When the doctors came to him on the Monday morning, they were pleased. The prognosis was good. "Home tomorrow if eating and drinking," his notes state. "TTA." That stands for "to take away," meaning the doctors had already prepared the documents for his discharge summary. The notes included the results of the latest blood test: his platelets and his white blood cells were low, but not worryingly so. The doctors were likely to have thought that, because of the irritation to his gut caused by the diarrhea, he may have bled a little into his intestine, which would explain the numbers they were getting back from the lab.

Doctors are detectives. They're always trying to rule out possibilities, to narrow down the number of potential causes for the condition they're looking at: exclude, exclude, exclude. New information comes in every day, but in this case the next day was no different. The first comment on Carter's notes states that he should be able to leave by the evening; but later there was bad news. Tests on his stool sample had picked up *Clostridium difficile* (which is often shortened to C. diff). C. diff is a nasty and opportunistic bug that afflicts people who've taken antibiotics, since the medicine wipes out the beneficial bacteria that protect us alongside the harmful ones that make us ill. Carter was clearly going to have to stay in for a bit longer, which was explained to the patient and his wife, although she was pushing a theory of her own.

"Patient and wife concerned about intentional infection of patient (?poison)," the notes record. "Reassured it's unlikely." And there at the bottom of the page is the cheerfully optimistic line "home tomorrow night." The doctors were confident their patient would be fine, even though Mrs. Carter was worried that someone had deliberately sought to harm her husband. Dr. Dean Creer, the senior doctor in charge of Carter's treatment, wrote later that this comment about poisoning hadn't been a one-off. There had been a second conversation when Mrs. Carter had asked about poison, but which he hadn't deemed important enough to include in the notes.

"I found this an unusual question and explained that we encounter diarrhea and vomiting commonly as well as C. diff and that intentional infection/poisoning was not likely," he wrote. "She explained that he was usually an extremely fit and healthy man who never got ill, or words to that effect, and that he had knowledge of dangerous people, although I forget the exact words, and that a friend of theirs had been killed by poisoning by these people hence her anxiety. I explained that Mr. Carter had only been in hospital a few days, that this remained our working diagnosis, and that we would expect a rapid improvement."

Again, this was entirely normal. Any doctor will tell you that, although it's important to listen to patients, it's also important not to be distracted by peculiar theories that they can sometimes come up with. Common things are common. Gastroenteritis is common. It would take a little while for Mr. Carter to get better, but some conditions take time. And so the days passed, with the doctors not quite sure what was wrong with him, but pretty sure he was about to get better.

November 11 was the weekend again, Carter's second weekend in Barnet

Hospital, and the duty team had a simple task—"check bloods and discharge patient." This job was so straightforward it was delegated to the most junior medic available, a preregistration house officer, only three or four months out of medical school. This was a routine task, but the junior doctor made a very disquieting discovery: Carter's white blood count had plummeted to 0.3, when it should never be lower than 4. "In view of above, patient not being discharged, will hand over for Sunday team to review," the junior doctor wrote. And that marked the end of the optimism about Carter being able to go home imminently. A white blood count that low is, in the later words of one of the doctors, "seriously, seriously abnormal." Something was wrong, but they had no idea what.

Carter, a healthy man, arrived in hospital with the symptoms of gastroenteritis, so the doctors gave him antibiotics. The drugs not only didn't help; they appeared to make his condition so much worse that he tested positive for C. diff. But that second diagnosis didn't really help their comprehension either. Had he suffered from two consecutive, different, unrelated conditions—a viral gastroenteritis, followed by an antibiotic-caused infection—but both with identical symptoms? That would be strange, though not impossible. But if that was so, why had Carter's white blood count dropped to an almost undetectable level? The medical detectives kept trying to exclude possibilities. What harms white blood cells? They sent some of Carter's blood off for an HIV test, which came back negative. No advances there. And there was something else odd: his mucous membranes were inflamed. The doctors put this down to thrush, a fungal infection that can affect those with weakened immune systems.

November 13 was bad: "Seen with wife. She is very upset and aggressive initially, but calms once explanation given. Explained that he had diarrhea likely secondary to viral illness ... Wife is concerned that he is not able to eat and vomiting with food. Explained that he will be able to drink/eat once much better." The doctors called in hematology experts in the hope they could understand what was happening with Carter's blood. By now it wasn't just his white blood cells that they were worrying about: his platelets had dropped to 21, which is the kind of level when the blood is so thin you begin to worry about spontaneous bleeding and the body being unable to stop it.

The hematologist came later that day to examine Mr. Carter and ask him about his life in slightly more detail than the emergency doctor had when he first arrived by ambulance. And that is why the notes now contained the sudden unexpected revelation that he was "ex-KGB." This wasn't just a medical mystery anymore, but a criminal one, too. Why had a former Soviet spy been taken ill in Muswell Hill? And why, suddenly, was his hair coming out in clumps? "I just tried to make some calm of his head and all of his hair was on my glove," as Mrs. Carter described it later, in her idiosyncratic English. "And that I realized all the same happened on his shoulder, on the pillow, it was all around. I said, 'What is this? Could you, anybody, tell me what happened to my husband?'"

Dr. Andres Virchis, the hematologist, was struck above all by Carter's appearance. He dealt often with patients with leukemia, cancer of the blood, who had had chemotherapy or who needed a bone marrow transplant. He thought Carter looked like someone who had had their body irradiated, so as to wipe out the existing bone marrow before it can be replaced. Perhaps Carter's wife had been right all along and there was some kind of poison here? He sent a sample of the patient's blood to colleagues at Guy's, another London hospital, which specializes in toxic substances; they in turn asked their radiology department to check if he could have somehow been irradiated. On November 15 the radiologists brought round their Geiger counter. The results are in the notes: "no radioactive emissions from patient." A Geiger counter would only be able to pick up a patient poisoned with one form of radiation, however: the high-energy electrons that are known as beta radiation. The note-taker added that it "would not detect anything if patient had been irradiated with gamma rays."

The note-taker did not mention that the Geiger counter also would not detect anything if the radiation in question was the naked helium nuclei that we call alpha particles, since they would not be able to break through the skin to be detected outside the poisoned person's body. But then, that would have been a pointless test. There were no recorded cases in history of anyone being deliberately poisoned with alpha radiation. Common things are common. If you see hoofprints, think horses; don't think hooved monsters from outer space.

The test results from Guy's came back on the evening of the next day, and revealed higher than expected levels of the heavy metal thallium, which is a known poison and which also causes hair loss. Could this be the cause of the problem? "Patient attended meeting November 1, believes poisoned then," Carter's notes say. They also record that the doctors started giving Carter the standard treatment for thallium poisoning: Prussian blue. But they clearly weren't satisfied with the diagnosis, partly because the symptoms weren't right, and also because Carter's thallium levels were too low to kill him. "Possible more than one poison (as thallium doesn't usually damage bone marrow unless radioactive)." And at the bottom of the page: "patient believes Russians do use radioactive thallium." Carter's white blood count was zero; his bone marrow had been completely destroyed. "Patient wants to know if he will die," the doctors wrote.

By this stage the doctors no doubt knew Carter's real name: Alexander Litvinenko. He was a refugee from Russia who had fled his homeland after exposing the inner workings of an FSB unit tasked with assassinating politicians and businessmen—a sort of Russian analog of the Treadstone program from the *Bourne* movies. He had adopted his new name almost immediately after he'd arrived in Britain in 2000, like someone on a witness protection scheme, but hadn't taken the logical next step of hiding himself away. During the six years he lived in Britain, he wrote extensively about the misdeeds of the Kremlin and told anyone who'd listen his theories about what Putin was up to. His patron and protector in London was the mischievous exiled oligarch Boris Berezovsky, who possessed a formidable publicity machine. Now that poisoning was confirmed, that machine started up. On November 19, the Sunday papers were full of the sensational news that an ex-FSB agent had been poisoned while attending a meeting in London. By now Litvinenko had been moved from Barnet to University College Hospital (UCH), which specializes in hematology. Reporters thronged outside its gates, desperate for updates.

His condition continued to worsen. He was moved to the UCH intensive care unit later that day. There is very little sign of frenzy in his notes, however, as the doctors continued their tireless attempt to understand what had happened to their patient, still puzzled by the fact that he was showing the

SCHU
CAT
xxxxxxxx3340
.
4/22/2022

Item: ï¿½2001009677 1547 ((book)

wrong symptoms for thallium, which would have stopped his nerves from functioning, but unable to identify any other problem. Litvinenko normally weighed a lean seventy-eight kilograms, but had lost fourteen of them in the three weeks since becoming ill.

In their quest for an answer, and struck by the fact that their patient looked like he had been irradiated, the doctors sent a sample of his urine to the Atomic Weapons Establishment (AWE), the body responsible for the design, manufacture and maintenance of Britain's nuclear weapons, and thus the institution best placed to find any rare signs of radiation poisoning. The results came back on November 22: Litvinenko's urine appeared to show a high level of one of the isotopes of polonium. The scientists tested a second sample, and the initial finding was confirmed: he had been poisoned with polonium-210. He was the first confirmed victim of deliberate alpha radiation poisoning in history.

It had taken them three weeks, but eventually these diligent doctors had discovered what was ailing their patient. The clues had been there all along. The inflamed mucous membranes weren't caused by thrush, but by rapidly dividing cells sloughing off tissue. The vomiting and diarrhea hadn't been gastroenteritis but the body's attempt to rid itself of this dreadful invader. The collapsing white blood cell count hadn't been HIV, but a result of the polonium gathering in the bone marrow, killing every cell within reach. The doctors had sought commonplace explanations for each of these symptoms, but never found one that explained all of them. Common things may be common, but very occasionally you are confronted with something no one has ever seen before.

Sadly, however, all that medical detective work was for nothing. Polonium-210 is perhaps the deadliest substance on Earth: a millionth of a gram, less than a speck of dust, will kill a human. The world's yearly output of the metal—about 100 grams—could kill everyone in Britain, with enough left over to kill most of France. The alpha particles it emits are like atomic artillery: they smash into everything around them with lethal force, destroying cells, shredding DNA, extinguishing bodily functions. It is a tribute to Litvinenko's physical fitness that he held out against it for so long. But he was doomed. He was as good as dead the moment he swallowed the few sips of polonium-laced tea that he drank. His body finally gave up fighting on November 23, within hours of the identity of the poison being confirmed. He was buried in a lead-lined coffin.

Where the medical detectives of the National Health Service left off, the criminal detectives of the Metropolitan Police took over. It had only been thanks to some inspired diagnoses by doctors, and some top-notch science from the experts, that Litvinenko's caregivers were ever able to tell what poison had been used. But, perversely, once he was dead, the murder weapon became the detectives' ally, because it had left an alpha-particle-emitting signature on everything it had touched, as well as everywhere those who had touched it had been. Police officers tested the offices, cars, hotel rooms, and clothing of everyone who had been near Litvinenko, and were able to make an unanswerably strong case against two Russians: Andrei Lugovoy and Dmitry Kovtun, who had met him on November 1 in the bar of a central London hotel.

Everywhere they went and everything they came into contact with was imbued with the ghostly polonium signature—plane seats, a hookah pipe, a teddy bear, rubbish bins, the teapot that delivered the poison itself—as if they were two atomic-era King Midases doomed to irradiate everything they touched. But their status as chief suspects merely created a new mystery. Lugovoy was a blond Muscovite whose private security company specialized in corporate protection rackets. He and Litvinenko were old friends from the 1990s, when they both allied themselves with Berezovsky and had been working together on due diligence projects. Kovtun, meanwhile, was a lazy-eyed drifter whose dreams of becoming a porn star had been derailed by a drink problem and indolence, and whose career had mainly involved washing up in German restaurants.

These were incompetent amateurs, rather than Moscow-trained assassins, and they launched not one, but three, missions to kill Litvinenko. On the first, in mid-October, he did ingest a very small amount of polonium-210, and might indeed have died of it, given time. The second trip was a total failure: Lugovoy appears to have knocked over his container of poison in his hotel bathroom, then mopped it up with a towel, which he left out for the maid to deal with. It was only on their third attempt, when they induced Litvinenko to drink some of that poisoned tea, that they succeeded in their aim. It appears that neither of them knew they were handling polonium-210; otherwise they wouldn't have splashed it around like cheap aftershave. Someone else must have given them the poison, and someone else must have sent them to kill Litvinenko. But who?

Litvinenko himself blamed Putin, in a deathbed statement ghost-written by Berezovsky's publicity people. Commentators later identified a range of sins that might have provoked the Kremlin's rage: Litvinenko had betrayed Putin's beloved FSB; he had defected; he was embarrassing the Russian state with allegations that Putin was a pedophile, and had staged terrorist attacks to win the presidency. But the problem with all of these reasons was that they made sense only in retrospect. Litvinenko's opinions gained traction after he was killed. When he was alive, he was dismissed as a conspiracy theorist, if he was noticed at all. In the early 2000s, I was working as a full-time specialist on the war in Chechnya, about which Litvinenko had written a book. I made a point of reading every significant work about Chechnya, but never even bothered opening this one. Nor did anyone else I knew. Litvinenko just wasn't influential.

Besides, if Putin was going to start killing people for having those opinions, he would have started with Berezovsky himself (whom Lugovoy met up with within hours of poisoning Litvinenko), rather than with this obscure former FSB hit man. So why had Litvinenko been chosen? It was a mystery, and one that appeared insoluble.

The British government clearly had no interest in revealing what it knew about the matter, primarily because to do so would embarrass Putin, and thus harm the bilateral relationship. "This case is obviously causing tension with the Russians. They are too important for us to fall out with," an anonymous cabinet minister told the *Sunday Times* on December 3, 2006, four days before Litvinenko was even buried. But Litvinenko's wife, Marina, was as forthright with the British government as she had been with the doctors of Barnet Hospital. She insisted on an investigation into her husband's murder, and continued to do so for years, even after Berezovsky stopped paying her legal bills. The British government finally abandoned its attempt to deny her justice in 2014. Post-Crimea there wasn't any relationship with Putin worth saving anyway.

I sat in the public seats during the inquiry in Court 73 of London's Royal

Courts of Justice, and the revelations that emerged explain why Litvinenko's murder belongs in a book about Moneyland. It was a worrying, if extreme, example of a way that the most violent Moneylanders can defend themselves. Like all Moneylanders, they exploit the tension between globalized financial flows and territorial legal systems, in order to secure their ownership of the money they have misappropriated. But they take the mismatch one step further. They prevent any information about their financial scams from leaking out, by sending assassins to kill whistle-blowers in foreign countries, then using their home countries' legal systems to protect those assassins at home. Without whistle-blowers, prosecutions are all but impossible. If a Moneylander is ruthless enough to kill any potential witnesses against him, he can keep his fortune safe forever.

The inquiry heard how Berezovsky had started cutting Litvinenko's allowance after he had been in the UK for five years, and how Litvinenko had looked around for new ways to make a living. He chanced upon the due diligence business, the private intelligence industry that collects information on companies and individuals, whether on behalf of passport-for-sale schemes or business rivals or prospective partners. Litvinenko lacked the on-the-ground sources necessary for up-to-date intelligence, but he had good historical knowledge of the people around Putin, from his days targeting corruption in the 1990s. He could combine this with information provided by an ex-KGB friend in America to create detailed reports on Kremlin insiders.

He had hoped Lugovoy would provide inside information from Moscow, which is why they had gone into business together, but he was disappointed by the results. Lugovoy's documents were always just a few paragraphs dredged off the internet. In an attempt to demonstrate what a report was supposed to look like, Litvinenko showed him his research into a Kremlin insider called Viktor Ivanov. Ivanov has worked with Putin since their KGB days and, according to Litvinenko and his colleague Yuri Shvets, is utterly corrupt. They said that Ivanov had worked closely with some of Russia's most notorious organized criminals, and had run the cocaine racket out of St. Petersburg under Putin's protection. "The best way to deal with Ivanov is to keep him at a distance and not let him get close because this closeness has good chances to develop into resentment on his part, and offended Ivanov can be the worst enemy," said the report, as entered as evidence into the inquiry proceedings. Shvets told the inquiry that, as a result of this report, the business deal that Ivanov was attempting had collapsed, costing the Kremlin man "between $10 million and $15 million."

Litvinenko sent the report to Lugovoy in late September 2006, intending him to keep it confidential. The first poisoning attempt came less than three weeks later, and Litvinenko was dead within two months. The coincidence in timing is too striking to be ignored. It looks extremely likely that the assassination was ordered to prevent Litvinenko from continuing to play the crucial role of whistle-blower and to stop him from revealing the secrets of the Russian kleptocracy. This interpretation is strengthened by a strange event that occurred when British police officers visited Moscow to interview Lugovoy and Kovtun later that year. The trip was largely fruitless from the British officers' perspective, not least because of the restrictions that Russian officials placed on their movements. When they met Lugovoy, only one British policeman was allowed to be present, and even then he was not permitted to record the interview, or to ask questions himself. When the time came for the two to go back to the UK, the Russians claimed the tape recorder had malfunctioned and there was no recording of the interview, which was naturally extremely annoying.

They did provide a transcript, which they claimed was a full record of the conversation, but the British officer who had been present noted that it missed out one crucial revelation. In the interview, Lugovoy had recounted a conversation he had had with Litvinenko about Russian criminals in Spain. Litvinenko had apparently told him how he was helping the Spanish secret services to investigate money laundering, and to prosecute criminals. But there was no sign of this revelation in the official transcript of the interview. Someone in a position of power in Moscow clearly did not want the Brits to know about dirty Russian money being used to buy property in Spain. It was all of a piece: some very wealthy Russians wanted the money they had stashed in Moneyland to stay there; were prepared to go to extreme lengths to neutralize any threat to that money; and were determined to shield the assassins who had protected it for them.

In 2007, Lugovoy won a place in the Russian parliament as a representative of one of Putin's tame opposition parties, and thus gained legal immunity from prosecution. During the course of the public inquiry into

Litvinenko's murder, the Kremlin awarded Lugovoy a medal "for services to the Fatherland," which is given to those who make "a great contribution to the defense of the Fatherland . . . for the preservation of state security." The inquiry lasted so long that those of us who were there every day became easy around each other. The security guards gave me a nickname, and we all became involved in the details of the murder, discussing them during the breaks. These were court employees, not lawyers representing one of the sides, but shock was visible even on their faces when Lugovoy's medal was revealed. Judge Robert Owen's complexion, meanwhile, turned from pink to brick red. And if that wasn't a clear enough signal that the Kremlin was taunting Western law enforcement, the inquiry heard how Lugovoy had sent Berezovsky a T-shirt bearing the legend "Polonium-210 . . . nuclear death is knocking your door [sic]" three years before Berezovsky's own death.

Owen, who wrote the report into the public inquiry, remained open-minded about why exactly Russia's Kremlin elite sent Lugovoy and Kovtun to kill Litvinenko (though he was in little doubt that the orders had originated in the Kremlin), but, as I sat in the inquiry day after day, I became increasingly certain that the reason was a simple one. Litvinenko threatened to expose the money trail. He needed to be eliminated.

In fact, Litvinenko's is just one in a whole series of suspicious Russia-linked deaths in the UK and elsewhere that have happened since Putin has taken power. They include that of Mikhail Lesin, a former government minister, who died in a Washington hotel room in what authorities have labeled an accident. It remains unexplained, however, what he was doing in Washington in the first place. Alexander Perepilichny, a healthy Russian businessman, collapsed and died while out jogging in Surrey in 2012. He was helping Swiss officials at the time with their efforts to trace dirty Russian cash in their banks. Sergei Skripal, a former Russian agent convicted of spying for the UK who had lived in Britain since being exchanged in a 2010 spy swap, was poisoned with a Soviet-developed nerve agent in Salisbury in March 2018, along with his daughter who was visiting him from Russia.

In these cases, and many others, suspicions have been raised that assassins from Moscow attacked ex-insiders to stop them from revealing the Kremlin's secrets. And in none of these cases have the Russian authorities provided genuine help to those seeking to investigate the crime.

This is where Moneyland is seen in its most troubling form. There has been a persistent feeling of complacency in rich Western countries that the world is moving in their direction, that development will gradually lead to the rest of the world becoming liberal capitalist democracies. But the case of Litvinenko reveals something very different. It is not in the Kremlin elite's interest for Russia to become governed by the rule of law, as Westerners fondly hope that it will be; instead, Kremlin insiders profit from the fact that they— and they alone—can earn vast fortunes in Russia, and export that money to safety in the West. Chaos and mismanagement not only allow them to earn further fortunes, but also provide them with the means to protect themselves and their friends from retribution. They can have those who threaten them killed, and protect the assassins in perpetuity behind a border that Western policemen cannot cross. This is another feedback loop: the profits made by Moneylanders give them an enduring interest in maintaining Moneyland. And if maintaining Moneyland requires dispatching amateur assassins to London with a vial of the world's deadliest chemical, then that's what must be done. They're offshore bandits.

Of course there are few, if any, politicians who have access to polonium-210 (the only place that makes it in commercial quantities is in Russia), but Moneylanders do not need specialized poisons to kill. You can silence a witness just as efficiently by chucking him out of a window, or pushing her in front of a train.

Dissidents have always fled abroad, and governments have always pursued them: think of Karl Marx in London, or Vladimir Lenin in Geneva. But those dissidents were enemies because of their ideas, which threatened the foundations of the Prussian, Russian or other states. Moneyland's dissidents are not hunted because of their ideas but because of their secrets. They know how the money moves. As Moneyland becomes more entrenched, and those secrets become more valuable, such murders will become more common. There might never be one as horrible as Litvinenko's, but the logic of his murder—to stop him from ever exposing his secrets—will not go away.

That means the cash stashed in Moneyland is safe, no matter how dubious its origins. The next question is what do Moneylanders do with it? That is what we will look at next.

14

SAY YES TO THE MONEY

The TV show *Say Yes to the Dress* first hit American screens in 2007 and, if you've never seen it, you're missing out. It features a procession of women—three per episode is standard—visiting the Kleinfeld Bridal store in New York to buy their wedding dresses. In some ways, it's the perfect reality television format: an endlessly repeatable scenario, into which women of different ethnicities, ages, body shapes, classes, backgrounds, sexualities, can be dropped, with guaranteed drama. And there's almost always a happy ending: the brides look gorgeous in white. The show has spawned multiple spin-offs and transformed Kleinfeld Bridal—formerly a well-regarded but unremarkable outlet on West 20th Street—into the world's most famous purveyor of dresses for the discerning bride-to-be.

On May 22, 2015, toward the end of the show's thirteenth season, viewers got a treat. In an episode called "V. I. Pnina," they watched the Israeli designer Pnina Tornai create special dresses for three "VIP" brides with unlimited budgets, while the rest of the boutique was closed for the day. Tornai, who has off-blond hair cascading down past her shoulders, and full lips, was little known before she started appearing on the show, but has since become a major celebrity, perhaps because her unsubtle style is well suited to television. If you're not familiar with her work, her creations look classy in the same way Donald Trump's interior décor looks classy, and she does not do understated. She specializes in semitransparent dresses with plunging necklines, adorned with drifts of crystals, topped off with veils and accessories, themselves crusted with sparkly things. "I live for bling, but bling is expensive. A bride with an unlimited budget is my dream, because I can focus on making the dress perfect at any cost," Tornai informs the camera during "V. I. Pnina."

The episode opens with a general flurry of preparation, centered around Ally McGown, the boutique manager. She has long hair, red lipstick and a rather harassed air, accentuated by permanently raised eyebrows and a wrinkled brow. "The daughter of an Angolan cabinet minister is about to arrive. She and her family have flown all the way from Africa to be fitted for nine dresses that she's purchased from Pnina," McGown intones, breathlessly.

The client is Naulila Diogo. She arrives in a vast Chevrolet SUV, her hair swept off her face, her eyes wide behind red-framed glasses. She speaks beautiful English, with a soft accent and a pleasant air. "It's always my dream to have a Pnina Tornai dress. The dresses are very glamorous, with a lot of crystals and I love it. I want to look like a princess, like a queen," she tells the camera, with unconcealed excitement. "I'm having a big wedding with 800 people. I want my wedding to be bigger and better than the other weddings I have seen."

To achieve this goal, she will need a number of dresses. First will be the ceremony where the marriage certificate is to be signed. That will be a modest occasion, attended only by family members, but she wants to look good all the same, and is spending $30,000 on a figure-hugging dress with bejeweled straps that look like hoarfrost. Made from a special silk tulle, it has a deep scoop out of the back and is embroidered with thousands of Swarovski crystals. Customization of the dress comes to a further $5,500 (the prices are laid out on the screen, so viewers can keep a running tally) and a "birdcage veil" is $500 more.

"Oh my gosh," Diogo says as she sees herself in the mirror. "I'm so beautiful."

She'll need another outfit for the main wedding ceremony, obviously, and this one is a ball gown, with skirts perhaps six feet across. Tornai explains that it takes about 300 hours of work to make a dress like this, and she holds her hands fully ten inches apart to show the size of the magnifying glass the seamstress will employ to check the quality of the work. Diogo's mother and friends gasp when the bride emerges from the dressing room. The corset contains a signature Tornai feature: a strip of translucent cloth between the breasts extending down almost to the navel.

And then comes the reveal: the giant fluffy skirt is lifted off over her head, to expose—beneath it—a figure-hugging mermaid dress with an explosion of froth around the feet. "Naulila is practically royalty in her country. I couldn't just make her a regular dress, so I made this one with a surprise skirt that comes off for the reception," Tornai explains to the camera, before producing a veil that stretches six feet along the floor behind the bride's back. "A veil like this is at least three days of work. The lace has been custom-made in France, hand-embroidered with hundreds of Swarovski crystals. This is one of a kind."

The veil costs $5,000.

"I'm so happy," Diogo says. "I don't have words."

The episode's final flourish is provided by Randy Fenoli, Kleinfeld Bridal's fashion director and the stand-out star of *Say Yes to the Dress*. The gloriously camp Fenoli intervenes to give advice to brides as well as to do any to-camera expositions the show requires. His summing-up of Diogo's starring role in "V. I. Pnina" is even more excitable than usual: "Naulila's spent more than any other bride in Kleinfeld history, walking away with a total of nine original Pnina Tornai dresses, a surprise skirt, customization, accessories, a total of over $200,000."

The episode was screened in the United States to the usual reception, with viewers marveling at the lengths the wealthy will go to when they want to make things perfect, and generally cooing at how beautiful Naulila and her fellow unlimited-budget brides looked.

And then the episode aired in Angola.

Angola is a country in West Africa that became independent from Portugal in 1975, and almost immediately plunged itself into a particularly nasty civil war, exacerbated by intervention from the two sides in the Cold War. The originally Maoist UNITA gained support from South Africa and the United States, while the Marxist-Leninist MPLA was backed by the Soviet Union and Cuba. The country has significant oil deposits, both on- and off-shore, as well as extensive diamond fields, which added the interests of corporations and traders to those of the superpowers. The Soviet Union's proxies emerged in the 1990s as the dominant force (although the fighting did not end until 2002). That did not much matter to the Western oil companies, which carried on as if nothing had changed.

The MPLA's leader, José Eduardo dos Santos, became president in 1979 and was, until he stepped down in 2017, Africa's second-longest-serving leader after Obiang of Equatorial Guinea. Although he was trained in the Soviet Union, and his government remained nominally socialist, this did not prevent his closest associates from becoming extremely wealthy. Dos Santos' daughter Isabel is Africa's richest woman, with a fortune estimated by *Forbes* magazine at more than $3 billion. She has a British passport, an extensive property empire in west London, and major shareholdings in telecoms, media, retail, hospitality and finance companies. In 2016, her father appointed her as chairwoman of Sonangol, the Angolan state oil company, which is the backbone of the country's economy. She lost the post when he stepped down.

The benefits from the Angolan oil industry have not been widely shared. The capital, Luanda, is rated as the world's most expensive city for expats, while two out of every three Angolans survive on less than $2 a day. According to the IMF, some $32 billion simply went missing from the state budget between 2007 and 2010 (the IMF attributed the loss to "quasi-fiscal operations undertaken by the state oil company"). British and American investigators have repeatedly accused Western companies of bribing Sonangol officials, and in 2017 Halliburton paid $30 million to settle a case brought in the US under the Foreign Corrupt Practices Act. In 2002, the governor of the central bank tried to transfer $50 million of the government's money to his own account in the United States. When the request was blocked by Western bankers, he tried again. Angola is, in short, an almost perfect case study of modern transnational kleptocracy.

Some of Global Witness' earliest reports detailed the link between corruption and conflict in Angola, with UNITA profiting from "blood diamonds," and MPLA dominating the oil industry. The NGO's 1999 investigation—entitled *A Crude Awakening*—described how international energy companies were paying off the government, thereby colluding in the despoliation of the country and the immiseration of its people. "Corruption starts with the head of state, surrounded by a clique of politicians and business cronies," the report stated. "Corruption pervades all sectors of the Angolan system, from access to medicines, to the provision of school books." According to the NGO's sources, dos Santos controlled a British Virgin Islands–registered company that "won" a $720 million contract to supply food to the army, just before the civil war resumed following unsuccessful peace talks in 1998. "The more the army consumes, the more those who are associated with these companies profit," the report noted.

The country was producing three-quarters of a million barrels of oil a day at the time, which made up 7 percent of US oil imports, yet the money was serving only to enrich the elite, to drive conflict and to make ordinary Angolans' lives dreadful. The average resident of the country survived for just forty-two years; 82.5 percent of the population lived in poverty; a quarter of children died before the age of five; child malnutrition was at its highest rate in twenty-five years.

Angola's government had previously rather approved of Global Witness, thanks to a report published a year earlier that had detailed how UNITA was funding its operations with the diamond trade, and so it saw *A Crude Awakening* as a betrayal. Police officers called newspapers in Luanda and demanded they remove any references to it, and a spokesman for dos Santos insisted he would sue the NGO in court (the effort tailed off after a few stern letters from lawyers).

In Luanda, a senior politician took to the radio to condemn the NGO's work as part of an anti-Angolan campaign designed to deprive the government of its ability to defend itself, to defend dos Santos, and to insist that its officials were honest. That politician was called Bornito de Sousa. He had been a part of the MPLA's politburo since the 1980s, and at the time headed its faction in parliament. A lawyer by training, he went on to write the new constitution. After leaving parliament, he became minister of territorial administration, and thus gained responsibility for compiling the electoral register: an important and influential job in any country.

Bornito de Sousa is Naulila Diogo's father, the "Angolan cabinet minister" whom McGown got so fluttery about at the start of the episode of *Say Yes to the Dress*.

After "V. I. Pnina" aired, Tornai posted a picture on Instagram showing Diogo and her new husband walking down the aisle in a storm of confetti, beads glistening on the bride's bodice and veil, a bouquet of lilies clutched in her left hand. An Angolan website called Club K wrote a news report on the episode, with the additional information that Diogo had been appointed a brand ambassador for Pnina Tornai, who had opened a new boutique in Luanda. The report was studiedly neutral, but the comments posted beneath it were not: "Where is this country going? Some can boast such wealth, while others live on rice and fish. God has given the country to the wrong people"; "a country where 90 percent of the people has neither water nor power, does not know what they'll eat the next day, litter, cesspools, sufferings. And a few people live inhumanly without worrying about the welfare of the people!!!"

De Sousa was furious. He took to Facebook to mock much of the criticism he had been receiving, as well as the demands that he resign. "People do not even look at the positive side of bringing to our country an internationally renowned stylist who thus puts Angola on the GLOBAL fashion scene, alongside New York, increases Angola's prestige, and provides high quality options to Angolan brides without them having to spend money on trips abroad," he wrote. It was not a convincing argument, not least because the two-thirds of Angolans who live in poverty would have had to save every cent they earned for almost nine millennia to afford the dresses that his daughter chose at Kleinfeld Bridal, whether or not they had to go abroad to buy them. Undaunted, de Sousa went on to insist that his official government income was more than enough to cover the expense of his daughter's wedding, and that any suggestion to the contrary was a disgrace. "The ones who should resign are those who deceitfully published such a gross and artificial lie," he wrote.

It is not known how much Bornito de Sousa earns, but the president's salary was approximately $6,000 a month back in 2014. That means that, in the unlikely event that the minister earned as much as his boss, he would have had to save up for more than two and a half years to afford his daughter's dresses. On top of that he would have had to pay for the flights to New York and accommodation in America, as well as the wedding party for 800 guests in Luanda. However much that adds up to, it's hard not to conclude that the money could have been spent more productively. The $200,000 or so he spent on his daughter's wedding dresses wouldn't solve the country's health problems on its own, but it would buy anti-retroviral drugs for more than 166 people for a year, which isn't a bad place to start.

(The scandal didn't do any harm to de Sousa's career, incidentally, and he became vice president in 2017 when dos Santos stepped down.)

It may well be that de Sousa did earn the money honestly, or that Diogo had her own successful and secret business career, or that she found another sponsor (she failed to reply to my requests for comment sent to her on Face-book), but what's extraordinary is why no one at the television company appears to have thought to ask. Kleinfeld Bridal and TLC, the production company that makes *Say Yes to the Dress*, both failed to respond to questions about whether they had checked the origin of Diogo's funds. In a statement, Michal Cohen, Tornai's head of operations, said that the company protected its customers' privacy. "We maintain only business relationships with our clients and do not engage in their personal matters," the emailed statement said. That is questionable; Tornai would surely not have referred to Diogo on camera as "practically royalty in her country" if she hadn't engaged with her as more than just a client, but it was all Cohen was prepared to provide.

Perhaps even more remarkable than their lack of interest or concern in the origin of her money is the fact that Diogo didn't seem to realize it was a bit crass to appear on television spending $200,000 on clothes in the first place, particularly when your father helps run a country with the world's eighth-worst infant mortality rate. It wasn't like she was caught in a hidden-camera investigative journalism sting; she agreed to take part in a reality television show, knowing it would specify exactly how much money she was spending on nine exceedingly vulgar dresses. She blew the whistle on herself. It's as if Marie Antoinette published a pamphlet detailing precisely how much she was spending on roast swan, then was outraged that the sansculottes didn't appreciate her investment in culinary technology.

No one comes out of this tale of bling and excess well, to be quite honest. But it does serve as the perfect metaphor for how shopping works in Moneyland. When there's big money on the table, no one asks too many questions. The offshore money has inflated house prices, art prices, fine wine prices, yacht prices. It has poured into the market for expensive watches, for luxury cars, for clothes and for shoes. There is now so much money washing around looking for something fun to be spent on that it has created a whole new field of economic study, which one bank analyst calls "plutonomy." And the idea of plutonomy explains a lot about how Moneyland manifests itself in the real world. But before we get to that, let's look at houses.

15

HIGH-END PROPERTY

The cities chosen by the superrich vary according to all sorts of factors—tax rates, immigration rules, language, legal system, time zone—but two cities always top the premier league: London and New York. One reason why London often edges ahead of its American rival is that it lacks co-ops, the New York apartment buildings where residents can veto would-be neighbors. This means cliquey old-money New Yorkers have long been able to deliberately block the flashy Moneylanders from moving into their buildings.

It was to sidestep this problem that 15 Central Park West, perhaps the swankiest apartment block in the world, was built. Completed in 2008, its developers shrugged off the nadir of the financial crisis, selling condos off-plan to tech and finance billionaires, oligarchs, sheikhs and the usual representatives of the global elite. It looks like a co-op, but it has none of the boring rules.

Known as 15CPW, it was built in deliberate imitation of the old-money mansions of uptown Manhattan. It is clad in limestone, with huge windows and high ceilings, and has two towers, the second one taller than the first so its residents can see over the top of its twenty-story twin and into Central Park. It redefined luxury property in the United States and created such a buzz that in 2014 journalist Michael Gross wrote a whole book about it, in which he echoed the overexcited society publication prose of a previous era. "Fifteen Central Park West is more than an apartment building. It is the most outrageously successful, insanely expensive, titanically tycoon-stuffed real estate development of the twenty-first century . . . it represents the resurrection and the life of our era's aristocracy of wealth," he wrote in *House of Outrageous Fortune*, which is a cracking read. "No longer dignified, unified, well-born, or even well-bred, they enjoy unheard-of incomes and the most extraordinary standard of living in history.

"The success of 15CPW consecrated a new, somewhat suspect, Global Super-Society," he went on. "Like them or not, these are individuals who have only one thing in common, staggering net worth, and have become the world's new ruling class. Typically in their first generation of wealth, they've made huge money in new ways . . . the newest of the new rich come from emerging markets such as the so-called BRIC nations of Brazil, Russia, India, and China."

Of course, most of the apartments are owned via anonymous corporate vehicles, so the precise identity of these aristocrats remains largely hidden, but Gross still identifies properties belonging to Israelis and Koreans, as well as to Russians, Greeks, Indians, South Americans, Italians and a Senegalese mobile phone tycoon. What Gross describes as "the looniest episode in 15CPW's short history" came in 2013 when Citigroup's ex-CEO Sandy Weill sold a penthouse for $88 million, having bought it for precisely half that just six years previously. The purchaser was the Russian fertilizer tycoon Dmitry Rybolovlev, who was at the time going through a messy divorce (which ended up costing him $6 billion) and who apparently decided that his daughter needed somewhere to stay in New York whenever she was taking a break from her studies in Massachusetts. It has four bedrooms, including a master suite with views over the park, as well as a library, a living room, a gallery, a dining room, a den, and en suite bathrooms for everyone. On top of that, there's a wraparound terrace extending around three of the flat's four sides.

Rybolovlev made his money from Uralkali, a fertilizer business in Russia, specifically from its potash mines on the edge of Siberia. It is hard to imagine anywhere less like the grand edifices of uptown Manhattan than the towns of Berezniki and Solikamsk, where those mines are located. They are ringed by enormous ruddy slag heaps that look like something from the surface of Mars, and which stretch for miles along the highway between the two towns. You reach them by a two-and-a-half-hour drive from the city of Perm, the kind of Russian journey that appears illusory, since you keep moving while seeming to stay in the same place: the same forests of birch trees, the same straight road, with only the occasional spiky conifer sticking out as a sign of progress.

The population of Berezniki has dropped by a quarter since the 1980s, and is housed in the same shoddy five-story apartment blocks thrown up by the Soviet government everywhere from Central Asia to the Arctic Circle. One school has a smart plaque on it testifying to the fact that ex-president Boris Yeltsin studied there, although that appears to be the only new thing added to the school in decades. A caretaker allowed me to take a picture of it, but not of the rotting brickwork or dirty windows. "The government treats us like we're livestock," she said.

Berezniki is built directly on top of the salt mines that made Rybolovlev's fortune, which is a problem because salt is soluble. When water flows into abandoned workings, it dissolves the pillars that support the tunnel roofs; the tunnels collapse; and sinkholes open up, taking houses, roads, trees, railway tracks, cars and factories with them. A hole that opened in 2007—nicknamed "The Grandfather"—is fifty stories deep and may be the largest sinkhole in the world. Much of Berezniki has therefore been evacuated, which gives it an even more woebegone air than provincial Russian towns normally have. Uralkali exports its fertilizers to dozens of countries, but precious little of the export earnings appear to stay here, and few ambitious locals stay either. Rybolovlev left long ago, and sold his stake in Uralkali to another billionaire in 2010. He bought a $95 million Florida mansion from Donald Trump in 2008, AS Monaco football club in 2011, and then the penthouse overlooking Central Park.

Jonathan Miller, a legendarily knowledgeable New York real estate consultant, said Rybolovlev's new penthouse was quite simply the best apartment in America. "I've been in probably 8,000 apartments in my life. I can't remember the names of people at cocktail parties, but I can remember the color of brick on the outside of a building and what the inside looked like," he told me in 2017, while sitting in an office lined with dozens of newspaper articles quoting him as an authority on the city's property market. "This building in my view, in my thirty years on the market, is the best condo ever built."

In Miller's analysis, luxury real estate has become in effect a new global currency, with very wealthy people using housing in the world's premier league of cities as a store of wealth, with the great advantage that they can then use their apartments as storehouses for all their other expensive stuff: their Monets, their Modiglianis, that kind of thing. "I don't want to stereotype and say they're all flight capital, because they're not, but the growth in their presence is flight capital. They're preserving capital. They're just getting it into something for an extended period of time because they want to preserve it." Some 30 percent of condo sales in large-scale Manhattan developments since 2008 have gone to foreign-based buyers, with the vast majority of them paying the full sum up front. It is a remarkable change, and one that accelerated in the early 1990s, when the collapse of communism created flight capital on a previously unknown scale—particularly in London.

The early 1990s was a tough time to be in the British property business. A bubble had inflated over the previous decade; then it was dramatically popped by a tax reform, interest rate rises and a recession. Where estate agents had previously epitomized the big-money 1980s culture of shiny suits and brick-sized mobile phones, now they sat and wondered where the next sale was coming from. The average London house price rose almost two-thirds in the second half of the 1980s; then the market dried up. The *Daily Mail* called it "the worst housing slump for 60 years," and prices were lower in 1993 than they had been four years earlier.

"The market at the bottom end stopped overnight," remembered one estate agent, who was working at the time in the tony west London borough of Kensington and Chelsea, which features some of London's most distinctive landmarks: the Albert Hall, the Natural History Museum, Harrods, the King's Road, the Saatchi Gallery.

"There were a lot of repossessions, even round here. I spent a lot of time doing repossessions in Kensington. I'd been working for ten years by then. In those days, I suppose our clients were mainly British, particularly in Kensington. It was a very residential British area," he recalled. Princess Diana and Prince Charles lived in Kensington Palace, which helped boost the borough, and gave its richer inhabitants a distinct identity; they were nicknamed "Sloane Rangers," after their favored haunt of Sloane Square, and Diana was their exemplar. They were said to be defiantly anti-intellectual, to love country sports, and to spend their money on Hermès scarves and Range Rovers. But even these wealthy Brits had stopped buying by late 1992, which is when a completely unexpected client walked into the estate agent's office.

"I'm trying to remember his name; it was Alex something-or-other. It turned out that he had two business partners; I think they had a bank," the estate agent told me. The three men bought a flat each, at prices ranging from £200,000 to £320,000, cash. The fact of the sale was unusual in those depressed times, but that wasn't what made him phone the papers to tell them about it; it was the clients' nationality that was newsworthy. They were Russians. "It's bugging me I can't remember his surname, but he's gone on to greater things. He's probably a billionaire by now."

This appears to have been the first sale of London property to private buyers from the former USSR in modern British history, and it opened the gate to many more. Within three months, the *Evening Standard* was reporting an oil tycoon had picked up a house in Hampstead for £1.1 million, while an Armenian had bought two properties nearby for £3.2 million. The paper quoted the estate agent as saying: "[We] will be seeing an increasing number of purchasers who recognize London as a safe haven for their money." Rarely has a prediction been proven quite so triumphantly correct, and the estate agent was delighted to be reminded of it, though he asked me not to use his name in the light of recent tensions between Russia and the UK.

"I had lunch with the Russian desk, which deals with the Russian market, earlier this week and I showed them the press release you showed me, and they were staggered," he said. The estate agent is pink-skinned, upper-middle-class and open-faced, like a jovial party guest from *Four Weddings and a Funeral*, and he laughed out loud at the memory. "What they were staggered by was the value of the property: £200,000. You'd probably add a nought to that now, literally, it's probably ten times the price. What they did say was that £200,000 was an extraordinary amount for a Russian to be spending."

Now, of course, it seems positively quaint. Between January 1995 and May 2017, the average price for a property bought in Kensington and Chelsea rose from £180,000 to more than £1.5 million. The average detached property in the borough now comes in at £3.8 million, and in March 2017 a run-down one-up/one-down house originally built as accommodation for gravediggers went for £713,823. That means every square foot of its diminutive footprint cost £1,717, even before its new owner renovated it.

The headline on that January 1992 *Evening Standard* article about the estate agent's pioneering deal was "Property—A Haven for Rich Refugees." In reality, however, it was more than that. Alex and his two business partners not only ended up finding a safe haven for their money in one of London's swankiest neighborhoods, but also earned a tenfold return on their original investment while doing so. Like a classic pyramid scheme, the earliest investors have earned sensational returns at the expense of their late-joining brethren. Meanwhile, wealthy foreigners like them have transformed much of west London into a place few Brits could ever afford to live in, as they spend their riches on the kind of luxuries only they can afford.

"It's an extraordinary market," said that lucky estate agent. "I always think of London as its own island which to some extent has sailed off from the rest of the UK. It's a truly international city, like no other city in the world, more so than anywhere. Why London? The time zone, the language, the legal system, the people, the food's improved enormously, and culture's another reason, the fact it's the financial capital of the world, on a par with New York, all of those reasons."

Savills, a London-listed company, publishes research into the spending habits of its clients, which provides fascinating insights into the kind of people who can afford to drop millions of pounds on a house in a city they don't even live in. In 2014 it published a paper showing how top-end London property had outperformed housing in the rest of the UK by 250 percent over the previous three decades. "With money the weapon of choice among those competing for space in the metropolis, it is hardly surprising house price growth has been so strong," Savills concluded. As cash has poured into Moneyland, its wealthy citizens have competed to buy a limited range of real-world assets in a limited number of locations, with inevitable results: staggering price inflation, which has in turn made them even wealthier.

In early 2014, Ukrainian oligarch Dmitry Firtash spent £53 million on an old Tube station, which had previously been used as offices by the Ministry of Defense, and which happened to abut his £60 million mansion. The mansion, which has a swimming pool in its second basement and was designed by mega-developer Mike Spink, is just a five-minute walk from Harrods. A minute or two from Harrods in the other direction is the four-part modernist edifice of One Hyde Park, Britain's smartest apartment block, built as a joint venture between its developers, the Candy Brothers, and a firm belonging to Qatar's former prime minister. According to one excitable media report, a penthouse in the development sold for £140 million in 2010, which would have made it the most expensive flat in the world. The development itself is owned offshore, as are most of the flats within it, so it is hard to say exactly how much living here would cost, or who the inhabitants are. However, if you walk past of an autumn evening, it's hard not to notice that few of the lights are burning. Whoever lives here does not appear to spend much time at home.

"More than ever before, these homes of the wealthy will be spread far and wide, across different countries and continents," noted a 2017 review of the global housing market jointly presented by Warburg and Barnes, two top-end US-based real estate agencies. "Property wealth was not always so far-flung or mobile. Three inter-related developments—all still ongoing today—have driven this change: the expansion of air travel, the technology revolution, and the globalization of business."

The review notes that one in ten of the ultra-wealthy (those who own more than $30 million in assets) has five or more homes, often in places handy for their business, as well as for their chosen leisure activities. The authors of the review become so excited by the earning potential inherent in a situation where a swelling number of very rich people buy multiple houses that they can't possibly ever need that their metaphors get hopelessly confused. "For these individuals, the world is their oyster, and they regard real estate as one of the pearls in their crown." And, this being Moneyland, a class of enablers has emerged to help them get what they want: people like Gennady Perepada.

Perepada is stocky and ebullient, his dark hair slicked straight back to reveal a pronounced widow's peak. He arrived in New York from Ukraine in 1990, and hustled like a true New Yorker, eventually finding a role as a fixer—he prefers to be known as a "Luxury Real Estate Broker and International Investment Consultant"—for wealthy Russian speakers looking to diversify into US property. His office on West 48th Street, in Midtown, is packed with souvenirs and memorabilia from all over the old USSR, as well as from farther afield: China, Israel, the Gulf. He speaks good, if accented, English but when we met, on discovering that I speak Russian, switched into a unique and bewildering hybrid that flipped backward and forward between the two languages, sometimes three or four times in a single sentence. (In the following quotations, italics represent when he was speaking Russian.)

"*I never condemn these people for the fact that they are traveling in a* handmade Maybach. *Or he's traveling in a* handmade Rolls-Royce, handmade. Anyway, I'm not sure it's handmade, but handmade with ostrich inside, or with a TV, or with a special something, you know. *But these are the same kind of people as you and me,*" he told me. "*It is all down to personal contacts. I don't know how you live with people, but I live by a very important understanding, you can't have too many friends or too much money.* Money and friends never enough. *Therefore,* criteria of my life my friends. *You have to befriend people,* do you know what I mean? *You have to be able to befriend people. My profession, do you know what it is, it is to befriend people.*"

Taking out his iPhone, he displayed the call record for the day. The first call had come in from Baku, the capital of Azerbaijan, at 1:24 a.m.; then others at 3:06 a.m.; 5:15 a.m.; 6:15 a.m.; 6:46 a.m.; 6:48 a.m.; 7:20 a.m.; 7:21 a.m. "*Every phone call is worth something, it could be a phone call of* something *or a call of* nothing. *But this* something *call could be worth a lot. My phone is never off. Ever.*"

He scrolled through the promotional materials for apartment blocks he was marketing, with their views over Central Park, paneled walls, multiple bathrooms, underground car parks. Among them was 520 Park Avenue, a limestone-clad needle on the Upper East Side still under construction, whose residents will be able to look over the world's head, directly across the park toward their comrades in 15CPW. "They are starting from $16 million, one six. *And* the penthouse, $130 million, one thirty. Fifty percent of it is sold. *I represent this building,* the whole *building.*"

It was impossible to tell how much of his fast-paced monologue was marketing patter, and how much was a reflection of what truly was happening, but you couldn't argue with the photographs. Luxury goods companies had sent him pictures of their products to check which would appeal to his clients, and he scrolled through multiple Rolex watches on his phone, picking out the ones he thought were most desirable. Finally, he ran out of Rolexes, and the next picture showed a party where guests were helping themselves to sushi from the body of a naked woman.

"*This is art, art. You see how rich people live. You fancy some sushi? She has sushi everywhere,* all over," he said, with a grin even wider than usual. It was the grin of an insider, because it is astonishingly difficult to see how rich people live; unless you are a rich person, which most of us are not.

Take Indian Creek, for example. It is a village in Miami-Dade County, Florida, that you approach through a quiet and pleasant residential neighborhood, all groomed lawns and bungalows; where the streets lack sidewalks, but where there is so little traffic that walking on the road feels fine. Eventually, there is a bridge, with cream guard towers on either side of it, and a wrought-iron gate between them. If you try to step onto the bridge, a voice booms out of an intercom, asking your business. If you have no business there, or if your business is (like mine) idle curiosity, then you will be told it is a private island and that you must go elsewhere.

To emphasize the point, there is a heavy police presence. At the last census, in 2010, Indian Creek had a population of eighty-six, which included four of America's 500 richest people, as well as the singer Julio Iglesias, Colombian billionaire Jaime Galinski (whose base is London, but who also has homes in New York and a couple of other places), and various others, all with a combined net worth—according to the *Miami Herald*—of $37 billion. That sum is approximately equal to the annual economic output of Serbia, which has a population of more than 7 million people. Indian Creek's police force employs ten full-time officers, plus four reserves, and four civilian public service aides, giving the community a police officer–to–resident ratio of around 1:5, which is significantly higher even than that of East Germany at its most paranoid. The village is an island, so cannot be approached except by the bridge, but the police are taking no chances in protecting what their website calls "America's most exclusive municipality," and they run a marine patrol unit day and night, seven days a week. It is, in short, a moated community, where Moneyland can become real. In 2012, one ten-bedroom, fourteen-bathroom house on the island sold for $47 million, making it South Florida's most expensive ever property, according to the agents who closed the deal. The local press reported that the purchaser was a Russian billionaire.

The photos of the house released by the agents show an airy, high-ceilinged mansion, modest yet enormous, with an infinity pool looking out on to Biscayne Bay, toward the sunrise. It has a dock with water deep enough for a superyacht, and is surrounded on the other three sides by the lush lawns of the island's golf course. It bears about as much resemblance to an ordinary person's house as a Bengal tiger does to a tabby cat, but it is simultaneously both tasteful and restrained. "Air flows in and out of the home like a deep, cleansing breath. In this open plan, where the line is eternally blurred between inside and out, entire walls part to allow the embrace of the refreshing bay breezes. Ceilings soar to incredible heights," the agents' brief declares. But the closest you or I will get to it is standing at the end of the bridge, looking at a photo of it on your phone, while being intensely eyeballed by a policeman in mirrored sunglasses.

Miami is not yet jostling for a playoff position in the premier league of global property hot spots, but it is pushing hard, alongside Sydney, Vancouver, Los Angeles, Tokyo and a handful of other places that have become magnets for the world's hot money, and which aim to supplant London and New York at the top of the table. The city's association of Realtors publishes figures showing where its clients come from and, though the information should be treated with caution since so many purchasers hide their identity behind shell companies, the pattern is one of a constant gush of foreign investment pumping up prices all along the sunny coastline of southern Florida. In early 2017, two-fifths of all the money invested in Miami property came from abroad, overwhelmingly at the top end of the market, with almost half of that originating in just four countries: Venezuela, Argentina, Brazil and Colombia. Venezuela had been the biggest foreign source of funds every year since at least 2011, despite the raging financial and economic crises in the country.

"That's suggestive of kleptocratic behavior," John Tobon, deputy special agent in charge of the Miami office at Homeland Security Investigations, told me in February 2017. He explained that even legal investment from Venezuela must have gone through the black market, thanks to restrictions on the export of dollars from the country. "The real kicker is that these legitimate individuals that have legitimate wealth that are trying to escape the political situation there, are giving their bolivares to buy dollars and those dollars actually come from kleptocrats, who are using this market to embezzle money."

And is Miami as bad as its reputation suggests?

"If you have some time off, go to Bayside, get on one of those boat rides and you can actually see Al Capone's home, it's still there, it's still advertised: this is a monument. I was on a money-laundering panel the other day: 'Oh, there's money laundering in real estate in Miami?' And I was like, have you not seen the house, the Al Capone house? This is where it started, this isn't new."

Of course, a majority of the investment in Miami still originates in the United States, and much of the foreign money is legal. The trouble is that, thanks to the obscuring effect of the non-transparent companies used to hold the property, we have no way of knowing what is legal and what isn't. In the early hysteria over President Donald Trump's Russia ties, a Reuters investigation into Russian investment in the Trump Organization found sixty-three Russians among the owners of 2,044 units in seven different Trump-branded developments in Florida. Far more remarkable was the fact that fully 703 of the units were owned via corporate vehicles, meaning there were no real people attached to their title deeds at all, and their ownership was completely obscure. They might have belonged to Vladimir Putin, for all anyone else could know.

Six of those seven developments were in the Sunny Isles Beach area, which lies to the north of Indian Creek, and is famous for its relatively high number of residents of Russian origin. The seafront is lined with towers packed full of condos that were once marketed to retirees from New England, but which now are more likely to be bought by wealthy Moneylanders keen to put their cash somewhere it can't be taken away from them. Just off Collins Avenue, which runs up the spine of Miami's biggest barrier island, is the showroom for a new tower being constructed on the beachfront. Visitors to the showroom have to fill in a questionnaire to ascertain what kind of property they are interested in, and my attempt to pass myself off as a legitimate investor didn't last long: the lowest option on the "amount to spend" box was $3–5 million, and I didn't have a thousandth of that. Thankfully, they were having a slow morning and a saleswoman called Monica, who was in her mid-fifties, lovely, warm and friendly, agreed to show me around as if I was something other than a rubbernecking intruder.

The Turnberry Ocean Club is a development of the Soffer family, which has built malls, hotels, clubs and more all across this section of Miami. Donald Soffer arrived from Pittsburgh in the 1960s and transformed a stretch of swamp into the city of Aventura, which is home to America's fifth-largest shopping mall, as well as tens of thousands of people. His children are now developers in their own rights, and legitimate members of the global elite, with daughter Jackie married to Craig Robins, who brought Art Basel to Miami. Son Jeffrey, at the time of Monica's and my conversation, was married to supermodel Elle Macpherson, although they split up shortly thereafter, amid a welter of tabloid speculation. Both Jackie and Jeffrey have homes in Indian Creek village.

The tower they are building in Sunny Isles Beach will have 154 residences over fifty-four floors, with swimming pools cantilevered out on both sides halfway up, as well as a pool at the ground-floor level for swimmers with vertigo. There will be a boardroom, and a conference room, and a stock-trading room, and a children's playroom, and a theater, and more, including an outdoor dog-walking area on the thirty-second floor, for those who can't be bothered to take their dog all the way down in the elevator. "You have a very nice sense of arrival. There'll be a Rolls-Royce or a Bentley, we haven't decided yet, a private car. We also have private aviation," said Monica, with a smile, to see how I was taking it. "We start as low as $3.9 million, on a lower floor. And you can go all the way up to $35 million, but the bulk of our business is in the fours and fives."

She walked me through a replica of one of those standard apartments—which will stretch all the way through the building, giving them both sunset and sunrise views—pointing out the bedrooms, bathrooms, terrace, the kitchen features and more. When it was time to go, I felt as if she had genuinely liked me and was sorry I was leaving, which is why she's a top-class salesperson and I'm not.

Some of the wealthy foreigners who buy properties in Western cities can afford—like the residents of London's One Hyde Park—to leave them empty, but many like to see a return on their investment, and to rent them out. That is a daunting proposition, however. If you're based in, say, Malaysia, and your tenant is in New York, you're barely going to be awake at the same time as each other, let alone able to communicate conveniently about any problems with the apartment. How will you know who to bring in to fix the dishwasher? And how will you know how to pay the local property taxes?

This is where Dylan Pichulik comes in. A young, lean, personable New Yorker, Pichulik worked in property development until 2012, when he noticed that foreign owners kept asking him to recommend someone who could manage their newly acquired properties for them, and he realized that person should be him. "We do literally everything from soup to nuts," he said. "We invoice for rent every month, we collect the rental income from the tenant. We pay the expenses: real estate taxes, insurance, we deal with maintenance and repair. So when the dishwasher breaks or there's a leak from above, the tenant calls us and we get it taken care of."

He uses his knowledge of the market to advise clients on renovating their apartments ("Don't worry, send me 400 grand and I'll do it for you"), to renting them out, to helping their children move house. It's a trust game: the clients trust him, so they ask him to do things for them, and then they recommend him to other rich people, and that's a lucrative business. He told a story about one client—a wealthy Israeli woman—for whom he did everything while she remained holed up in her hotel room, up to and including buying her cigarettes, nine packs at a time. Her son had trouble with his visa, and so was unable to accompany her on the flight back to Ben Gurion Airport. She paid for Pichulik to sit up in first class with her, which was a weird experience.

"She wears a diaper, because she can't be bothered to go to the bathroom," he told me, with a grimace, as he remembered getting onto the plane. "It was all well and good until three hours later I look over and hear this 'ding.' The stewardess comes over: 'I need you to change my diaper.' So they look at me . . . like, 'Let your son do it.' I'm like, 'That's not my mother.' They made the flight attendant do it. So, yeah, we go above and beyond."

That was, however, an outlying case. Most of his clients are ordinary wealthy people—"Fortune 500 CEOs, former presidents, really big-name people." One Russian client owns a $14 million condo to stay in for the two weekends a year when she comes to New York to do her shopping; one time he picked up a magazine at the hairdresser's and saw one of his clients on the cover. The biggest share of the investment comes from China, with significant chunks from South America, the Gulf states, and, of course, the countries of the former Soviet Union. The wave of foreign investment has transformed the city. "Five years ago, if you wanted to spend 20 or 30 grand a month, you had a handful of options," he said. "Now I have a whole portfolio of $20–30–40,000 a month apartments, and I have hundreds of apartments for $15–20,000 and rental values will go all the way up to $110,000 a month. You can spend $80,000 a month easily and still be kind of under the radar."

Pichulik was funny and thoughtful about his curious career, and clearly concerned by the kind of inequality he has witnessed. That gave him sufficient insight to realize that spending his days looking at apartments worth $50, $60 or $70 million was doing strange things to his mind, and to wonder about the mind-set of people who live their lives surrounded by that kind of luxury: "You wake up in an apartment like that when you pretty much command the city, and you have this sort of castle to yourself. What does that do to your life on a daily basis, just waking up with that feeling and seeing that?"

And, more importantly, what is it doing to our world, to have whole chunks of our most important cities annexed by Moneyland? Some of the world's cleverest financial analysts have been mulling over this same question for more than a decade, and their conclusions are startling. We need to talk about plutonomy.

16

PLUTOS LIKE TO HANG OUT TOGETHER

Ajay Kapur is someone who thinks a lot about money, and how to make it. In autumn 2005, he started thinking about why the rise in oil prices was not affecting the US equity market in the way that conventional thinking predicted that it should. Oil was yet to hit its record highs of 2008, when Brent crude exceeded $140 a barrel, but the price had still doubled in three years, which was startling enough. Since US taxes on fuel are low, increases in the crude oil price were passing quickly into matching increases in the pump price, with an inevitable effect on consumers' disposable income. Drivers were angry; politicians were asking questions; the government was fretting. And, yet, there had been no apparent knock-on effect on the stock market. It was puzzling, and it was the sort of puzzle that analysts love to unpick.

At the time, Kapur worked for Citigroup as director of Global Strategy Research, and his job was to find assets for his clients to invest in, which meant it was important for him to understand what was going on. He and his colleagues looked into the situation, and concluded that it was too early to be concerned. And then they thought some more, and read some more, and inspiration came: which they revealed to the world in an October 2005 report entitled "Plutonomy, Buying Luxury, Explaining Global Imbalances." The footnotes to the report are packed full of works by academics who were then or who have since become heroes to the political left—particularly Thomas Piketty and Emmanuel Saez—but the bank's analysts brought them into the service of the very wealthy. The report's message was a simple one: the rich are getting richer, and that can make you rich.

Kapur's insight was that, if the majority of a country is owned by very few people, it doesn't necessarily matter what the oil price does. The oil price is important to people who are on a budget. If the cost of a daily commute doubles in the space of a couple of months, then inevitably that will reduce the amount of money you have to spend on other things: holidays, trips to the cinema, even food. But if you are very wealthy, then the proportion of your income that you spend on travel is very low, so your spending will barely be affected at all. If your customary purchases are Birkin bags, Sunseeker yachts, or a fourth home, perhaps in Miami, then changes to the oil price don't matter, which has important consequences for the profitability of the companies that make those products.

Kapur thought too many of his fellow analysts were looking at the average consumer, when, in an age of inequality, the average consumer's role in the economy was increasingly marginal. He used the word "plutonomy" to describe economies where the wealthy have a disproportionate share of the assets (he claimed to have invented it, although it dates back to at least the mid-nineteenth century, when it was used as a synonym for economics), places like Britain, America or Canada. His analysis was original, and provided a fascinating insight into how the kind of luxury spending detailed in the previous two chapters is affecting the world.

"In a plutonomy there is no such thing as 'the US consumer' or 'the UK consumer,' or indeed 'the Russian consumer,'" Kapur wrote. "There are rich consumers, few in number, but disproportionate in the gigantic slice of income and consumption they take. There are the rest, the 'non-rich,' the multitudinous many, but only accounting for surprisingly small bites of the national pie." According to the Citigroup analysts' research, the top million households in the United States had approximately the same wealth as the bottom 60 million households. And rich people have relatively little of their wealth tied up in their homes, meaning that a far higher proportion of that wealth is disposable. If you looked at just financial assets, and exclude housing from the calculation, the top million households held more of the sum total of American wealth than the bottom 95 million households put together. This was a new phenomenon, and one with lucrative possibilities for a canny investor. If you could find a way to invest in the companies that produce the kind of products favored by Naulila Diogo (the newlywed Angolan princess with the $200,000 dresses) or Dmitry Firtash (the Ukrainian tycoon with the

London Tube station), then you could profit from inequality, and perhaps with time become a plutonomist yourself.

Not all of Kapur's analysis has stood the test of time. He speculated that the reason the United States, Canada and Great Britain have greater inequality than continental Europe and Japan is because of their immigrant heritage, and suggested this might be because immigrants have higher levels of dopamine ("a pleasure-inducing brain chemical ... linked with curiosity, adventure, entrepreneurship") than those whose forebears happily stayed in their ancestral villages. But his economic approach was rigorous. He identified a basket of stocks that have benefited from the kind of purchases favored by Moneylanders: companies like Julius Baer, Bulgari, Burberry, Richemont, Kuoni and Toll Brothers. His report traced the prices of the shares of the companies in the basket back to 1985, and showed they cumulatively yielded an annual rate of return of 17.8 percent, far higher than the stock market as a whole. That outsized return had only accelerated with time, particularly since 1994, when wealthy Russians and others began to develop their taste for Western luxuries.

"The emerging market entrepreneur/plutocrats (Russian oligarchs, Chinese real estate/manufacturing tycoons, Indian software moguls, Latin American oil/agriculture barons), benefiting disproportionately from globalization are logically diversifying into the asset markets of the developed plutonomies," he wrote. "Just as misery loves company, we posit that the 'plutos' like to hang out together ... the emerging markets' elites often do their spending and investment in developed plutonomies rather than at home."

It was an obvious point to make. Two years previously, Russian billionaire Roman Abramovich had sensationally bought Chelsea Football Club, so it should have come as no surprise that the world's wealthy like to spend their money in just a handful of cities. But the consequences of this behavior had not been teased out before.

Kapur credited the key insight into what this all meant to his "fashion-loving colleague Priscilla," who apparently told him: "Wow, I can get rich by owning the plutonomy stocks, and then spend my money on these products." Priscilla was arguing that, if inequality keeps increasing, rich people will buy more luxury goods, so shares in companies producing luxury goods will keep outperforming the broader market. If Kapur's clients keep investing in those shares, they can keep making money out of the rise in inequality, which they can spend on luxury goods, which will boost those shares, which will increase inequality further, so more luxury goods will get bought, which will boost those shares, and so on. It was a virtuous circle, for anyone clever enough to invest in it. The basic message was the same one as that learned by Pnina Tornai's wedding dress boutique, or by the estate agents of west London: there's a lot of money to be made from those who don't ask too many questions about where money comes from.

Kapur stuck with the subject, producing several more investigations into his theme. In March 2006 came a report called "The Rich Getting Richer," and in September he hosted a London symposium called "Rising Tides Lifting Yachts," in which he summarized his investment advice with the short but memorable formulation "Binge on Bling." The website for the symposium is still live and, although the links to its presentations are no longer working, the report paraphrases the words of some of its participants, who had unrivaled insight into what the citizens of Moneyland like to buy.

"The general message was that the rich wanted great service, uniqueness, quality and that the traditional concept of cost was far less than value. Time is of great value, rather than money. The rich value personal attention and uniqueness," the report's authors concluded. "Our own view is that the rich are likely to keep getting even richer, and enjoy an even greater share of the wealth pie over the coming years."

In this aspect of the research, they were not entirely correct. The financial crisis that began in 2007 and engulfed the world economy wiped out the fortunes of some very rich people. But they were not entirely wrong either. After the crisis, banks were reluctant to lend money as freely as before, meaning those with spare cash were in an even better position than before; which is why developers in places like London, Miami and New York were so keen to build properties for wealthy foreigners to invest in. If cash buyers are dominating the market, it's natural to build the properties that cash buyers want. And if cash buyers want a dog-walking area on the thirty-second floor, then that's what they must have.

As Kapur and his team of analysts said back in 2006, in what now sounds like a perfect description of the citizens of Moneyland: "the ultra-rich plutonomists, they don't tend to be part of a specific geography, but tend to be very global, hanging out in plutonomy destinations with fellow plutonomists. For example, in London 60 percent of houses costing over four million pounds are now sold to non-Brits." After the financial crisis, these nomadic Moneylanders inherited the earth.

There are a lot of banks like Citigroup, and those banks employ a lot of analysts, and those analysts produce a lot of reports, and those reports describe a lot of asset classes—stocks, bonds, commodities, land, anything else that can yield a profit. The vast majority of the reports vanish after a couple of days, having served their rather limited purpose. Kapur's plutonomy papers have lasted longer, however. Reuters ran a long article based on his first report within a week of its publication, and was followed by most of the world's most prestigious media outlets. Follow-up papers found their way into articles in the *Economist*, *Barron's*, the *Financial Times* and the *Atlantic*. His insights made their way into books, including Michael Gross' engrossing tale of 15CPW, and into a 2009 film by the polemical documentary maker Michael Moore, who cast Kapur as one of the bad guys in *Capitalism—A Love Story*.

This is unfair. Kapur has never exulted in the situation he and his analysts described, and explicitly stated in the plutonomy paper that he took no moral position on the matter at all ("our analysis here is based on the facts, not what we want society to look like"). He was just doing his job of seeking profitable investment opportunities for his clients. He primarily focused his macroeconomic analysis on developed countries, particularly the United States, and mentioned the wealth coming out of corrupt kleptocracies largely in passing, so he can't be criticized for conniving in the kind of egregious theft that led the Obiangs to buy so many supercars from Californian dealerships, or the diminutive ex-president of Zambia to buy bespoke suits and shoes with lift heels.

In fact, his analysis of poor countries is perhaps the least convincing part of his work, since it largely boils down to a belief that their economies will become increasingly law-abiding, more like the United States. In reality, the rule of law is deteriorating in many of the countries he mentioned, so they are developing in precisely the opposite direction. Be that as it may, Kapur and his team do not deserve the reputation they have earned in some of the shadowier reaches of the internet, which casts them as a sort of morals-free cabal of high priests to the kleptocrats.

If there is criticism, it should not be directed at them, but rather at the structure of the Moneyland ratchet, which inspires highly intelligent people like these analysts to restlessly scan the world for ways the very rich can get very much richer. In a world dominated by the wealthy, whether you call them plutonomists or Moneylanders, no ambitious businessperson can afford to ignore the financial might of the very rich, even if their fortunes are of dubious origins.

This has curious consequences for once-staid concerns. In 2015, the accountancy firm Deloitte published a study of Swiss watches headlined "Uncertain Times," which described how leading manufacturers of exclusive timepieces were gloomy about the future. The reason for the misery came not from a recession, or from any problem with the products, but rather from the fact that the government in China was cracking down on corruption, which was harming sales of the kind of lavish gifts that crooked officials had previously accepted in return for favorable decisions. "The pessimism about China and Hong Kong can be explained by the lower rates of growth in the economies of many emerging markets, and also the anti-corruption and anti-kickback legislation in China: these developments have led to a fall in the sales of luxury products," Deloitte's analysts wrote; "81% of watch executives indicated that demand in China has fallen over the past 12 months due to anti-corruption legislation."

Luxury watches are popular among officials, since they provide a discreet but effective way of advertising their power. In 2009, the Russian newspaper *Vedomosti* mischievously published a compilation of photographs of the watches worn by top officials at public events, noting each one's price and contrasting that with the declared income of the official in question. The cheapest watch belonged to the head of the Audit Chamber, costing a mere 1,800 Swiss francs. The majority were in the $10,000–50,000 range, beyond which a handful of officials had really splashed out. The deputy mayor of Moscow won both first and second place, with watches costing $1.04 million and $360,000; while Chechen president Ramzan Kadyrov's watch came third, with an estimated price of $300,000. The article caused some embarrassment to top officials, which is perhaps why the official photographer photoshopped a $30,000 Breguet timepiece off the wrist of the Patriarch of Moscow as he sat at a highly polished table in 2012. The photographer neglected to remove the watch's reflection, however, which both made the Patriarch look ridiculous and also rather undermined his attempts to argue for a return to asceticism and traditional values under the moral leadership of himself.

The watch controversy has not led to any concerted anti-corruption campaigns in Russia (perhaps to the relief of the manufacturers of luxury products), but a serious Chinese anti-corruption campaign began in 2012, with tens of thousands of people indicted, including members of previously untouchable classes—leading figures in the military, central government and provincial administrations. Officials stopped flaunting their wealth almost instantly, with dramatic consequences for the kind of businesses that Kapur had suggested his clients invest in, including businesses that produce luxury food and drink. France's Bordeaux region had exported a mere 12,000 hectoliters of wine to China in 2005 but, within seven years, that had increased almost fiftyfold, to 538,000 hectoliters, with the ostentatious buying patterns of wealthy Chinese people utterly transforming the economics of French wine production. When the anti-corruption campaign started, and Chinese officials were no longer quite so willing to publicly imbibe bottles of Château Lafite, the region's exports dropped by a quarter in two years. "Certainly, we are seeing fewer wealthy Chinese arriving on private planes and buying up €50,000 of wine in one go," a wine merchant rather laconically told a trade publication.

The same thing happened to other Western manufacturers who had profited from booming sales of the kind of prestigious products popular among China's Moneylanders. In 2014 the Scotch Whisky Association blamed what it euphemistically referred to as the "Chinese government's austerity campaign" for the fact that sales to China and Singapore (which often reexported to China) had dropped. By the end of 2016, sales to these two Far Eastern markets were down by almost 50 percent. Any investors who had bought into wine or spirits producers in the hope of riding Kapur's plutonomy wave would have had a very rude shock.

Kapur had warned his clients about this risk, however. He might not have analyzed the ways that politicians and businessmen in emerging markets exploit the rules to get rich, and he might have mistakenly predicted that places like Russia would become more, rather than less, law-driven; but he did at least recognize the danger to his basket of plutonomy stocks posed by anti-corruption campaigns. "High income inequality, projected to get worse and associated corruption perceptions, often centered around [state-owned enterprises], is likely to bring about a strong anti-corruption policy," he wrote in a follow-up paper for Merrill Lynch Bank of America (his new employer) in 2014. "Luxury sales with a strong Emerging Market angle, or with high visibility (watches, wine, cars, jewelry, etc.) are likely to be at risk in the short term."

He took the opportunity to reexamine his calculations from a decade earlier, but saw no reason to revise them: "in Russia, Malaysia, Israel, the Philippines, Taiwan and Chile, the uber-plutonomists account for a much larger share of their economies than their compatriots in the US. Given that larger fortunes enjoy larger pre-tax returns, we expect this wealth concentration to grow."

Note his use of the word "compatriots" there. It was presumably supposed to be something like "comrades," since very rich people from around the world do not actually share citizenship. But it's a psychologically telling slip nonetheless. The subtext is that Kapur's plutonomists are all citizens of the same country, whatever passport they hold.

Anti-corruption campaigns by governments are not the only risks to the profitability of Kapur's plutonomy investment strategy, however. Since his very first paper in 2005—and he has kept publishing them, through a series of different employers—he has highlighted the fact that, in its essence, plutonomy is about inequality. His investment strategy will only keep yielding outsize profits if the wealthy can keep gaining an outsize share of the world economy. If the societies where they live and spend their money decide to stop that excessive accumulation of wealth, then the situation could be reversed. "A backlash against plutonomy is probable at some point," he concluded back in 2005. And that is what happened, under the leadership of the United States.

17

BREAKING SWITZERLAND

In early 2007, two Washington attorneys got in touch with the Department of Justice to offer them a case. They had a client, they said, who wished to remain anonymous, but who could expose tax dodging and rule breaking by thousands of America's wealthiest people, all arranged by one of the world's most powerful financial institutions. Bradley Birkenfeld had walked into the office of the attorneys, Paul Hector and Rick Moran, almost a year earlier and told them he had "inside information on a worldwide conspiracy," which he wanted them to take to the DoJ, and the attorneys had spent months collating it. "We're telling you," they wrote to DoJ prosecutor Karen Kelly, "this is a once-in-a-lifetime case."

Birkenfeld wanted immunity from prosecution in return for telling federal prosecutors everything he knew, but he didn't get it. Quite the reverse, in fact. Although he sat in long meetings with them over the summer of 2007, and shared documents and memories, the DoJ prosecutors felt he was holding out on them. In May 2008, he was arrested on arrival in his home town of Boston and charged with Conspiracy to Defraud; a month later, he pleaded guilty, and faced a sentence of five years in prison. The statement of facts published alongside his guilty plea is a remarkable insight into the lengths that private bankers like him would go to in their quest to help their clients keep their cash out of the government's clutches.

Birkenfeld admitted to having advised his clients to "place cash and valuables in Swiss safety deposit boxes; purchase jewels, artwork and luxury items using the funds in their Swiss bank account while overseas; misrepresent the receipt of funds from the Swiss bank account in the United States as loans from the Swiss bank; destroy all off-shore banking records existing in the

United States; and utilize Swiss bank credit cards that they claimed could not be discovered by United States authorities." In one instance, which caught the imagination of journalists covering the case, Birkenfeld admitted to having bought diamonds on behalf of an American client, stashed them in a toothpaste tube, and smuggled them into the United States so his client could enjoy his wealth without the Internal Revenue Service (IRS) knowing. It was like the old Goldfinger scam from the 1960s, but better: why go to the trouble of attaching heavy plates of gold to a customized Rolls-Royce that James Bond can follow all the way to Switzerland, when you can stash millions of dollars worth of diamonds in your sponge bag?

Birkenfeld later published a book about his experiences, *Lucifer's Banker*, which makes clear that the revelations in the statement of facts were barely the start of what he'd got up to. He described how he had stalked rich Americans at yacht regattas, motor sports events, classical music recitals, art galleries, and then pitched for their money over vintage brandies with a straightforward boast. "What I can do for you is zero," he'd say, enjoying their surprise, before going in for the kill. "Actually, it's three zeros. Zero income tax, zero capital gains tax, and zero inheritance tax."

When they flew out to see him in Geneva, he'd take them to a top-class restaurant, then a strip bar, where he'd pay for their prostitutes. That would get them in the right frame of mind for business, so the next morning he'd escort them to the bank, where they would sign over their money. And every dollar that he brought in—all of the Net New Money, as the bank called it— would inflate his bonus, which he spent on enjoying himself. "Maybe it wasn't so special, unless you're partial to magnums of Laurent-Perrier champagne, fresh beluga caviar, or boxes of Churchill cigars just flown in from Havana. I guess it was nice if you like Frigor Swiss chocolates, Audemars Piguet watches, Brioni suits, and gorgeous girls who care only about pleasing you and having a great time," he wrote with inch-thick sarcasm in his memoir. "I'd perfected my game, flying first-class all over the world, staying in five-star resort hotels, and seducing scores of one-percenters into stashing their fortunes in Swiss numbered accounts, no questions asked."

The prosecutors denied Birkenfeld immunity because, they said, he had tried to shield himself from prosecution, and had not been entirely candid with them. They accused him in particular of covering up his relationship with the billionaire Igor Olenicoff, a long-term client of his who had hidden $200 million in secret Swiss accounts, which were supposedly owned by a Bahamas shell company, rather than by the property developer, with the details obscured by corporate structures in Denmark and Liechtenstein. "We cannot have people, US citizens, engage in that kind of fraud scheme come back here and put half the leg in the door," prosecutor Kevin Downing told the judge at Birkenfeld's sentencing hearing.

He had a point. You have to earn immunity from prosecution, by giving up everything you know, which is why the judge jailed Birkenfeld for forty months. But it's true also that if anyone was going to be cut a little bit of slack, it should have been Birkenfeld. The banker didn't just manage to incriminate himself when he came to reveal his conspiracy in Washington; he provided a priceless and unprecedented window into the heart of Swiss banking, the inner sanctum of Moneyland. And that changed the world, as Downing— perhaps a little reluctantly—conceded. "Without Mr. Birkenfeld walking into the door of the Department of Justice in the summer of 2007, I doubt as of today that this massive fraud scheme would have been discovered," the prosecutor admitted. "That investigation now has resulted in not only changing the way in which we obtain foreign evidence from banks in Switzerland, it has caused the Swiss government to come and enter into new tax treaties with the United States."

Few people have done more to strike at the foundations of Moneyland than Bradley Birkenfeld, whose revelations caused a revolution in the way offshore finance works. When he came to Washington, he didn't just share his information with the Department of Justice; he also took it to the Internal Revenue Service and the Senate's investigations subcommittee, which published a report on the matter in July 2008. According to the investigators' conclusions, the US Treasury was losing around $100 billion a year in tax revenues, thanks to offshore schemes of the sort revealed by Birkenfeld. And the report laid out just how Birkenfeld's employers—the Swiss banking giant UBS—had done it.

The scam was partly a continuation of the hallowed Swiss tradition of ripping off other countries, as enshrined in the banking secrecy laws of 1934, which were originally passed to protect French clients from a government that was trying to maintain its revenue base in the midst of the Great Depression.

This was the same secrecy that came to be much loved by Nazi war criminals and other kleptocrats, and then exploited by London's pioneering offshore bankers. But this was an updated version of the old scam, since it followed an agreement designed to prevent precisely such behavior. In 2001, Birkenfeld's former employer UBS agreed to become a Qualified Intermediary (QI), under which it promised either that its American clients would declare all their income from Swiss-held assets, or that the bank would itself withhold tax from that income, and provide it to the Treasury if the clients refused to do so. The essence of the deal was that the Swiss banks could keep their secrecy as long as they promised to collect tax on the Treasury's behalf.

It was an elegant plan, but it had one small flaw: it required the banks to be honest. Quite naturally, therefore, it failed. In fact, not only did it fail, but UBS actively subverted it. While banks from other jurisdictions agreed to close their Swiss private banking operations, UBS aggressively expanded, marketing undeclared accounts to as many rich Americans as it could. The reason is obvious: facilitating tax evasion is extremely lucrative. "Undeclared accounts held more assets, brought in more new money, and were more profitable for the bank than the declared accounts," the Senate concluded. "Soon after it joined the QI program, UBS helped its US clients structure their Swiss accounts to avoid reporting billions of dollars in assets to the IRS."

Birkenfeld told the Senate committee how he had been part of a "formidable force" of around seventy private bankers who used to attend UBS-sponsored events like Art Basel in Miami with the goal of picking up wealthy attendees. The bankers quadrupled the amount of US-originated money they held between 2004 and 2006, and were looking to quadruple it again in 2007. "You might go to sporting events. You might go to car shows, wine tastings. You might deal with real estate agents. You might deal with attorneys," Birkenfeld told the subcommittee. "It's really where do the rich people hang out, go and talk to them."

When asked why someone would want a bank account in Switzerland, Birkenfeld's reply was blunt: "tax evasion. And ... people always like the idea that they could hide some from their spouse or maybe a business partner or what have you."

Unsurprisingly, the Department of Justice did not react well when it heard quite how methodically UBS has been abusing its trust. In July 2008, the US government demanded that the Swiss banking giant hand over the names of all of its US account holders, something that would destroy the Swiss tradition of banking secrecy. In normal times, UBS would have ignored the demand, or obfuscated, or come up with some work-around like the QI deal which would end up giving it new earnings opportunities. But this was during the depths of the banking crisis. By the end of October that year UBS would have offloaded $60 billion-worth of toxic assets onto the Swiss banking regulator, and written down $49 billion worth of losses linked to the US mortgage market. Its shares had lost two-thirds of their value, and there was speculation over whether it could survive as a bank at all. It simply did not have the ammunition for a battle with the US government, on top of its life-or-death struggle with the financial markets. So it started handing over its clients' data. It was a first crack in the mighty fortress of Swiss banking secrecy.

In February 2009, UBS came to a Deferred Prosecution Agreement, agreeing to pay $780 million in fines to various US government agencies. It admitted that 17,000 of its 20,000 American private banking clients had used its services to hide assets totaling $20 billion (that's more than $1 million each), which earned $200 million in revenue for the bank each year. The indictment makes it clear that, while UBS might have looked like a staid buttoned-up banking operation, in reality it ran its private bank like something out of a thriller. "Executives, and managers . . . referred to the United States cross-border business as 'toxic waste' because they knew that it was not being conducted in a manner that complied with United States law and the QI agreement," the government prosecutors stated. "Executives, managers, desk heads, and bankers utilized nominee entities, encrypted laptops, numbered accounts, and other counter surveillance techniques to conceal the identities and offshore assets of United States clients."

Five years later, UBS's great rival Credit Suisse (between them, they controlled about half of all the money in Switzerland) admitted to similar charges, though its punishment was far harsher. It had to plead guilty (rather than cop to the more lenient DPA), and pay a fine of $2.6 billion. The prosecution revealed yet more details about what Credit Suisse admitted had been an "illegal cross-border banking business," which had lasted for decades, and which had serviced 22,000 Americans with $10 billion in assets. Half of those assets were controlled by a relatively small number—just 1,234, according to a Senate investigation—of extremely wealthy tax dodgers who hid their identity behind shell companies.

Perhaps the most telling aspect of the prosecution was the revelation that Credit Suisse had initially tried to comply with the QI agreement it signed up to, and even established a new private bank called CSPA with which to do so. The plan never took off, however, because its American clients were not interested. "The CSPA initiative ultimately failed as a business, in part due to US clients' unwillingness to pay a premium for an account in Switzerland if their accounts were declared and tax compliant," the statement of facts stated. In other words, the whole point of banking in Switzerland was to dodge taxes; if a client couldn't do that, she saw no value in the bankers' exorbitant fees. Credit Suisse would rather break the rules than forgo those fees. Welcome to Moneyland.

It was not all high-tech. Credit Suisse had a branch in Zurich airport, so clients could access banking services without having to trek into the middle of town. Among its services was helping Americans get around the $10,000 limit on bringing cash into the United States, by breaking the total up into smaller packages. UBS was in this game, too. In the prosecution of multimillionaire UBS client Ernest Vogliano, lawyers revealed that he moved his money from Switzerland to the United States by using travelers' checks, which he endorsed in Zurich, then put in the mail to be picked up on his return home to New York. That was not only absurdly low-fi, but also an almost exact copy of the first eurobond scam, all the way back in 1964, except the travelers' checks did not even provide any income. They just sat there until he wanted to spend them. If ever proof had been needed that Swiss bankers simply couldn't be trusted to look after anyone's interest but their own, the humiliation of Credit Suisse and UBS was it. As Birkenfeld told me during a long chat in a wood-paneled drawing room in his London private members' club, complete with a vintage car in the lobby, this was just how the Swiss do business.

"I think what these banks have done historically, and UBS in particular, is they've just said, 'Fuck you, we're Switzerland, we're big, try us,'" he explained, with a laugh. He's an extremely affable conversation partner, big and boisterous, with a huge diamond-studded knuckleduster ring on the middle finger of his right hand, but he's disconcertingly direct as well. "Was I part of it? Of course I was. It wasn't like the janitor's going to come in and be able to expose this ... I will continue to expose it, because they're still in denial, like an alcoholic that can't admit they have a drinking problem."

Incidentally, although Birkenfeld was jailed for helping his clients dodge taxes, he came out on top in other ways. New legislation designed to encourage whistle-blowers earned him a cut of the fine that UBS paid to settle its case. His share came to $104 million. At one conference I attended, he was giving away laminated facsimiles of the government check, to be used as bookmarks. The Treasury had deducted tax at source, so the check was only for $75,816,958.40, but that's still enough to set him up for life in the style to which he had been previously accustomed.

Thanks to the UBS revelations, and other related scandals (Wegelin, Switzerland's oldest bank, was forced to close in 2013 after pleading guilty in a similar case), in 2010 Congress passed the Foreign Account Tax Compliance Act (FATCA), which was like QI but with big sharp teeth. "For too long, individuals have taken advantage of the system by hiding money in accounts overseas, while millions of families and small businesses here at home pay the price," Treasury Secretary Tim Geithner said at the time.

Under FATCA, if foreign financial institutions declined to reveal the identity and assets of American clients, the government would impose a 30 percent tax on any investment income received from the United States. It was a pretty compelling offer, particularly when combined with the ongoing criminal investigation into Credit Suisse and other Swiss institutions. Foreign banks could continue to help Americans break the law but, if they did so, they would be cut off from the US market, and under constant threat of a multibillion-dollar fine. Where the QI scheme had failed, this succeeded. By 2013, five years after Birkenfeld was arrested and the UBS scandal broke, Credit Suisse had closed the accounts of 18,900 of its 22,000 US clients, and their assets had dropped to just $2.6 billion (the exact same amount as the fine it paid to the US government a year later, funnily enough). FATCA came into full operation in 2015. It still has some loopholes, but essentially it has killed the easiest form of tax evasion for Americans.

A 2017 study showed that the number of Americans reporting foreign accounts had risen by a fifth after FATCA entered into force, with an additional

$75 billion of wealth disclosed. "US banks lost out to foreign banks selling secrecy. It was as simple as that. Then FATCA changed the rules," said Elise Bean, formerly the chief counsel at the Senate Permanent Subcommittee on Investigations, and one of the driving forces behind senators' efforts to expose tax evasion. "FATCA has already begun discouraging offshore tax evasion, causing more US taxpayers to disclose their offshore accounts, report their offshore income, and pay the taxes they owe."

The United States is perhaps the only country that could have done this. Its tax code requires all citizens to file a tax return even if they don't live in the United States, so Americans can't easily escape the rule's provisions by moving abroad. On top of that, the weight of the US economy, and the unique global role of the dollar, has given the government more leverage in standing up to the banks than any other country could have. And where the Americans led, the rest of the world followed. European countries agreed to swap information with each other; and the various British tax havens agreed to exchange data with the UK. All these efforts culminated in 2014 with the Common Reporting Standard (CRS), under which countries agreed to automatically swap information about all the assets that each other's residents hold in each other's banks. Previously, countries had exchanged information, but only on request, which meant tax authorities had to know what they were looking for before they looked for it. Now that information flowed automatically, they could cross-check financial data with tax returns and see who was breaking the rules. The agreement threatened to stymie the most potent motivating force behind Moneyland, the fact that law enforcement stopped at national borders, but money did not.

Philip Marcovici, a Swiss lawyer who has counseled the wealthiest people in the world for decades, told me in 2016 that these new international agreements have completely changed the picture for the superrich. "Families have only two choices: play by the rules of your country, or get out of your country. It used to be that there was a lot of abuse, that people could hide money, using bank secrecy, using complicated structures, all that," he said. "What does it mean to play by the rules of your country? It means you need to understand what the tax laws of your country are. In some cases, people are living in countries where playing by the rules is not even an option, because they're living in a country that may have political instability; there may

240

be corruption in the tax system; there may be lots of reasons why in some cases playing by the rules is simply not safe for the family. And then you also have countries where taxes are so high that playing by the rules for some families is just not acceptable, because it's too expensive, and they don't want to live in that kind of society. You have a choice, though; you play by the rules, or you get out."

This new prohibition on cheating has been bad news for many offshore centers. The island of Jersey, for example, has seen its banking sector's contribution to the economy fall from more than £1.8 billion at the turn of the millennium to £800 million now. In Jersey and elsewhere, assets have returned onshore, now that the traditional advantages of the old offshore centers have vanished. Jersey's whole financial sector is far smaller than it was at the start of the financial crisis, and is showing few signs of recovery. This has had a brutal impact on the budget for the island's government, which has been forced to bring in a sales tax to make up for the corporation tax cuts it passed in a bid to keep businesses from leaving, driving up the cost of living for ordinary islanders.

Some US citizens have sought to escape the provisions of FATCA by renouncing their citizenship, since that means they no longer have to file a tax return. In 2016, 5,411 Americans gave up their passports, up 26 percent on 2015, which was in turn 58 percent higher than in 2014. Only 235 passports were renounced in 2008, before FATCA was conceived of, which shows how steep the increase has been. The arrival of CRS has also been a boon for the residency-for-sale business, with companies like Henley & Partners boasting of ever greater volumes of business. After all, as Marcovici said, there are now only two options for those who want to keep their wealth out of the hands of the taxman: pay up or get out. If you take up residency outside your country, it will be your new home that gets the information about your assets, rather than your old one, which is an incentive to move somewhere with low taxes and/or honest bureaucrats.

So, is this a happy ending? Is Moneyland doomed? If you've read this far, you won't be surprised to discover that it isn't; predictions of its demise always prove premature. There are two reasons for this.

The first has been highlighted by many campaigning charities, such as Oxfam and Christian Aid. They have repeatedly pointed out that the CRS was created by the G20 and the Organisation for Economic Co-operation and Development (OECD), both of which are clubs for wealthy countries, and its terms are designed for well-resourced tax departments. Countries can choose which other places they think are sufficiently honest and competent to make use of their information: Switzerland has so far agreed to share data with only nine other countries (plus the members of the EU), all of them wealthy. To really make a difference, poor countries need to see the information about their residents, and if they are cut out of the exchange, they cannot tax them. Here is another one of those unfortunate Moneyland feedback loops: if a country's rulers steal its wealth and stash it offshore, that country will almost certainly be deemed too corrupt to be included in information exchange programs. That means the details of its rulers' theft will never be revealed, so no one will ever be able to seize it back. Once again, the incentives surrounding the international financial system prevent a sustained assault on the way Moneyland works.

But anyway, that's by the by. Even if the world's poorest countries did receive all of the data, most of them would lack the resources to analyze what they'd gain. According to Christian Aid, the countries of sub-Saharan Africa would need to hire 650,000 new tax administrators to reach average global staffing levels, which is a number almost twice as large as the population of Iceland. And they would have to hire, train and maintain those employees before they earned any new taxes, which would naturally lead to a significant cash flow problem. So that's the first reason why it's too early to talk of CRS as a solution to the Moneyland problem. CRS is a first step, but the journey toward making the world's wealthiest people obey the same laws as everyone else will still be long and fraught with dangers.

It'll be a stroll, however, compared with problem number two.

If you think back to how offshore first appeared in the immediate postwar period, it was thanks to bankers identifying and exploiting a small but important loophole: dollars in the City of London could not be controlled by the US Treasury, and did not interest the Bank of England. The two jurisdictions' regulatory regimes didn't quite overlap; rich people squeezed their money through the gap, and down the tunnel into Moneyland.

The new post-Birkenfeld regulatory regime, in which tax authorities automatically exchange information with each other, has a structural weakness, too—one that was baked into it at the very start. CRS involves—as an aspiration, if not yet as a reality—everyone exchanging information with everyone else. But the United States is not part of CRS; it has its own system. Unlike CRS, FATCA, the US law that first broke the back of Swiss secrecy, only works in one direction. Financial institutions from more than 100 countries have to share information on assets held by US citizens or residents, but US institutions don't have to send anything back in return. US institutions will be fully informed about what's going on elsewhere in the world, but their counterparts in other countries will be completely blind as to what's happening in the United States. If you think how much money could be made out of a small loophole like the one that gave birth to the City of London's eurobonds, just imagine how much can be made from a yawning gap like this one, in the very heart of the world's new financial architecture.

"If the Americans ask the Brits which Americans have accounts here in England, the Brits will give them the information. If they ask the Germans, same thing. If the Germans ask the Americans, however, the Americans say, 'Buzz off.' Are you kidding me? This is the biggest hypocrisy on the planet," said Birkenfeld. "It's a big problem, and they're part of it."

Moneyland is not a geographical location, it is a system, which emerges wherever conditions allow it to. The rules of Moneyland dictate that, if the money is no longer left undisturbed in Switzerland, its guardians will shift it somewhere it will be. Thanks to Birkenfeld, conditions are no longer so great in Zurich and Geneva, which have been losing business to rival financial centers now that their banks are not the impenetrable fortresses of old. But conditions are perfect in America: in places like Reno, "The Biggest Little City in the World," Washoe County, northern Nevada.

18

TAX HAVEN USA

If you're arriving on the bus from San Francisco on a snowy February day, Reno looks like a scene from the 1970s. The cars are huge, the roads are wide, the casinos are concrete edifices with square corners and negative charm. If you walk into the gambling halls, you are confronted by ranks upon ranks of slot machines, positioned on tired-looking carpets, illuminated by energy-sapping fluorescent lights. Punters are few and unenthusiastic. On the streets outside, pawnshops offer you loans secured on your jewelry; and sell off the guns of those who've been unlucky at the tables.

My only previous knowledge of Reno had come from Johnny Cash, who sang about murdering someone there just to watch him die. After a day or two wandering through the place, I began to see how it might have that effect.

Nevada's state motto is "Battle Born," which reflects the fact that it gained statehood during the American Civil War, as part of a rushed effort by the Union to conjure new states into existence and thus gain extra votes for Abraham Lincoln. It was, at the time, the third-largest state in the Union (after California and Texas), and yet had only 40,000 inhabitants. It therefore struggled to pay for itself, particularly when output from its silver mines started to decline a decade or so after the war ended, which is why it has been constantly casting around for new sources of revenue ever since. One lucrative vein of business has been undercutting the regulations of California, its larger, more populous and much richer neighbor. Las Vegas has long made a handsome living by offering services to residents of nearby Los Angeles that they couldn't get at home, and Reno has done the same for its neighbors in San Francisco: quickie divorces, shotgun weddings, gambling, low taxes, marijuana. Even prostitution is legal in Nevada, which makes it unique in the United States.

This Nevadan form of deregulation came to affect Moneyland in 1986, when Congress set out rules for the taxation of "generation-skipping transfers." The precise details of the rules (it involves grandparents passing assets to their grandchildren) don't matter; what is important is that they had loopholes. One loophole affected trusts, the legal structure created when you give property away to a professional trustee, who then follows the instructions you agreed to at the time of the gift. If you owned an oil company, and put it in trust for your grandchildren, the 1986 rules were supposed to ensure that they would pay tax on the generation-skipping transfer that occurred when the trust ended. So far, so good. But Congress made a crucial mistake. It left it up to individual states to decide when trusts ended, rather than setting a single standard itself, with predictable results. Thanks to the Moneyland ratchet, states began to compete with each other, to the benefit of wealthy people and to the detriment of everyone else.

Under the common law that America inherited from England, you could not put property in trust forever, but were limited to a period equal to twenty-one years after the death of anyone alive at the time you created the trust (in practice, this works out at about a century). This was based on the principle that it's wrong for future generations to be bound indefinitely by the wishes of dead people. The whims of capricious ancestors might have made for good plots in nineteenth-century novels, but the judges who shaped the common law thought they would be disastrous if followed slavishly in real life.

In America, the states could decide for themselves how long a trust could last, and some of them—Wisconsin, South Dakota, Idaho—had already diverged from the common law and abolished this so-called limit on perpetuities before 1986, but with little effect. There was at the time no tax advantage to a trust that lasted longer than the traditional duration, which would at any rate long outlast the grantor herself. As soon as there was a tax on generation-skipping transfers, however, the incentives changed completely. Congress had, inadvertently, created an advantage for trusts that could last forever and thus never be taxed, meaning the desires and wishes of dead people will go on binding future generations for centuries, if not until the end of time.

By 2003, at least $100 billion (and probably much, much more) had poured into states with these long-lasting so-called dynasty trusts, creating a powerful incentive for other states to change their laws to abolish their own limits. This is a new phenomenon, in historical terms, but it is likely to have profound consequences, because forever is an extremely long time. If a trust persists for just 350 years, its beneficiaries could be fifteen generations removed from the original grantor, and there could easily be more than 100,000 of them. Every one of these beneficiaries will have the right to bring a lawsuit against the trustees and, were they to want to hold a meeting, they would have to rent a stadium to do it in. These distant cousins will be essentially as unrelated to each other as they would be to anyone else in the general population, yet they will be linked together by the zombie wishes of their common ancestor.

Thanks to some Massachusetts genealogists, we have some great examples of quite how distant those cousins can be. If George Allen, who died in the state in 1648, had been able to establish a perpetual trust for the benefit of his descendants, those would have included both Barack Obama and Winston Churchill. If Samuel Hinckley, who died in Massachusetts fourteen years later, had done the same, both Obama and George W. Bush would have been beneficiaries. No one has really thought through what this is likely to mean for future wealth distribution. Instead, perpetual trusts are a curious and under-explored consequence of a small and apparently inconsequential quirk in tax law.

And that is not the only way that US states have attempted to tweak their law to undercut each other and attract the wealthy to their law firms. Nevada does not have perpetual trusts, but in 2005 it passed a law deeming that they can extend for 365 years, which is still a remarkably long time (that is approximately how long ago New York City was founded; imagine if someone had put Manhattan in trust for their descendants when it was just a swampy island).

Nevada is also particularly proud of its asset protection ordinances, which mean that—providing two years have passed since you put your property in trust—your creditors have no way of getting hold of it, just like in Nevis. If a man owns a company, puts it in trust, then gets divorced, his ex-wife has no claim on those assets at all, and nor do his children. And, thanks to the generosity of Nevadan law, you can even be a beneficiary of your own trust, which means you've given your property away, so it can't be taken away from you, and yet you retain all the benefits of owning it. "The theory behind an asset protection trust is to provide the client with an extra layer of protection between the client and his/her future predators and creditors. We use the example of a bullet proof vest. You could get shot/sued, and it will hurt, but you will walk away" is how Premier Trust, which has offices in both Las Vegas and Reno, puts it on its website. There has not been a single case of a creditor ever managing to pierce a Nevada trust.

This has long been a potentially attractive prospect. Even so, for decades, it wasn't enough to bring in the kind of wealthy foreigners who kept their money in Switzerland, not least because of the proactive approach of US law enforcement. Putting your money in America looked worryingly like keeping your honey in a cave inhabited by a large bear. This means Moneyland in America was largely the preserve of Americans; foreigners preferred to keep their money out of the reach of the Internal Revenue Service. "Look, I used to work for an English investment bank, and no one who wasn't a US person wanted to deal with the US at all, because of the IRS and the complexity, they just didn't want to be next to the US," said Greg Crawford, president of the Alliance Trust Company in Reno. "That has all kind of changed ... We have money from overseas now, we have significant money from overseas."

Crawford's office is on the ground floor of 100 West Liberty Street, a smart building a few blocks from Reno's rather depressing cluster of casinos, and which used to house the US headquarters of Porsche. Alliance Trust arrived here in late 2016, having outgrown its previous home, thanks to the surge in demand. "Alliance Trust has seen a rise in interest around Nevada trusts from international families. While more countries are taking measures to decrease privacy, Nevada is one of the few locations left in the world where the privacy of families is still respected and protected," said his company's press release at the time of the move. With Switzerland knocked out of the secrecy game by FATCA, Nevada (and several other states) is rushing to take up the slack.

Upstairs from Alliance Trust, on the twelfth floor, is the office of Rothschild & Co., one of the world's most venerable financial institutions. Rothschild arrived here in 2013, but it does not advertise its presence on the board in the lobby (the section for the twelfth floor is entirely blank). This may be a result of a small furore that followed a Bloomberg article published in 2016, which recounted how wealthy clients were moving money into Nevada from traditional tax havens like Bermuda and the Bahamas. That article quoted a draft presentation by Rothschild managing director Andrew Penney (which he insists he amended before he delivered it), which referred to the United States as "effectively the biggest tax haven in the world," and which attracted considerably more attention than anyone was comfortable with.

He was telling the truth, though. What we are seeing in Reno, and we could just as easily see in other states like South Dakota, Delaware and Wyoming, which also have thriving trust businesses of their own, are the perverse results of the world's failure to agree to consistent standards. These are the visible signs of wealth slipping out of democratic supervision, just at the moment when governments thought they had the upper hand—and of US financial institutions getting rich from it.

Peter Cotorceanu has seen this up close. He joined UBS in January 2007, as part of the bank's wealth structuring department. A New Zealand–born lawyer, he advised anyone with more than $50 million in liquid assets how they might want to invest them, although he insists he only worked with money that had been declared to the relevant authorities, which made him something of an outlier. "I was actually mocked at the bank for that, because it was all about undeclared money," he told me by telephone from his home in Pennsylvania in 2017. "At the time, at the bank, the number that was floating around was 70 percent undeclared money, and if you didn't deal with undeclared money, then what the hell were you doing at UBS?"

Then the Bradley Birkenfeld scandal broke, and everything changed. Suddenly, UBS needed to find clever ways for its clients to manage their money that didn't offend the American authorities, and the straight-laced Cotorceanu was the man to find them. He assessed the relative merits of forty different jurisdictions, and created the templates for an entirely new way of doing business. As such, he became an expert in the relative merits of FATCA and CRS, and that's when he made the same discovery made by a handful of other clever lawyers. The United States had bullied the rest of the world into scrapping financial secrecy, but hadn't applied the same standards to itself.

"When people ask, 'What did the US do to become the new secrecy jurisdiction?' I say they didn't do anything, that's the point. They always were a secrecy jurisdiction, but everyone else was as well," Cotorceanu told me. "I liken it to Warren Buffett's expression: 'You only know who's not wearing a bathing suit when the tide goes out.' There were lots of people not wearing bathing suits at the time, the US among them. The tide went out, and everyone else scurried to put on bathing suits. The US is the only one without a bathing suit on. It's always been without a bathing suit, but now it's alone by itself."

The reasons for why this happened are complicated, and partly stem from differences in the ways different countries administer taxes. US authorities only collect information on interest and dividends, meaning that this is the only information they can share with foreign counterparts, whereas CRS regulations require other countries to share information on the actual assets that are earning the income. But there is more to it than that—and this reflects a tension at the heart of offshore wealth that goes back to the very beginning of Moneyland, and which was reflected in the creation of the first eurobond, the transaction that circumvented the official plumbing of the oil tanker of the world economy.

As you will recall, back in the 1960s, Swiss banks held money for Nazi war criminals, but they also held money for tax dodgers and for refugees. These groups of people all sought secrecy/privacy/confidentiality (delete as applicable), meaning the evil money washed around with the naughty money, which washed around with the scared money. All three groups of people benefited from those first eurobonds, because they provided an income on money that had previously been static, but not all three were advertised equally prominently.

Swiss banks loved to claim that their bank secrecy had been designed to protect Jewish wealth from Nazi confiscation, and kept quiet about all the dictators whose money they also hoarded, or the tax dodging they facilitated. In effect, the refugees were being used to run interference for the others, and to make the Swiss banks look high-minded, rather than like the criminogenic institutions that they were.

Swiss banks insisted that the reason they didn't want to reveal the details on their clients was because that would endanger the legitimate interests of people seeking protection from rapacious governments. That excuse died for Switzerland with the revelations about diamonds in toothpaste tubes that resulted from the Birkenfeld scandal, meaning the tax dodgers and the kleptocrats finally got exposed. But it hasn't died for the United States, where bankers still like to claim they're acting as a refuge for the money of the world's huddled masses, rather than for the wealth of greedy businessmen and crooked officials.

In 2011, the Obama administration was seeking to expand the information it collected on foreigners' bank accounts, so it could exchange it with those foreigners' home governments. This was a crucial plank of the anti–tax evasion agenda, since the United States looked hypocritical if it demanded services from foreigners and provided nothing in return. The response from bankers, however, was furious. "At a time when we are trying to create jobs and reduce the burden on businesses, this is the wrong issue at the wrong time," fumed Alex Sanchez, president of the Florida Bankers Association, in testimony to Congress. "This proposal could result in the flight of tens to hundreds of billions of dollars of capital."

All twenty-five members of Florida's House of Representatives backed the association with letters of their own, using an argument familiar to anyone who's followed Swiss banking over the years. Sanchez admitted that the owners of the $60–100 billion of foreign-owned deposits in Florida banks paid no tax, but said that was not why they kept their money in the state. They banked in Florida, he claimed, because they were worried about their safety. "Their personal bank account information could be leaked by unauthorized persons in their home country governments to criminal or terrorist groups," Sanchez argued. "Which could result in kidnappings or other terrorist actions being taken against them and their family members in their home countries, a scary scenario that is very real." Similar letters came in from bankers' associations in Texas, California and New York, all insisting that they were providing a safe haven for people who feared for their lives, if information about their wealth leaked.

If you believed these associations, their member banks were almost charitable institutions. It may well have been true that their account holders were scared of their governments, but that was of minimal importance compared to the Florida banks' real concern. If they weren't allowed to sell secrecy anymore, and all the Latin American money found a new home, just as the undeclared money fled Switzerland when Birkenfeld broke UBS open, then they would go bust, just like Wegelin, Switzerland's oldest bank, did. Some Florida banks relied on foreign deposits for up to 90 percent of their capital, which meant almost none of the banks' clients were paying tax on their interest at all.

The bankers' publicity offensive was joined by right-wing think tanks like the Heritage Foundation, which was at least more honest in its reasons for opposing the attempt to expose foreign tax dodgers hiding their cash in the United States. Daniel Mitchell, a Heritage senior fellow, insisted that the proposals to exchange information between countries were "fiscal imperialism . . . our government has no obligation to help enforce the bad tax laws of other nations." Since the United States was at the time obliging other nations to help it enforce its own tax laws, this argument did not persuade the Obama administration, but it did ensure that the passage of this rather technical amendment became much trickier than it might otherwise have been. There is now no political appetite to expand FATCA's requirements to mesh with those of the rest of the world, which means the mismatch that has brought all that money to Reno is here to stay.

"Until the Democrats control both houses of Congress, and the presidency, I don't see it changing. Stranger things have happened, but I do think—for the near to mid-term—we're stuck with it," Cotorceanu said. "I don't see who's got the leverage to put on the US to make them comply."

So, how does this loophole work? "It's extremely straightforward," Cotorceanu assured me, before launching into an explanation that was extremely complex. Essentially, it comes down to where a trust is based, for tax purposes. Since a trust—unlike a company—is not registered with the authorities, and instead exists as an agreement between a settlor and her lawyers, its jurisdiction is not a straightforward matter, and interpretations differ from country to country. The lawyer's goal is to exploit those mismatches, to create a trust that exists in the gap between the regulations.

"The simplest way to do it, and there are lots of others, is just to give one foreign person, a non-US person, one of a laundry list of powers: for example, give a foreign protector the right to remove and replace the trustee. Bang, that's a foreign trust," Cotorceanu said. "It doesn't matter that the trustee is in the US, that it's governed by Nevada law, that all the assets are in the US, that all the investments are in the US, that the bank account is in the US. If one power on the laundry list is held by a non-US person, that makes it a foreign trust for tax purposes." If it's a foreign trust for US tax purposes, then the United States cannot give information about it to foreign governments even if it decides it wants to, so that's good.

But here's the better bit. If it has a US trustee—such as Alliance Trust Company of Reno, Nevada, for example—then it is American for the purposes of the CRS, and thus immune to its provisions. That means it doesn't have to exchange information with foreign governments under CRS, which means a rich Chinese businessman, or a Russian, or whoever, can park their money here with no fear that information about it will drift back to his home country's authorities. The trust is American under foreign law, and foreign under American law: it doesn't exist anywhere. Nevada's magical trusts have played jurisdictional Twister in a way that would have warmed Siegmund Warburg's heart: it's American when it wants to be; and foreign when it doesn't. "It's incredibly useful," said Cotorceanu.

So who's taking advantage of it? "Latin Americans, Russians, Saudis, these people aren't worried about taxes. Saudi doesn't have an income tax, but information about wealth can be used against people, and if you've got a regime that's not to be trusted, then you want to keep that data confidential. You've got a lot of people from the Middle East and these sort of oppressive regimes that want privacy as well," Cotorceanu continued. "I require that the clients be declared, because I don't want to assist in hiding undeclared money. For me, it's all about privacy for declared money. However, a lot of people are using these structures now for undeclared money. The old offshore world has been brought onshore to the US."

Nevada does not appear to publish data on the amount of assets held by its trust companies, but its rival South Dakota does. In 2006, before the UBS storm hit, the state's trustees held an already impressive $32.8 billion—that's around $42 million per head for every South Dakotan. By 2015, that total had reached $175.1 billion; and then rose by almost a third in just the next twelve months. In 2016, the state's recorded total was $226 billion, which was $261 million for every resident of this prairie tax haven. "Many of the off-shore jurisdictions are becoming less appealing for international families looking for secrecy. The stability of the US combined with its modern trust laws catering to international families may be more appealing to many international families than an offshore trust based in a less powerful country," one South Dakota trust company states on its website. Translated into normal English, that means that tax havens can be bullied into coughing up information about their clients, but the United States cannot.

"South Dakota and Nevada are basically identical," said Crawford as we approached Carson City, Nevada's capital, where the legislature was scheduled to discuss some changes to tax law and he had been asked to give evidence. "We copy some of their ideas, they copy ours. It's a constant process to stay competitive." That's the Moneyland ratchet.

We were zooming down the interstate, passing through the scrubby desert landscape that has featured in thousands upon thousands of Westerns, and it was strange to think that this was now home to billions of dollars. Although Americans are only able to place a limited amount of assets in a trust—around $5 million—that does not apply to foreigners, so the boom in international business has brought in a disproportionate amount of money. "The influx from overseas has been fun. It's nice to go to Zurich and Hong Kong and such, and those trusts tend to be fairly large. If you think the average trust we have in our office is, say, $8–10 million dollars; the ones that come in from overseas have been probably on average $50 million. So that is one aspect of the business that is enjoyable," he told me. "Because of the CRS, there's a lot of money coming out of the traditional money centers: Switzerland, Singapore, Hong Kong, to a certain extent Dubai, a little bit of the Caribbean ... they'll call up and say, 'My grand-dad set this up in many of those places, and now all of a sudden this information is going to be sent back to Bangladesh or Uzbekistan, so let's move it to the States.'"

Was America being hypocritical in demanding other countries close down these schemes, while simultaneously creating some more itself? He looked troubled for a moment. "It's not like there was some grand plan behind this," he said. "It truly evolved accidentally. But that is the case, you can put your money in the States and, in all honesty, we don't know if they've reported things or not. We get affidavits, and we try to make sure the money is at least clean coming in, but we can't verify."

The Nevada State Assembly is a handsome building, with rounded arches about its windows, and broad lawns. We passed beneath the pillars around its grand entrance, and climbed the stairs to a committee room where Crawford and others gave their opinions about a rather technical point of law, which would allow companies like his to expand into other states, while allowing out-of-state trust companies to come to Nevada. They were in favor and so, it appeared, were the various representatives asking their questions. After the hearing ended, Assemblyman Al Kramer (whose district number 40 spreads from Carson City up toward Reno, and which I had just been driving through) hung back and chatted to George Burns, commissioner from the financial institutions division of Nevada's Department of Business and Industry.

Kramer was full of enthusiasm about all the jobs that this influx of foreign money would bring to his constituents. "I'm looking at, what, twenty-one or twenty-five companies in Nevada, and they'll all add five or six people over the next few years. Regardless of what you say, that's over a hundred employees, and they're probably with benefits and on over $100,000 each," he gushed. "If you had a hotel with a hundred employees and they were all going to make a hundred grand a year, all based on people coming to Nevada, you'd think this was the greatest success in the world, and that's what I'm looking at. I think we're set up; this is going to be big."

Reno might look run-down now, but if only a few more trust companies arrive, it will gain a financial district, which will drive regeneration of the whole town. Burns—who licensed Rothschild & Co. when it opened its office there—shared his passion, and the two men gloated a little about all the jurisdictions they were outcompeting for business.

"You've got the Isle of Man, you've got some of those places in the Caribbean, you've got a couple of places in the Pacific Ocean, islands and that, which have their own rules on stuff like this. Quite frankly the US government, the IRS, is quite capable of putting pressure on some of these places to change some of their rules. So, by being in Nevada, they aren't subject to whims of what might happen," said Kramer.

"Where it's a little more volatile," chipped in Burns. "Cyprus, for example, has some pretty good rules, but who in the heck wants to put his money in Cyprus?"

They both laughed uproariously.

Who indeed? If your wealth is protected from the United States government by the United States government, then what protection can an island in the Mediterranean offer? As Cotorceanu wrote in an article in *Trusts & Trustees*, an industry magazine, in 2015: "[T]hat 'giant sucking sound' you hear? It is the sound of money rushing to the USA to avoid [CRS] reporting. Unfortunately, much of that money will be undeclared."

It is also the sound of Moneyland reasserting itself. This is not a conspiracy—it never is—but a natural consequence of the laws of the anthill. When the incentives are right, everyone acts in the same way. Nevada becoming a tax haven is just the natural consequence of bright people seeking ways to make money for themselves (and save money for their clients), in a world where money moves freely but laws do not. If Nevada and the other popular trust-friendly states have as much money booked in at their law firms as South Dakota does, that means more than a trillion dollars is hiding from sight, avoiding taxes and oversight, and will be able to do so until long after even our great-grandchildren are dead; until perhaps the end of time.

New York State's department of taxation and finance estimated in 2013 that it was losing around $150 million a year in taxes because its residents were putting assets into trust in other states, but there is no estimate for how much the rest of the world is losing. CRS hasn't even been fully implemented yet, so the consequences of the traditional wealth havens losing their secrecy haven't played out, yet already the effects are clearly visible in official statistics. According to some recent research from Gabriel Zucman (the French economist at Berkeley), Swiss institutions' share of the world's offshore wealth has dipped from around 50 percent to barely a quarter over the last decade. Asian tax havens are creeping up to join them. But is "offshore" even a useful concept any more? If the best tax haven is now the United States, we may need a whole new term for the places that adapt their laws to accommodate the needs and whims of the nomadic Moneylanders.

Curiously, perhaps the person I met who best appreciated what was happening was Mark Brantley, prime minister of the little Caribbean tax haven of Nevis, who spent fully ten minutes responding to a question about the importance of financial services to his island with a full-blooded condemnation of the United States. He is a fluent and convincing speaker, and his passion was genuine, particularly when he described how Nevis had been obliged to sign up to FATCA and CRS, yet Washington had done nothing in return. "I once attended a conference many years ago and I recall that the speaker opened with a very explosive comment, that the most money laundering in the world occurred on an island," Brantley told me in early 2018. Apparently, most of the Caribbean jurisdictions were represented in the room, and they looked at each other in alarm. "I held my breath hoping the island was not Nevis. And he said the island of Manhattan . . . what is happening now is that money that was traditionally offshore is now flooding onshore, and is going to Delaware and Nevada and places like that."

He had plenty of wrath left over for Britain, too.

"It is no secret that the UK, and London in particular, has a disproportionate number of wealthy Russians, and wealthy oligarchs from all round the world. The question is why? It can't be for the weather. So, why are people flocking to London?" he asked. "There is clearly a deliberate policy to attract people of a certain net worth because of the added value those people can bring. So if the United Kingdom can do that, then what is the issue with other countries, not as endowed as the UK, trying to stand on their own two feet?"

Like Simeon Daniel, the prime minister at Nevis' independence from Britain, Brantley is faced with trying to help his island earn a living, despite all the disadvantages of being small, remote and surrounded by water, and he thinks America and the European countries are being extremely hypocritical in insisting on standards that they don't keep to themselves. "I think a lot of the time, the suggestion is that we operate in some murky Shangri-La," he said. "When I practiced as a lawyer, we dealt with and did work with all the major law firms in London, all the big City firms, and all the major law firms in New York and Zurich, big cities such as those. It's not as though we are somehow cut off. In fact, there is a fallacy in trying to divide us into offshore and onshore; there is no divide."

He has a point. The same tricks played by Nevis are equally available in Nevada, yet the State Department criticizes his country rather than its own; imposes rules on foreigners that it does not obey itself. "One wonders whether some of this zealous regulatory oversight is not really a money grab . . . You have this anomalous notion that's sometimes being promoted that these rules are for the good of everyone, and I'm not convinced at all," he said.

Brantley recalled a speech that President Barack Obama made in 2009, in which he criticized Ugland House, an office block in the Cayman Islands that is home to thousands of companies, and which the president called either the largest building or the largest tax scam in the world. "I was surprised, you know, for a Harvard-educated lawyer not to know how the financial services sector works," he said. "There's no money in Cayman, that money is in London, that money is in New York, that money is in the big money centers of the world. Cayman is not a big money center; it is a facility."

Brantley was elected in December 2017, and had only been in office for a few weeks when we spoke, so he is fresh from the private sector. He has a law degree from Oxford University, and has acted in some major commercial litigation processes, which gives him a strong understanding of the business he oversees. "A lot of time when we strip away all the furore about regulation, and 'This is bad for the world,' and you pare it down to the bare minimum, you see that those making the most noise are really doing some very interesting things themselves, which kind of look like what we're trying to do. And that is a major concern."

Perhaps he's right; it certainly seems a convincing argument to me. But there is only one certainty in all this, and that is that Moneyland will continue to evolve, its protections will continue to strengthen, as its imaginative and well-motivated defenders think of new ways for its citizens to hide and multiply their money, in whatever jurisdiction is most welcoming to them, whether that's Nevis, the United Kingdom, the United States or somewhere else entirely. And this is a very worrying thought for anyone attached to the idea of democracy and the rule of law.

19

STANDING UP TO MONEYLAND

There is an enduring point of view that none of this matters: Moneyland is the price of globalization, and it's a net gain for the rich countries and the offshore havens that enable it. Yes, much of the world is being looted by greedy thugs posing as politicians; yes, rich people are minimizing their taxes through elaborate offshore structures—but as long as the Moneylanders spend their money in our countries, then we come out on top.

This argument is the basis for the economy of Jersey and of Nevis, as well as for the kind of economy Nevada would like to become. It also underpins a lot of the discussion around the London and New York property markets: it may be true that few Brits or Americans can afford a house in large sections of their own cities, but that doesn't matter because real estate agents and lawyers and accountants make a good living assisting the people who can. Once upon a time—before Andy Murray spoiled it by being both British and good at tennis—this could have been called the Wimbledon hypothesis: it doesn't matter if you don't win the trophy, as long as you host the tournament.

Obviously, the degradation that offshore-enabled venality causes in places like Ukraine, Afghanistan and Nigeria is worth caring about on its own terms, but if you are unswayed by such naïve humanitarian concerns, you should note too that the misery in distant countries will become our misery if we don't act to stop it. Corruption radicalizes Islamists in Afghanistan, Nigeria and the Middle East, and helps them defeat underfunded and demoralized government soldiers. But groups like the Taliban, Islamic State or Boku Haram don't stop at national borders once they're on the march: indeed, their violence is already spreading. This is why the US Marine Corps general John

Allen, whom I quoted in Chapter 1, believes corruption to be the most potent threat his forces faced in Afghanistan. And corruption does not only empower terrorists. It also prevents the treatment of epidemics in sub-Saharan Africa, helping deadly diseases to gain a foothold. It incentivizes doctors in ex-Soviet countries to use the wrong courses of medicine, thus helping viruses gain resistance to the drugs we use to treat them. These diseases don't stop at national borders any more than terrorists do.

Furthermore, the corrupt elites that we allow to buy property and influence in Western countries don't stop being crooks just because they've flown over an ocean. They are polluting public life here, just as they did in the countries where they earned their fortunes.

For reasons of national security, public health and public order, we should all care about Moneyland.

***

I recognize, however, that these arguments are unlikely to spur government action, for the understandable reason that it is difficult to persuade people of the merits of a course of action that will cost them money. Moneyland's enablers pay taxes, and tackling them will give public finances a short-term hit. That's why, when governments have taken action, enforcement has often been lackadaisical at best.

Just look at the response by US banks to the White House's modest attempt to make them report foreigners' interest payments to those foreigners' home countries. "Kidnapping is not just a theoretical concern for these depositors. Having their deposit information leaked is a real threat to them," said Gerry Schwebel, executive vice president of a Texan bank, who predicted "massive capital flight" if the regulations took effect, as well as the collapse of many banks.

The regulations took effect anyway, in 2011, and in the years since not only has IBC Bank of Laredo, Texas, not gone under, but its stock price has tripled. His bank's resilience may be a result of the fact that his and other objections persuaded the US authorities to limit the number of countries they were willing to exchange information with. Mexico and Brazil are on the list; Venezuela, Colombia, Panama, Equatorial Guinea, Afghanistan, Nigeria,

Malaysia, China, Russia and most other places plagued by kleptocrats are not, which makes the whole thing rather pointless.

Another country not on the list is Ukraine, which has produced so many stories of high-level egregious corruption, from people claiming such different political beliefs, over such an extended period, that you could be forgiven for concluding that this is simply what Ukrainian politicians do. Antipodean bowerbirds just happen to make elaborate displays of beetle wing cases; the moon just happens to fit precisely over the sun during a solar eclipse; ministers in Kiev just happen to steal.

Paul Manafort's conviction reveals that view of corruption—as a form of behavior specific to a particular culture—to be nonsense, however. Manafort is a veteran Washington operator, and Donald Trump's successful election bid was the fifth presidential campaign he had been involved in; yet it is striking how closely the behavior he was found guilty of tallies with that of Ukrainian politicians over the decades since independence. He even had a British company, Pompolo Ltd (which we met in Chapter 1), just like his boss did. It was not registered at the address on Harley Street used by Yanukovich, but it did exactly the same job as the ex-president's shell companies. It helped hide his identity while he spent money on luxury goods and property in the United States, in the same kind of upscale neighborhoods favored by the clients of Gennady Perepada, the ebullient bilingual broker I met in New York. The expenditure breakdown could have come from a Senate investigation into a luxury-loving African politician.

Manafort's conviction makes clear that people steal not because of something intrinsic to the culture they grew up in, but because they think they'll get away with it. They are more likely to steal in countries with poorly developed or corrupted institutions, like Ukraine, but that is a function of the opportunity, not the individual. And there are disquieting signs that the dirty money sloshing around the world, seeking safe Moneyland investments, is beginning to besmirch the places that have been so happy to provide it with a haven. The anguish in the United States over Russia's involvement in the 2016 presidential election is a remarkable testament to the destabilizing impact of a relatively small amount of dirty money, even in a developed democracy. There is similar concern in Britain, over murky donations into the Leave campaign during the Brexit referendum, and equivalent worries in other leading Western countries, particularly France and Germany.

In one of the Harry Potter books, Mr. Weasley warns his children: "Never trust anything that can think for itself if you can't see where it keeps its brain." He was referring to a diary that magically replied every time his daughter Ginny wrote in it, and which turned out to be possessed by the spirit of the evil Lord Voldemort, but the principle is equally sound in the Muggle world. Anonymous companies act rationally, but have no clear controlling intelligence, and that should perturb anyone who comes across them. It is striking that even their defenders struggle to come up with a justification for their existence. The most frequent argument I have heard is one based on the Disney Corporation's quest to buy up land in Florida, which it did via multiple small companies, rather than in its own name. Had it been unable to hide its identity, the argument goes, the sellers would have increased the sale price because of their knowledge of its wealth, which would have been unfair. If that is the best case that anonymous companies' defenders can make, then it's clear there really is no argument for them. At the very least, political parties should refuse to accept money from an entity if they can't see where it keeps its brain.

The widespread acceptance of this anonymous money into politics is contributing to a broad loss of trust in democratic processes. More than two years has passed since the Brexit referendum, and we still do not know who gave £425,000 to a body called the Constitutional Research Council, which passed it to Northern Ireland's Democratic Unionist Party, which spent most of it on advertisements urging Britons to vote Leave. No rules were broken—because of the special circumstances of Northern Ireland, where party donors have their identity hidden for security reasons—but rules were very definitely bent. Almost all of the money was spent in England and Scotland, where the DUP fields no candidates, and where the money would normally have had to declare its provenance.

As with the eurobonds, those magical pieces of paper invented in London in the 1960s and which set hidden wealth free, when naughty money ran interference for evil money and helped make offshore tricks look acceptable, it was an example of Westerners bending rules that are later broken by kleptocrats. If indeed Vladimir Putin perverted the US democratic process by hiding dirty money behind elaborate corporate structures, he was only following a path long taken by wealthy Americans (and revealed in the journalist Jane Mayer's excellent book *Dark Money*) reluctant to act in their own names. Disapproval of these surreptitious payments should not depend on whether they are benefiting your own side or not. They are inherently harmful. Without trust, liberal democracy cannot function.

When representatives of the Allied powers met in Bretton Woods, New Hampshire, in 1944 to design the post-war financial architecture, they had a keen awareness of the danger posed by the flow of uncontrolled money, and the power it had to spread instability and damage democracy. "A breach must be made and widened in the outmoded and disastrous economic policy of each-country-for-itself," wrote the US delegate, Harry Dexter White, in a memo to Treasury Secretary Henry Morgenthau in 1942.

Morgenthau himself addressed the opening conference of the International Monetary Fund two years later, and reflected the same theme: "The thread of economic life in every nation is inseparably woven into a fabric of world economy. Let any thread become frayed and the entire fabric is weakened. No nation, however great and strong, can remain immune." It was this reasoning that persuaded them of the merits of locking speculative wealth behind national borders, where democratic governments could keep an eye on it.

The system that the Allies created did not last as long as its creators hoped, and it was frequently criticized during its lifetime for, among other things, the high tax rates the participating governments imposed, but its achievements look remarkable in retrospect. As the British journalist Ed Conway points out in *The Summit*, his history of the Bretton Woods event and its aftermath, between 1948 and the early 1970s, the world enjoyed progress and stability never rivaled before or since. The world's gross domestic product expanded by an average of 2.8 percent a year, more than the equivalent rates for the preceding and succeeding periods. For those charmed two and a half decades, there was not a single global recession. Since the system collapsed, with Richard Nixon's abandonment of the dollar's peg to gold in 1971, there have been four.

The Bretton Woods participants' dream of locking speculative money behind national borders is dead. Globalization is here to stay, so we must seek other solutions to the problems they identified. If we accept globalization, however, we don't need to accept its dark side: the profusion of anonymous money, which is nosing into our politics, our economies and our major institutions. The simple fact about offshore is that it only exists to allow people to do things they can't do onshore. Offshore structures allow people to hide their ownership of money, which benefits those with something to be ashamed of, and bewilders everyone else. This abuse of corporate structures is all the more peculiar when you think back to what limited liability companies were created for: to encourage entrepreneurs to invest without fearing personal bankruptcy. Giving the owners of companies the right to secrecy quite clearly runs counter to the law's intentions: secrecy encourages fraud, not entrepreneurship.

There are, of course, people with legitimate reasons to disguise their identity: film stars at risk of being stalked; political refugees pursued by rogue regimes; children with fortunes left to them by wealthy parents. Their privacy should be respected, but it should be provided systematically and consciously, for clear reasons, and to anyone who needs it, not just to the rich. It would be perfectly reasonable to prevent the details of people with a legitimate need for anonymity from being published on open registers, while denying that privilege to everyone else. But at present, the favors of Moneyland go only to those who can afford them, not to those who need them. Once those with legitimate fears of exposure have been given privacy, everyone else should be treated in exactly the same way.

I came across one example of why our failure to do this is a problem while researching an article about lobbying in the UK. (It was never published, for legal reasons.) The European Azerbaijan Society (TEAS) had spent tens of thousands of pounds flying members of parliament to Baku, putting them in top-class hotels and showing them around. When those MPs came back, they almost invariably spoke favorably about Azerbaijan in the House of Commons, which seemed strange, since this former Soviet republic is a hereditary dictatorship that, among other things, jails journalists who reveal the business dealings of the country's ruling family.

Azerbaijan "has made tremendous strides forward both politically and economically in recent years. That should be recognized and rewarded," said

Tory MP Mark Field in 2011; at the time, he was earning £4,000 a month from TEAS. Across him on the opposition benches, there was equivalent enthusiasm. "We discovered that the trade unions there enjoyed better relationships and more employment rights than we do here in the UK. Azerbaijan is a young democracy," said Jim Sheridan, a Labour MP, six months after returning from a £3,100 trip of his own.

There appeared to be a fairly direct link between the all-expenses-paid trips to Azerbaijan and the on-the-record praise heard in the House of Commons, which is no doubt why Tale Heydarov, who ran TEAS, paid for those trips. "Such visits have great effectiveness," he boasted at a conference in March 2012. (Anar Mammadov, the son of Baku's transport minister, did the same job in the United States, with equally impressive results.)

So where did the money come from? Heydarov, who is fluent and charming and who speaks the kind of beautiful English you'd expect from a graduate of the London School of Economics, told me at a drinks reception (when I had the bad manners to ask him) that TEAS raised money from members' subscriptions. But it did not appear to have enough members to pay these kinds of expenses; and that explanation did not tally with the words of Göran Lindblad, a Swedish politician who was on the TEAS payroll for a while. "Very often the documents that followed the money show a transaction starting in the Marshall Islands, via Estonia," he told me. "Every banker and taxman will directly think about money laundering . . . It's lucky no bank reported it to the tax authorities." It is surprising that TEAS would route members' subscriptions earned in Britain via the Marshall Islands and Estonia before spending them on MPs' travel expenses.

And this is not the only mystery. Tale and his brother Nijat, who has also been involved in running TEAS, are not short of cash. They have both owned property in highly desirable parts of central London, as well as a café and a restaurant, but it is not clear where the money comes from. Meanwhile, their father, Kamaladdin, has been head of Azerbaijan's Ministry of Emergency Situations (MES, which wags have called the Ministry of Everything Significant) since 2006. In a US embassy cable revealed by WikiLeaks, an American diplomat told his superiors in Washington that Heydarov Sr. had earned a vast fortune by exploiting his powers. "Only one name—Kamaladdin—is regularly whispered as the most powerful man in Azerbaijan," the cable said.

"Heydarov expanded Customs income by systematizing bribery within the organization, in effect creating an extensive pyramid scheme."

It may well be that TEAS does raise all its income from members, or that Tale Heydarov has another source of earnings. But if that is so, the evidence has never been presented, which leads to corrosive speculation that money embezzled from Azerbaijan's state budget could have found its way to London, been spent on MPs, and thus persuaded them to praise the Azerbaijan government in the House of Commons. This is clearly a very worrying thought, and not the kind of speculation that helps expand faith in democracy.

And similarly opaque money trails can be found in the United States. A Ukrainian friend alerted me to the existence of Aveiro, a Northern Ireland–registered limited partnership that is listed on its corporate registration documents as involved in "international trade and investment." In reality, it was spending money on Washington lobbyists on behalf of unidentified Ukrainian interests, and there was no way of finding out who they were. Aveiro's two partners were offshore companies—Montfler SA and Nisbett Invest SA—and the documentation didn't even reveal what jurisdiction they were based in, let alone who their shareholders were. You might trust in the good intentions of Aveiro's owners, but in reality no one would employ such a roundabout approach to spending their money, unless they had something to hide.

There have been efforts to address this problem in some parts of the world. Ukraine now insists that all companies identify their real owner. The database is poorly managed and hard to access, but it did allow me—when searching for the oligarch Mykola Zlochevsky, whose $23 million was temporarily frozen by a London court—to track down Zlochevsky's mother in a flat in central Kiev and have a very nice chat with her. He had listed himself as living at her address, and she said she had got accustomed to journalists popping by occasionally. Other countries have insisted on disclosure, although so far with the same kind of problems. Denmark is one of several European countries that has insisted that companies publish their "beneficial owners," which puts paid to any repeats of the scams run by Bradley Birkenfeld before he blew the whistle on UBS, and for which he liked to use Danish companies.

Britain now requires companies to report a "person with significant control" (PSC), which means we can sidestep the clever ownership structures used by Formations House, the company factory on Harley Street, and see who really owns its shares. The new PSC register shows that the company is owned by Charlotte Pawar, the evasive woman whom I briefly met (and who emailed to complain after I wrote an article about the long record of companies created by Formations House being involved in fraud).

Campaigners who have analyzed the data point out that it shares the same problems with all of Britain's corporate information, in that it is self-reported and not checked. There are rules against deliberately falsifying information, but enforcement is weak or non-existent: the only man who has ever been convicted of this crime—a company formation agent named Kevin Brewer—created two companies in politicians' names, specifically to alert them to how easy it was for fraudsters to abuse British corporations. It was a publicity stunt, designed to shock them into action, but it achieved the opposite response. When he told them what he had done, he was prosecuted himself, and in March 2018 was fined £22,800, in a farcical legal proceeding that the British government's own anti-corruption coordinator, an MP named John Penrose, called "a bone-headed exercise in shooting the messenger."

Despite the failure to adequately enforce this law, its existence is still a step forward in the quest to stop people from hiding behind British companies and other legal structures. In 2018, Parliament, despite opposition from the government, passed a law forcing the UK's Caribbean offshore territories to reveal the true owners of their companies. Since these tax havens already had to exchange information with UK authorities, police officers were able to see behind the veil of secrecy erected by the British Virgin Islands, Jersey, Anguilla, Gibraltar and others, and the number of companies being created in them has fallen sharply.

Without the secrecy provided by corporate structures and numbered bank accounts, the central section of the Moneyland pathway—steal it, hide it, spend it—falls away, and tracking the theft becomes far easier. Remember: John Tobon of Homeland Security Investigations in Miami said that fully half of his time was spent just working out who owns stuff. Other investigators said that was an understatement. If real names can be attached to property, it becomes very obvious, very fast, what property has been stolen.

All efforts to move in that direction are welcome, but the problem so far is that those efforts have all been partial, and do not address the root cause of Moneyland, which is that money is international while laws are not. As long as some jurisdictions allow things that other jurisdictions do not, Moneyland's gatekeepers will always find a way of exploiting the mismatches, just as they have with the differences in the information exchange requirements between the United States and the rest of the world. The companies that sell residency are now marketing their product to wealthy Russians and others, with the promise that their jurisdictions will keep financial secrets, since information is exchanged with the country of residence, not the country of origin. Loopholes provide opportunities, always.

Heidi-Lynn Sutton, the supercilious regulator in Nevis who found my concerns about corruption so amusing, made it clear her island would not be following the British territories' example and giving foreigners automatic access to its registries. "We are an independent country," she said. "So if law enforcement officials here in Nevis want to look at our register that's a different matter for us. But for another jurisdiction to do that without a warrant, that might be of concern."

Her concerns are understandable, of course, but they need to be overcome. If the world is to stop billions upon billions of dollars draining into Moneyland, and away from oversight, it needs to act as one. This was understood at the Bretton Woods conference, where participants believed they were acting to keep democracy safe. Ironically enough, however, their actions required a certain disdain for democracy for them to be successful. The International Monetary Fund and indeed Keynes' proposal for an international currency were both dominated by a supposedly enlightened technocratic elite. In a democracy, the argument appeared to be, some things are too important to leave to the people. Any argument of this nature is inevitably vulnerable to a backlash from politicians able to whip up public distrust.

Some US politicians are sufficiently concerned by the dynamics of Moneyland to risk this, and a number of bills have been introduced in the House of Representatives, including a bipartisan proposal from the Financial Services Committee in 2018 and a Corporate Transparency Bill in 2017, which would oblige states to collect true ownership information for companies created under their laws.

The Trump administration has moved in the opposite direction, however. In his first six months in office, the White House scrapped two crucial measures that prevented US companies from bribing foreign officials: the Extractive Industries Transparency Initiative and the related Cardin-Lugar Amendment, both of which required energy companies to publish what they paid to foreign governments.

Oil companies had argued that the requirements put them at a disadvantage with their foreign rivals, which was preventing them from expanding. "The energy jobs are coming back. Lots of people going back to work now," said Trump after signing the documents to scrap the rules, a clear example of a democratic imperative clashing with an international initiative.

He may have been influenced in his thinking by the fact that members of his administration, most notably son-in-law Jared Kushner, have long profited from the flow of anonymously owned foreign money into the United States, particularly into the real estate market. The Kushner family companies, after a wave of media attention, are currently being investigated for how they've benefited from the EB-5 visa program, under which foreign citizens can apply for a green card if they invest at least $500,000 in eligible US projects. But in reality, property developers from all over the country have been using the program as a useful source of capital ever since the financial crisis, and indeed before.

In a way, it's odd there hadn't been scandals around the EB-5 program before, considering how poorly managed it is. A Government Accountability Office report from 2015 identified a truly startling catalogue of vulnerabilities, which US Citizenship and Immigration Services (USCIS) did not appear to be taking seriously at all. Applications are still entered on paper, rather than electronically, which means the kind of basic automatic searches that banks do to check for fraud are unavailable.

"It can be difficult to verify the source of investors' funds," the report noted. "Some petitioners may have strong incentives to report inaccurate information about the source of their funds on their applications in instances when the funds came from illicit—and thus ineligible—sources, such as funds obtained through drug trade, human trafficking, or other criminal activities."

Applicants were using skilled intermediaries to prepare their documentation, and USCIS was totally unequipped to assess the reliability of the information they were providing. A follow-up report the next year included the startling information that the program receives 14,000 petitions and applications a year (the total number of visas available under the program is capped at 10,000, and routinely hits that limit annually), each of around 1,000 pages. That comes to a total of 14 million pieces of paper, all of which have to be reviewed manually, and all of which are presumably stored in a huge shed somewhere in Washington. The archive is likely to be better organized than that of St. Kitts and Nevis, but even so, with documents piling up at that rate, it would be difficult to keep monitoring their accuracy.

In 2012, USCIS employees complained that their director, a political appointee called Alejandro Mayorkas, was "exerting improper influence" on applications under the EB-5 program. An investigation by the Office of the Inspector General reveals the specific risks created by any program of this nature, and the workings of the Moneyland ratchet in microcosm.

Rich foreigners were investing money to the benefit of influential locals, and that created a powerful incentive against scrutinizing the origin of the funds. In one case, Mayorkas, at the request of a powerful senator, intervened to overturn a decision not to approve a project in Las Vegas, causing one staff member to note in an email: "I fear we are entering a whole new phase of yuck."

A special agent from the Department of Homeland Security named Taylor Johnson gave evidence to a Senate investigation in 2015 in which she reported being subject to harassment and retaliation after investigating that same Las Vegas project. "I had discovered ties to organized crime and high-ranking officials and politicians, who received large campaign contributions that appeared to have facilitated the EB-5 project," she wrote. "I discovered that EB-5 applicants from China, Russia, Pakistan and Malaysia had been approved in as little as 16 days and in less than a month at most. The files lacked the basic and necessary law enforcement queries . . . During the course of my investigation it became very clear that the EB-5 program has serious security challenges." (These allegations have not been tested in court, and are disputed by her employers.)

Even before the Kushner family's involvement in effectively selling visas to wealthy Chinese citizens, tens of thousands of wealthy Moneylanders had settled in the United States, and billions of dollars' worth of under-checked money had come with them. At least one kleptocrat has been shown abusing the system: Jianjun Qiao embezzled a fortune from the state grain warehouse in Zhoukou City, Henan Province, China, then used the money to invest in the EB-5 program and to buy a house in Washington State. Qiao's ex-wife Shilan Zhao pleaded guilty in 2017, but he remains on the run. It was clearly a taxing investigation, particularly since so much of the evidence had to be prized out of China, and it raised more questions than it answered: how many other scandals are buried in those miles of files in a storage facility in Washington DC?

China is the source of the vast majority of EB-5 applicants, so the pattern of the Qiao/Zhao crime could be repeated thousands of times. How many of the 10,000 successful primary applicants for EB-5 visas are buying US residency with stolen money? More worryingly, how many of them are purchasing entry to the US in order to subvert it from within? Answering these questions requires transparency as to the source of the money involved, and the property that it's buying. Any efforts to answer them are therefore clearly doomed while Trump remains president, thanks to his opposition to efforts to shine light into the inner workings of the economy.

Similarly, after the Brexit referendum, the UK government's agenda to open up the offshore world to fight both tax dodging and corruption almost entirely halted. "The anti-corruption phone just stopped ringing," said Jon Benton, an ex-policeman who worked in the Cabinet Office as a senior adviser for the pre-referendum prime minister, David Cameron. In a country focused on its own troubles and concerns, there is little appetite for leading a global quest to rebuild the world's financial architecture. It is possible to cheer this development, as a reassertion of one country's democracy against the snares of international bureaucracy, which of course it is. But it is ironic, too, that a democratic outburst sparked by anger over the arrogance of a distant elite should have destroyed an initiative designed precisely to rein in that very elite.

***

The slogan of the winning Leave campaign in Britain's referendum on EU membership was "Take Back Control," which was a superb way to encapsulate so much of the frustration people all over the world feel when confronted by the misdeeds of the unaccountable Moneylanders. But the slogan was pointed at the wrong target. The EU was helping countries work together against unaccountable wealth, thus stopping crooks and thieves from keeping their fortunes. If Britain acts alone, it will only increase the number of loopholes that are created when each country institutes its own regulations.

So far, too many citizens have believed the claims of the likes of Donald Trump or, in Britain, Nigel Farage, who argue that if we just tighten our borders against immigrants, we can make our countries great again. The real threat to the liberal order is not the poor immigrants, but unaccountable money. Offshore bandits are looting the world, and this looting is undermining democracy, driving inequality and sucking ever-greater volumes of wealth into Moneyland, where we can't follow it.

The solution is not to pull up the drawbridge, or to demonize foreigners who flee their collapsing countries in the hope of a better life in the lands where their nations' money has found a home. The solution is to solve the root causes of the instability that is driving the refugee crises in the first place. If we can stop the ruling elites of Nigeria, or Russia, or Syria, or Central America from stashing their stolen wealth offshore, we can help stop them from stealing it. Remember, corruption is a crime of opportunity, and people are far less likely to steal if they know they won't get away with it.

We need to shine light onto this dark side of globalization, impose transparency on the ownership of wealth and property and find out who really owns what. Once we have done that, the Moneyland pathway will collapse, and we'll be able to prosecute the corrupt and identify them as the thieves that they are.

So what do we as citizens need to do? We need to know who owns what; we need to put crooks in jail; we need to stop our cities from laundering the stolen wealth of the world. And we need to support any politicians prepared to build the coalitions required to do this patient, taxing, technical and unglamorous work. Only by doing this can we truly take back control of our economies and our societies, and halt the wholesale looting of the world that threatens us all.

ACKNOWLEDGMENTS

Many of the ideas and stories in this book grew out of articles I have written, and I am very grateful to the editors who commissioned them. In particular, thanks to Anne Applebaum, Jonathan Shainin, David Wolf, Sigrid Rausing, Jonathan Heaf, Ryan Kearney, Charles Davidson, Brent Kallmer, Francis Wheen, Stephanie Giry and Nathan Thornburgh. Thanks also to Havana Marking—perhaps one day our film will even be shown somewhere. Melissa Aten was extremely helpful in finding me people to talk to in Washington and elsewhere. Courtney Ransom, Sofia Millham and Simon Ostrovsky could not have been more hospitable. Thanks, friends!

It has been great to have a group of friends happy to exchange thoughts on the minutest aspects of how money moves around, particularly Roman Borisovich, Arthur Doohan, Richard Smith, Ed Caesar, Chido Dunn and Sue Hawley.

Karolina Sutton has been the dream agent, full of advice and encouragement. Ed Lake at Profile was enthusiastic about the project from the first moment he heard about it, and has been a fantastic editor. I've really enjoyed our working together.

Rosie has tolerated my absences with grace and perfection. And thanks to Tobin and Cai for barging into my office whenever they feel like it, and thus regularly reminding me why it's important to care about the future of the world. I wrote this book for them.

NOTES ON SOURCES

I recorded all on-the-record interviews conducted for this book, and the recordings and transcripts are in my possession. I have, however, anonymized people when asked to do so (and have indicated in the text when I have done so). I did not record off-the-record interviews, but wrote them up either contemporaneously or immediately afterward. Most people who asked to be off the record did so because of fears about their safety, although in a small number of cases it was because they were not authorized to talk to the media. If you are one of the very many people who shared their time, experiences and thoughts with me but whom I didn't end up quoting in the book, please accept my apologies.

I also relied on primary sources gathered by other investigators, as well as academic papers, books and television programs. I have used reliable media reports extensively, and have identified them as the source where appropriate. It would take too long to list all the books I have read, but here is a brief summary of key texts used in researching different chapters, with suggestions for further reading.

1—Aladdin's Cave

Mancur Olson's theories on bandits are set out in *Power and Prosperity: Outgrowing Communist and Capitalist Dictatorships* (New York: Basic Books, 2000). I also found Francis Fukuyama's *The Origins of Political Order: From Prehuman Times to the French Revolution* (New York: Farrar, Straus & Giroux, 2011; London: Profile Books, 2011) very helpful. Sarah Chayes lays out the connection between corruption and terrorism in unanswerable detail in *Thieves of State: Why Corruption Threatens Global Security* (New York and London: W. W. Norton & Co., 2015).

The John Allen quote is taken from evidence he provided to the US Senate's Committee on Foreign Relations, and is available on its website, alongside statements from diplomats and others, at https://www.foreign.senate .gov/hearings/a-transformation-afghanistan-beyond-2014.

Thomas Piketty's monumental work *Capital in the Twenty-First Century* (Cambridge, MA, and London: Harvard University Press, 2014) is surprisingly readable. Gabriel Zucman's *The Hidden Wealth of Nations: The Scourge of Tax Havens* (Chicago, IL: University of Chicago Press, 2015) is fascinating and gloriously brief. Walter Scheidel's *The Great Leveler: Violence and the History of Inequality from the Stone Age to the Twenty-first Century* (Princeton, NJ, and Oxford: Princeton University Press, 2017) is also very interesting. James S. Henry's assessment of how much money is hidden offshore is contained in his paper "The Price of Offshore Revisited," published by the Tax Justice Network in 2012.

2—Pirates

The history of the City of London is laid out in loving detail in David Kynaston's epic four-volume history of the place. *The City of London, Volume 4: A Club No More, 1945–2000* (London: Chatto & Windus, 2002) is the relevant volume for all things eurobond. For anyone intimidated by the sheer heft of that book, Kynaston also wrote the single-volume *City of London 1815–2000* (London: Chatto & Windus, 2011) and co-wrote (with Richard Roberts) the snappier *City State: How the Markets Came to Rule the World* (London: Profile Books, 2001).

The meeting at Bretton Woods has not received as much attention as it deserves, although Ed Conway's *The Summit: The Biggest Battle of the Second World War—Fought behind Closed Doors* (London: Little, Brown, 2014; New York: Pegasus Books, 2015) helps make up for that, as does Benn Steil's *The Battle of Bretton Woods: John Maynard Keynes, Harry Dexter White, and the Making of a New World Order* (Princeton, NJ, and Oxford: Princeton University Press, 2013). There are also too few biographies of John Maynard Keynes himself, although I enjoyed Richard Davenport-Hines' *Universal Man: The Seven Lives of John Maynard Keynes* (New York: Basic Books; London: William Collins, 2015).

The definitive take on Siegmund Warburg is *High Financier: The Lives and Time of Siegmund Warburg* by Niall Ferguson (New York and London: Penguin Press, 2010). Ian Fraser's autobiography is *The High Road to England* (Norwich: Michael Russell Publishing, 1999). The Jim Keogh quote comes from *The Bankers* (New York: Weybridge and Talley, 1974) by Martin Mayer.

The eurobond market has been well served by historians. Ian M. Kerr's *A History of the Eurobond Market: The First Twenty-one Years* (London: Euromoney Publications Ltd, 1984) is interesting, as is *Bonds without Borders: A History of the Eurobond Market* by Chris O'Malley (Chichester: John Wiley & Co., 2014). I found the transcript of the 1990 witness seminar that Kathleen Burk chaired for the Institute of Contemporary British History invaluable.

Ronen Palan is a crucial authority on the development of offshore, and I am grateful to him for chatting to me, as well as for writing so many excellent papers. His books *Tax Havens: How Globalization Really Works* (cowritten with Richard Murphy) (Ithaca, NY: Cornell University Press, 2009) and *The Offshore World: Sovereign Markets, Virtual Places, and Nomad Millionaires* (Ithaca, NY: Cornell University Press, 2003) are excellent. Nicholas Shaxson's *Treasure Islands: Uncovering the Damage of Offshore Banking and Tax Havens* (Basingstoke: Palgrave Macmillan, 2011) is very good as well.

The quote from Bradley Birkenfeld comes from *Lucifer's Banker: The Untold Story of How I Destroyed Swiss Bank Secrecy* (Austin, TX: Greenleaf Book Group Press, 2016). I chose to illustrate the widespread awareness of corrupt money in Switzerland by reference to Hergé's *Flight 714 to Sydney* (London: Methuen, 1968) rather than to Goscinny and Uderzo's *Asterix in Switzerland* (London: Hodder & Stoughton, 1973) in the forlorn hope it might finally convince my wife that Tintin is better than Asterix, since the Tintin book made the point first, and better. Ian Fleming's *Goldfinger* was first published in London by Jonathan Cape in 1959.

3—Queen of the Caribbees

Much of the information on Nevis came from documents I found in the is-land's public library, which was helpfully located within sight of several of its company factories. Statistics on company formations are available on the Nevis government website. The history of Nevis is told in *Swords, Ships & Sugar: A History of Nevis to 1900* (Corvallis, OR: Premiere Editions, 1992) by Vincent K. Hubbard, although he sadly didn't consider his own time as an offshore lawyer on the island worthy of recording in the book.

Information on the Russian "laundromat" money-laundering schemes can be found on the website of the Organized Crime and Corruption Re-porting Project (OCCRP), which has been doing extraordinary work for years.

The quotes from debates in the States of Jersey come from the transcripts in the island's version of *Hansard*, which is published on the assembly's web-site. Statements from the former police officers can be found on the website of the Independent Jersey Care Inquiry. I'd also draw your attention to the Voice for Children and Rico Sorda blogs, which kept publishing informa-tion when many of Jersey's other media outlets had stopped.

Jersey historians have not paid much attention to the island's develop-ment as a tax haven, although Geoffrey Colin Powell's *Economic Survey of Jersey* (St. Helier: States of Jersey, 1971) is fascinating for those of us who like that kind of thing. The two novels *Marigold Dark* by Paul Bisson (St. Helier: Jayplate, 2015), and *What I Tell You in the Dark* by John Samuel (London: The Overlook Press, 2014) give a good insight into the peculiar atmo-sphere of Jersey.

4—Sex, Lies and Offshore Vehicles

I found *The Piratization of Russia: Russian Reform Goes Awry* by Marshall I. Goldman (London and New York: Routledge, 2003) extremely useful, as was Karen Dawisha's *Putin's Kleptocracy* (New York: Simon & Schuster, 2014). The Richard Palmer quotes are taken from testimony he gave to 1999 hearings into Russian money laundering held at the US House of Represen-

tatives' Committee on Banking and Financial Services, available at https://
archives-financialservices.house.gov/banking/92199pal.shtml.

5—Mystery on Harley Street

Most of the research into 29 Harley Street was for an article I published in
the *Guardian* in April 2016.

6—Shell Games

There are several fantastic books on the role shell companies play in facilitat-
ing crime. *Global Shell Games: Experiments in Transnational Relations, Crime,
and Terrorism*, by Michael G. Findley, Daniel L. Nielson and J. C. Sharman
(Cambridge: Cambridge University Press, 2014) is indispensable. Stephen
Platt's *Criminal Capital: How the Finance Industry Facilitates Crime* (Basingstoke: Palgrave Macmillan, 2015) is very interesting. And Brooke Harrington's
Capital without Borders: Wealth Managers and the One Percent (Cambridge,
MA, and London: Harvard University Press, 2016) lays out the role of the
finance industry in driving inequality. *The Destructive Power of Family Wealth:
A Guide to Succession Planning, Asset Protection, Taxation and Wealth Management* (Chichester: John Wiley & Sons, 2016) by Philip Marcovici is more
amusing than a book of its nature has any right to be, and I'm sorry it didn't
make it into this book.

Global Witness published its investigation into the willingness of American lawyers to bend the rules in 2016 on its website under the title *Lowering
the Bar: How American Lawyers Told Us How to Funnel Suspect Funds into
the United States*.

There are excellent databases of historic corruption cases on the website
of the World Bank's Stolen Asset Recovery Initiative, and Stanford University Law School's collection of prosecutions under the Foreign Corrupt Practices Act. Please can other countries start archiving court judgments in such
an excellent way?

The Senate Permanent Subcommittee on Investigations dredged out the unsavory details of Citibank's activities, and published them on its website in November 1999, along with a trove of other material.

7—Cancer

This chapter is based on my own work in Ukraine. Case studies on corruption can be found on the website of the Anti-corruption Action Center (AntAC), a small group of brave and determined activists who have been extremely helpful to me in my investigations.

8—Nasty as a Rattlesnake

I first read *The Dogs of War* (London: Hutchinson, 1974) by Frederick Forsyth when I was a teenager, and it remains one of my favorite thrillers. Chinua Achebe's novels *Things Fall Apart* (London: William Heinemann, 1958) and *No Longer at Ease* (London: William Heinemann, 1960) are magnificent. His essay *The Trouble with Nigeria* was first published by Fourth Dimension Publishing in Nigeria in 1983, but was reissued in 2010 alongside *An Image of Africa* as part of Penguin's Great Ideas series. A modern-day Nigerian novelist grappling with some of the same themes is Chibundu Onuzo, whose *Welcome to Lagos* (London: Faber & Faber, 2017) is fantastic.

If you want an in-depth study of the origins of the word kleptocracy, you can find it in an essay I wrote for the *Journal of Democracy*'s January 2018 issue called "The Rise of Kleptocracy: The Dark Side of Globalization." Stanislav Andreski explored the idea most interestingly in *The African Predicament: A Study in the Pathology of Modernization* (New York: Atherton Press; London: Michael Joseph, 1968). Sinnathamby Rajatnaram's lecture on kleptocracy is printed in Arnold J. Heidenheimer's *Political Corruption: Readings in Comparative Analysis* (New York and London: Holt, Rinehart and Winston, 1970).

For Equatorial Guinea, *Tropical Gangsters: One Man's Experience with Development and Decadence in Deepest Africa* by Robert Klitgaard (New York:

Basic Books, 1991) is key. The US Senate's investigation into the Obiang family is also highly interesting, as has been the ongoing court case in France, brought by activists from Sherpa, a campaigning legal group.

The International Monetary Fund's research paper "Institutionalized Corruption and the Kleptocratic State," written by Christian Harm and Joshua Charap in 1999, lays out a convincing theory of how corruption works.

9—The Man Who Sells Passports

Christian H. Kälin's thesis *Ius Doni: The Acquisition of Citizenship by Investment* (Zurich: Ideos Publications Ltd, 2016) gives a thorough summary of the principles behind the passport industry. Atossa Araxia Abrahamian described the business in her *The Cosmopolites: The Coming of the Global Citizen* (New York: Columbia Global Reports, 2015). If you want to delve into the murky beginnings of the St. Kitts and Nevis program, you need to read Ken Rijock's *The Laundry Man* (London: Viking Press, 2012), not least because it's great fun.

The International Monetary Fund's working paper "Too Much of a Good Thing?: Prudent Management of Inflows under Economic Citizenship Programs," which analyzes the success of the St. Kitts program, was published in 2015.

I wish I had had more space to write about Anguilla's curious path to becoming a tax haven, since it has been under-documented. The story of its anti-independence revolution, however, is well told in Donald E. Westlake's hilarious *Under an English Heaven* (London: Hodder & Stoughton, 1973).

10—"Diplomatic Immunity!"

The misuse of diplomatic immunity by extremely wealthy people has gone under-remarked, *Lethal Weapon 2* excepted.

11—Un-write-about-able

The story of Bill Browder's life as a fund manager in Russia, and his conversion into a human rights activist, is told in his *Red Notice: How I Became Putin's No. 1 Enemy* (New York: Simon & Schuster; London: Corgi, 2015). The film that was never shown was directed by Havana Marking, and it was really good. Thanks to Daria Kaleniuk and others for appearing in it.

12—Dark Matter

The 2015 Deutsche Bank paper "Dark Matter: The Hidden Capital Flows That Drive G10 Exchange Rates" by Oliver Harvey and Robin Winkler is available online, and links much of the secret money moving into Britain to Russia. It is ironic that two years later, that same bank paid fines of $630 million to settle US and UK charges that it had moved $10 billion of hidden capital out of Russia in so-called mirror trades.

The Mark Pieth–edited essay collection *Recovering Stolen Assets* (Basel: Basel Institute of Governance, 2008) lays out many of the difficulties faced by anyone trying to return money to its proper owners. The World Bank's StAR initiative published *Few and Far: The Hard Facts on Stolen Asset Recovery* by Larissa Gray, Kjetil Hansen, Pranvera Recica-Kirkbride and Linnea Mills in 2014, to bring the rather depressing story up to date.

13—"Nuclear Death Is Knocking Your Door"

Most of the information in this chapter derives from evidence given to the inquiry into the death of Alexander Litvinenko, which was held in London's Royal Courts of Justice between January and March 2015, and which I attended thanks to a commission from British *GQ*. A certain amount of evidence was later redacted after legal objections from lawyers for the Russian government. This means some of the information related to Litvinenko's work with the Spanish intelligence services is no longer visible on the inquiry's website. With a bit of clever Googling, however, you can find the originals.

Luke Harding wrote *A Very Expensive Poison: The Definitive Story of the Murder of Litvinenko and Russia's War with the West* (London: Guardian Faber, 2016; New York: Vintage, 2017) after the inquiry, drawing on the work he had done on the murder over the previous decade. Marina Litvinenko and Alex Goldfarb wrote *Death of a Dissident: The Poisoning of Alexander Litvinenko and the Return of the KGB* (London and New York: The Free Press, 2007) and Litvinenko himself wrote (with Yuri Felshtinsky) *Blowing Up Russia: The Secret Plot to Bring Back KGB Terror* (London: Gibson Square, 2007) which was reissued after his death and again in February 2018.

14—Say Yes to the Money

Nicholas Shaxson's *Poisoned Wells: The Dirty Politics of African Oil* (Basingstoke: Palgrave Macmillan, 2007) and Tom Burgis' *The Looting Machine: Warlords, Tycoons, Smugglers and the Systematic Theft of Africa's Wealth* (London: William Collins; New York: PublicAffairs, 2015) are both excellent accounts of how offshore finance has savaged Africa. The groundbreaking 1990s Global Witness reports on Angola, "A Crude Awakening" (1999) and "A Rough Trade" (1998), are still available on its website.

15—High-End Property

Michael Gross' history of 15CPW, *House of Outrageous Fortune: Fifteen Central Park West, the World's Most Powerful Address* (New York: Atria Books, 2014) is excellent. For anyone interested in the New York property market, Jonathan Miller runs a weekly newsletter called "Housing Notes," which you can subscribe to on the Miller Samuel Inc. website.

The Miami Association of Realtors provided the information on foreign buyers of property in southern Florida.

My friend Sasha drove me from Perm to Solikamsk and Berezniki when I was researching *The Last Man in Russia: And the Struggle to Save a Dying Nation* (London: Allen Lane; New York: Basic Books, 2013). Thanks, Sasha!

16—Plutos Like to Hang Out Together

Although Ajay Kapur's plutonomy reports are infamous, they're quite hard to get hold of, so thanks to Jules for finding them for me. I repeatedly tried to contact Kapur, but he never got back to me. If you're reading this, Ajay, please get in touch.

17—Breaking Switzerland

Bradley Birkenfeld's memoir *Lucifer's Banker: The Untold Story of How I Destroyed Swiss Bank Secrecy* (Austin, TX: Greenleaf Book Group Press, 2016) was a key source for this chapter, as was the Senate report into the behavior of UBS, for which he gave evidence. Gabriel Zucman's *The Hidden Wealth of Nations: The Scourge of Tax Havens* (Chicago, IL: University of Chicago Press, 2015) was important for the history of the Swiss banking industry.

18—Tax Haven USA

I found Lawrence M. Friedman's *Dead Hands: A Social History of Wills, Trusts, and Inheritance Law* (Stanford, CA: Stanford Law Books, 2009) useful as an introduction to US trusts. Peter Cotorceanu's 2015 paper for Anaford Attorneys (Zurich), "Hiding in Plain Sight: How Non-US Persons Can Legally Avoid Reporting under Both FATCA & GATCA," helped me understand what was going on.

19—Standing up to Moneyland

The quotation from Arthur Weasley comes from *Harry Potter and the Chamber of Secrets* (London: Bloomsbury, 1998) by J. K. Rowling, and can—in my opinion—be applied to pretty much everything.

Jane Mayer's *Dark Money: The Hidden History of the Billionaires behind the Rise of the Radical Right* (New York: Doubleday, 2016) is an eye-opening account of how the gravitational effect of US oligarchs' money has been bending reality for longer than Vladimir Putin has been around. Nancy McLean's *Democracy in Chains: The Deep History of the Radical Right's Stealth Plan for America* (New York: Viking, 2017) is perhaps even more extraordinary.

INDEX

Abacha, Ibrahim, 128
Abacha, Maryam, 125
Abacha, Mohammed, 128, 177–178
Abacha, Sani, 97, 125, 128, 177–178
Abercia, Ralph, 76–77
Abercia, Ralph, Jr., 76–77
Ablyazov, Mukhtar, 160
Abramovich, Roman, 227
Achebe, Chinua, 120–122
Adada, Loujain, 154
advanced fee fraud, 77, 125
Afanasiev, Dmitry, 133
Afghanistan, 11, 13, 14, 134, 258–259
Africa, 13, 16, 19, 34, 48, 66, 87, 115–123, 130.
    See also individual countries
Alabama, 92
Alamieyeseigha, Diepreye, 85
Alison-Madueke, Diezani, 160
Aliyev, Ilham, 8
Allen, George, 246
Allen, John, 14, 258–259
Alliance Trust Company, 247, 252
Allseas, 77–78, 81
Andreski, Stanislav, 119, 122, 130
Angola, 12, 13, 205–209, 226
Anguilla, 140–143, 266
Anthony, Kenny, 157, 160
Antigua and Barbuda, 149, 150, 152, 160
Anton (driver), 5–6, 10, 14
Arab Spring, 10, 189
Ardern, Danielle, 80–81
Argentina, 42, 220

arms smuggling, 11, 90, 143
asset protection, 50–53, 56, 246–247
asset recovery, 10, 26, 54, 179–181, 186,
    188–190
    Stolen Asset Recovery (StAR) initiative
        (World Bank), 87, 189
Astaforova-Yatsenko, Nina, 165
Astaforova-Yatsenko, Nonna, 165
Astaphan, Dwyer, 139, 141, 144
Astute Partners Ltd, 73
Australia, 18, 144, 161
Austria, 18, 145, 150
Autonomous Nation of Anarchist Libertar-
    ians (ANAL), 20
Aveiro, 265
Azerbaijan, 8, 13, 55, 56, 218, 263–265
    The European Azerbaijan Society
        (TEAS), 263–265

Bahamas, 23, 31, 47, 86, 235, 248
Bailhache, Philip, 63
Baku, 8, 218, 263
Bank Commerciale pour l'Europe du Nord,
    65
Bank of New York, 67
banks
    City of London, 32–37, 39–41, 43, 45–46,
        146
    eurobonds, 40–43, 45, 53, 69, 99, 146, 238,
        243, 249, 261
    eurodollars, 35–37, 40, 44, 65
    FATCA, 239–241, 243, 247–248, 251, 256

banks (*continued*)
  and secrecy, 235–243, 248–253, 262–263, 266–267
  and sources of funds, 95–100
  Switzerland, 26, 38–39, 41, 43, 46, 61, 96–97, 233–239, 242–243, 247, 249–251, 255
  United States, 32, 35, 44–46, 67, 240, 259–260
Baring, Rowland, 32
Barnard, Bill, 49–50, 56
Barrington, Robert, 168
Basseterre, St. Kitts, 55, 135, 141, 146, 151
Bates, Robert, 117
BBC, 36, 118, 132
Bean, Elise, 240
bearer bonds, 41, 46
Beatles, 32, 34, 39–40
Beckwith, Tamara, 153–154
Belgium, 18, 40, 42, 43, 69
Belize, 11, 143
Benson, Richard, 76–77
Benton, Jon, 270
Berezniki, Russia, 212–213
Berezovsky, Boris, 164, 196, 198–200, 202
Berger, Henri, 77
Berger, Michael, 128
Bermuda, 95, 181, 248
Bhatia, Lal, 77
Biden, Hunter, 187–188
Biden, Joe, 187
Bin Mahfouz, Khalid, 169
Birkenfeld, Bradley, 39, 233–236, 238–239, 242–243, 248, 250–251, 265
Blake, Nicholas, 185, 186
blood diamonds, 207
Bloody Money, 166–167
Blum, Jack, 55, 123
Blythe (Europe) Ltd, 73–74
BNP Paribas, 182, 183–184
Bond, James, 30–32, 35, 234
bonds, 29–30, 37–43, 45, 50, 65, 89. *See also* bearer bonds; eurobonds
Bongo, Omar, 128–129
Borisovich, Roman, 19
Brantley, Mark, 255–257
Brazil, 11, 17, 125, 144, 148, 179, 212, 220, 259
Bretton Woods system, 28–35, 37, 43–45, 69–70, 262–263, 267
Brexit referendum, 133–134, 260–161, 270–171
BRIC nations, 212. *See also* Brazil; China; India; Russia

Britain. *See* United Kingdom
British Virgin Islands, 11, 21, 77, 86, 95, 99, 183, 184, 207, 266
Browder, Bill, 172–175
Bryant, Fitzroy, 138, 148–149
Buffett, Warren, 249
Burisma, 182–187
Burns, George, 254

Caines, Richard, 136–137
Cambridge University Press (CUP), 167, 168, 174
Cameron, David, 270
Canada, 85, 134, 143, 151, 173, 226, 227
Cancer Institute, Ukraine, 101–108, 112–114, 123–124
Candy Brothers, 216–217
Cane Garden Services Limited, 21
Cantrade, 61–62
Capitalism—A Love Story, 229
Capone, Al, 68, 167, 220–221
Cardin-Lugar Amendment, 268
Carter, Edwin. *See* Litvinenko, Alexander
Cash, Johnny, 244
Catch-22 (Heller), 163
Cayman Islands, 21, 65, 86, 96, 98, 99, 257
Central African Republic, 126, 160
Charles, Prince of Wales, 214
Charlestown, Nevis, 56–57
Chastanet, Allen, 160
child abuse, 62–63
Chile, 18, 232
Chiluba, Frederick, 88
China, 23, 160, 233
  and American manufacturing sector, 45
  anti-corruption campaign, 238, 239–240
  and BRIC nations, 212
  and EB-5 applications, 22, 269–270
  flight capital, 11, 176
  and globalization, 25
  and Japanese surrogacy, 83–84
Christensen, John, 60–61
Christian Aid, 241–242
Christophe Harbor, St. Kitts, 146–148
Citibank, 36, 96–97, 128–129
Citigroup, 212, 225–226, 229
citizenship, 83–84, 132–139, 146–148, 151, 232, 241
City of London, 32–37, 39–41, 43, 45–46, 143, 242–243
  eurobonds, 40–43, 45, 146
Club K, 208

Coales, Edwina, 80
Cohen, Michal, 210
Cole, Julia, 191, 192
Colombia, 143, 219–220, 259
colonialism, 34, 56, 116–120, 124–125, 140, 144–145, 179
Common Reporting Standard (CRS), 240–243, 248–249, 252–253, 255–256
companies, 67–71, 72–82
    information on, 79–80, 85–86, 90
    shell companies, 12, 19, 21, 23, 53, 65, 67, 70, 71, 85–86, 90–96
Constitutional Research Council, 261
Conway, Ed, 262
Corporate Nominees, 80, 82
corruption, 3–19, 241–242, 258–260
    in Angola, 13, 207–208
    in China, 83–84, 230–231
    in healthcare, 101–108, 112–114, 123–124
    in Kenya, 179
    and kleptocracy, 85, 94, 97, 99, 101, 109, 119–123, 126–130, 207, 220, 229–230, 261–262
    in Nigeria, 84–85, 120–122, 125–128, 179
    in Russia, 55, 57, 64–66, 167–168, 172, 200, 230–232
    in Ukraine, 1–2, 4–17, 19, 22, 55, 74, 101–108, 112–114, 123–124, 164–165, 181–182, 186–189, 250
Corruption Watch, 87
Cotorceanu, Peter, 248–249, 251–252, 255
Crawford, Greg, 247, 253–254
Credit Suisse, 17, 237–239
Creer, Dean, 193
Crimea, 11, 13, 103, 133, 161, 199
Cyprus, 3, 11, 16, 19, 68, 254
    citizenship, 22, 132, 134, 150–151
    and Ukraine, 11, 106, 182

Daniel, Simeon, 49, 51, 256
Darby, Buddy, 148
Dawisha, Karen, 167–168, 174
de Botton, Alain, 132
de Sousa, Bornito, 208–210
Delaware, 3, 21, 50, 75, 90–93, 248, 256
Deloitte, 230
democracy, 4, 7, 13, 17, 25–29, 51, 114, 118–124, 174–175, 203, 260–271
Democratic Unionist Party (DUP, Northern Ireland), 261
Denmark, 18, 40, 235, 265
Depardieu, Gerard, 95

Diana, Princess of Wales, 214
Diogo, Naulila, 205–206, 208–210, 226
diplomatic immunity, 141, 143, 156–160, 201
Disney Corporation, 261
divorce settlements, 51–53, 58, 157–160, 212, 246
Dogs of War, The (Forsyth), 115–116
Doing Business (World Bank report), 89–90
Dom Lesnika, 10, 73
Dominica, 139, 145, 149–150, 160
dos Santos, Isabel, 207
dos Santos, José Eduardo, 206–208
Downing, Kevin, 235
dynasty trusts, 246

Eaton Square, London, 20–22
Egypt, 11, 90
Ehrenfeld, Rachel, 169
Elliott, Amy, 96–97
Equatorial Guinea, 10, 11, 115–116, 126–127, 178, 207, 259
Eritrea, 89
errors & omissions (E&O), 176–177
Estonia, 264
Estrada, Christina, 153–159
eurobonds, 40–43, 45, 53, 69, 99, 146, 238, 243, 249, 261
eurodollars, 35–37, 40, 44, 65
Evening Standard, 215
Extractive Industries Transparency Initiative, 268

FATCA (Foreign Account Tax Compliance Act, US), 239–241, 243, 247–248, 251, 256
Fenoli, Randy, 206
Fenwick, Edward Henry, 73
Fenwick, Samuel, 72
Feynman, Richard, 23
Field, Mark, 264
15 Central Park West (15CPW), 211–212, 218, 229
FIMACO, 65–67, 69
Financial Conduct Authority (UK), 87
Financial Services Authority (FSA, UK), 97–98
Finkel, Amy, 15
Finnegan, Hugh, 87
First World War, 28, 29, 33
Firtash, Dmitry, 216, 226–227
Fisher, Jeffrey, 53
flags of convenience, 49

Flash Crash, 53–54
Fleming, Ian, 30, 35
Flight 714 to Sydney (Hergé), 38–39
flight capital, 11, 176, 213–214
Florent, Gerry, 76–77
Florida, 1, 3, 51, 52–53, 76, 85–86, 213, 219–221, 250–251, 261
Foreign Corrupt Practices Act (US), 87, 108, 207
Formations House, 75–76, 79–82, 85, 266
Forsyth, Frederick, 115–116
419 scams, 125–126, 128
France, 13, 18, 32, 35, 38, 59, 87, 112, 145, 206, 231, 261
Fraser, Ian, 40–43
Freedom House, 116
Frontline Club, 165–166, 174, 183
Fukuyama, Francis, 7, 124
Fyodorov, Boris, 66

G20, 242
Gabon, 128–129
Galinski, Jaime, 219
Geithner, Tim, 239
generation-skipping transfers, 245
Geneva, 12, 38, 42, 153, 169, 203, 234, 243
Gerashchenko, Viktor, 65–66
Germany, 19, 28, 33, 37, 99, 132, 134, 219, 243, 261
Gherson, 189
Gibraltar, 21, 23, 94–96, 266
Giles, 141
Global Financial Integrity, 176, 180
Global Shell Games, 92
Global Witness, 87–88, 207–208
globalization, 25, 263
Gluzman, Semyon, 110
GML, 94
gold, 28–32, 35, 44–45, 51, 55, 56, 68
Goldfinger (Fleming), 30–32, 35
Goldman, Marshall, 66
Goncharenko, Andrei, 20–21
Gould, Richard, 183–185
Government Accountability Office (US), 92–93
Grant, Valencia, 135
Great Britain. *See* United Kingdom
Greenaway, Karen, 90, 94, 180
Grenada, 150
Grieve, Dominic, 181, 185
Gross, Michael, 211–212, 229
Guernsey, 21

Hadid, Zaha, 8
Halliburton, 207
Hamilton, Alexander, 56
Harley Street, London, 72–79, 81–82, 85, 125, 260
Harper, Lenny, 62–63
Harrington, Brooke, 99–100
Harris, Robert, 90–92
Harris, Timothy, 144, 149, 151
Harrison, George, 32
Harry Potter, 261
Haslam, John, 167–168
Hayden, Justice, 158
Hector, Paul, 233
Heller, Joseph, 163
Hello!, 153
Henley & Partners, 132–135, 145–146, 151–152, 241
Henry, James, 47
Herbert, William "Billy," 140–144
Hergé, 38–39
Heritage Foundation, 251
Heydarov, Kamaladdin, 264
Heydarov, Nijat, 264
Heydarov, Tale, 264–265
Holder, Eric, 181
Hong Kong, 21, 47, 68, 82, 84, 95, 139, 160, 230, 253
Hoppner, Harald, 133
Human Rights Watch, 116
Hydra Lenders, 54
IBC Bank of Laredo, 259

Idaho, 56, 245
Iglesias, Julio, 219
incorporation agents, 92
India, 25, 30–31, 34, 212, 227
Indian Creek, Florida, 219–222
Indonesia, 11, 12
inequality, 17, 99–100, 122, 271
and plutonomy, 26, 210, 224, 225–232
International Maritime Organization (IMO), 155, 157
International Monetary Fund (IMF), 127, 262, 267
on Angola, 207
on corruption, 130
creation of, 29
on illegal money, 176
"Institutionalized Corruption and the Kleptocratic State," 130
and Poland, 35

and Russia, 64–66
and St. Kitts and Nevis, 146
and Ukraine, 187
Isle of Man, 21, 23, 181, 254
Ismaylova, Khadija, 55
Israel, 41, 108–109, 111, 150, 204, 212, 217,
223, 232
Italy, 18, 38, 40, 78, 132, 139, 160, 212
Ivanov, Viktor, 200–201
Ivanyushchenko, Yuri, 189

Jackson, Michael, 178
Japan, 83–84, 99, 148, 161, 227
Jersey, 21, 23, 27, 45, 47, 54, 59–64, 73, 87, 129,
179, 241, 258, 266
and Christensen, 60–61
and FIMACO, 65–67, 69
and Harper, 62–63
and Power, 62–63
al-Juffali, Walid, 153–160

Kadyrov, Ramzan, 161, 230
Kalin, Christian, 131–133, 135, 145–145, 151
Kaplin, Sergei, 113
Kapur, Ajay, 225–232
Karimova, Gulnara, 95–96
Karpov, Pavel, 173–174
Kasko, Vitaly, 184–187, 189
Kazakhstan, 12, 90, 178, 179
Kelly, Karen, 233
Kensington and Chelsea, 214–215
Kenya, 11, 179
Keogh, Jim, 36
Keynes, John Maynard, 29, 45, 267
Khan, Nadeem, 81
King, Eleanor, 52, 158
Kleinfeld Bridal, 204, 206, 209–210
kleptocracy, 85, 94, 97, 99, 101, 109, 119–123,
126–130, 207, 220, 229–230, 261–262.
See also corruption
Klitgaard, Robert, 126–127
Knight, Paul, 79
Korner, Eric, 42
Kovtun, Dmitry, 198, 201, 202
Kramer, Al, 254
Kushner, Jared, 268, 269
Kyrgyzstan, 8

Labour Party (St. Kitts and Nevis), 137–140,
148–149
Landscape of Lies, 78–79
Las Vegas, 76–77, 79, 125, 244, 247, 269

Latvia, 55, 56–57, 95, 182, 183, 188
Lawrence, Laurie, 52
Legal Nominees Ltd, 80, 81–82
Lenin, Vladimir, 203
Lesin, Mikhail, 202
Lethal Weapon 2, 156, 158
libel tourism, 164, 173–174
Liberia, 21, 49
Libya, 11, 13, 89, 150, 189
Liechtenstein, 10, 16, 21, 23, 45, 74, 177,
182, 235
Limited Liability Companies (LLCs), 50,
53, 55, 87–89, 263
Lindblad, Göran, 264
Litvinenko, Alexander (Edwin Carter),
191–203
Litvinenko, Marina, 191, 193, 194–195, 199
Lombard Odier, 96
London, 12–13, 258, 256–257, 264–265
and diplomatic immunity trade, 153–160
Harley Street, 72–79, 81–82, 85, 125, 260
Kleptocracy Tours, 19–22
Litvinenko murder, 191–203
One Hyde Park, 216, 222
Pompolo Ltd, 1–3, 260
private banking, 97–98, 236
property, 18–22, 211, 158, 207, 214–216,
219, 220, 222, 227–229
See also City of London
London Kleptocracy Tours, 19–22
Los Angeles, 12, 220, 244
Low, Jho, 151
Lugovoy, Andrei, 198–202
Luxembourg, 19, 40–42, 46, 47, 69, 115,
129, 182
eurobonds, 40–42, 69

McGown, Ally, 205, 208
Macias Nguema, Francisco, 116, 126
McLean, Andrea, 79
Macpherson, Elle, 222
Macron, Emmanuel, 55, 59
Magnitsky, Sergei, 55, 90, 173–174
Mainichi Shimbun, 83–84
Malaysia, 10, 11, 16, 151, 222, 232, 260, 269
Malta, 77–78, 132, 134, 150–152, 170
Manafort, Paul, 1–4, 8, 15–16, 18–19, 21, 68,
260
Marchenko, Oleg, 109–110
Marcos, Ferdinand, 177
Marcos, Imelda, 118
Marcovici, Philip, 240–241

Marshall Islands, 264
Marx, Karl, 203
Marxism-Leninism, 206
Mauritius, 21, 22
May, Theresa, 182
Mayer, Jane, 262
Mayorkas, Alejandro, 269
MC Brooklyn Holdings LLC, 15–16
MCA Shipping, 21
Merrill Lynch Bank of America, 232
Mexico, 96–97, 108, 132, 259
Mezhyhyria palace, 4
Miami, 12, 55, 85–87, 143, 159, 219–222, 226, 228, 236, 266
Miller, Jed, 20–21
Miller, Jonathan, 213–214
Mishcon de Reya, 157
Mitchell, Daniel, 251
Mitchell, Don, 141–142
Moghadam, Alizera, 151
Monaco, 11, 12, 21, 26, 47, 181, 213
Moneyland, 3, 23–27
    creation of, 27, 28–48, 69–70
    defending, 22, 26, 131–203
    fighting back, 26, 239–251, 258–271
    hiding wealth, 12–13, 25, 26, 49–100, 244–257, 266
    spending, 12–13, 15, 20–23, 26, 204–210, 211–232
    stealing, 1–3, 17, 24–26, 101–130, 161–162, 180, 242, 260, 266, 271
Montana, 92
Montenegro, 132
Montfler SA, 265
Moore, Michael, 229
Moran, Rick, 233
Morgenthau, Henry, 85, 262
Morning Star, 49–50, 56
Moscow, John, 61
MPLA, 206–208
Mueller, Robert, 1, 3, 14–16, 68
Murray, Andy, 258
Musy, Oleg, 111–113

NAV Sarao Milking Markets Fund, 54
Nazarbayev, Nursultan, 178
Netherlands, 40, 88, 95
Netherlands Antilles, 43
Neufeld, David, 50
Nevada, 258
    company formation, 90–93
    trusts, 243, 244–248, 252–256

Nevis, 49–60, 66, 90, 93, 123, 148, 246, 255–257, 267, 269
Nevis International Trust Company (NITC), 57
New York, 12, 26
    and banking, 34, 36–39, 67, 95, 96, 98, 129, 257
    and diplomatic immunity, 159
    Kleinfeld Bridal, 204, 206, 209–210
    and Manafort, 2–3, 15–16
    property, 47, 60, 211–224, 228, 258
New York Times, 52–53, 151
New Zealand, 18, 54, 89–90, 177, 248
Nigeria, 11–13, 19, 22, 258, 259, 271
    Achebe, Chinua, 120–122
    advanced fee fraud, 125
    asset recovery, 54, 177–178
    corruption, 84–85, 120–122, 125–128, 179
Nisbett Invest SA, 255
No Longer at Ease (Achebe), 120
Nobre, Luis, 78, 81
Nominee Director Ltd, 81
North Korea, 18, 89
Northern Ireland, 261, 265
Norway, 78
Novaya Gazeta, 71

Obama, Barack, 246, 250, 251, 257
Obiang, Teodorin, 127–129
Obiang, Teodoro, 116, 178
Obiang family, 116, 127–129, 178, 207–208, 229
Oesterlund, Robert, 52–53
offshore finance and schemes, 1, 11–12, 16, 21–25, 36–37, 44–46
    eurobonds, 40–43
    eurodollars, 37, 242
    sharing data, 240, 242, 243, 249, 252
    See also Moneyland
offshore radio stations, 36
O'Flaherty, Victoria, 136–137
Okemo, Chrysanthus, 179
Olenicoff, Igor, 234–235
Olson, Mancur, 23–24
Olswang, 173
One Hyde Park, 216, 222
Onipko, Natalya, 102, 106–107
Orange Revolution, 4–6, 9, 13, 74, 103–104, 112–114, 180
Oregon, 93
Organisation for Economic Co-operation and Development (OECD), 242

Organized Crime and Corruption Reporting Project (OCCRP), 57, 278
Orwell, George, 118
Owen, Robert, 202
Oxfam, 129, 241

P&A Corporate Services Trust Reg, 73–74
Pakistan, 14, 151, 269
Palmer, Richard, 67, 69
Panama, 21, 23, 68, 142–143, 259
Panoceanic Trading Corporation, 21
passports, 14, 22, 23, 25, 26, 131–152, 156, 160, 170, 200, 207, 241
Paton, Leslie, 73
Pawar, Charlotte, 81, 266
Penney, Andrew, 248
Pennsylvania, 93, 248
People's Action Movement (PAM, St. Kitts and Nevis), 137–141, 144
People's Prosecutor (television program), 113
Perepada, Gennady, 217, 260
Perepilichny, Alexander, 202
person with significant control (PSC), 266
Peru, 9
Peters & Peters, 166, 183, 185–186
Philippines, 9, 11, 118, 177, 232
Pichulik, Dylan, 222–224
Piketty, Thomas, 16, 225
pirate radio stations, 36–37
plutonomy, 26, 210, 224, 225–232
Poland, 35, 122
Politically Exposed Persons (PEPs), 97–98
polonium-210, 197–199, 202–203
Pompolo Ltd, 1–3, 260
Power, Graham, 62–63
PR agencies, 170–171, 173
Premier Trust, 247
privacy, 263
    bank accounts, 122, 233–243, 250–252
    corporate structures, 85–86, 235, 262–263, 266
    trusts, 251–253
private banking, 96–98, 128–129, 233, 236–238
Professional Nominees, 80, 82
Proksch, Reinhard, 74
property, 12, 60, 211–224, 235, 246–247, 259–260, 266, 268, 270–271
    New York, 47, 60, 211–224, 228, 258
    London, 18–22, 158, 207, 211, 214–216, 219, 220, 222, 227–229
Purnell, Jon, 95
Pursglove, Sarah, 52–53

Putin, Vladimir, 7, 17, 18, 133, 221, 262
    and Browder, 172
    and Litvinenko, 196, 199–202
    and organized crime, 167–168
    and Skuratov video, 70–71
    and Ukraine, 161
Pyatt, Geoffrey, 187

Qualified Intermediary (QI) scheme, 236–239

Rajatnaram, Sinnathamby, 118–119, 122
Raven, Ronald, 73, 78, 81
Rejniak, Marek, 77–78
Reno, 91, 243, 244–245, 247–248, 251, 252, 254
Riggs Bank, 127
Rijock, Kenneth, 142–143
Robins, Craig, 222
Rolling Stones, 32
Romania, 78
Rothschild & Co., 247–248, 254
Rowling, J.K., 261
Russia, 11, 121, 270
    Bentley cars, 8
    Berezniki, 212–213
    and Browder, 172–175
    corruption, 55, 57, 64–66, 167–168, 172, 200, 230–232
    and Crimea, 11, 13, 103, 133, 161, 199
    FIMACO, 65–67, 69
    inequality, 7, 16–18, 232
    and Litvinenko murder, 196–202
    Magnitsky affair, 55, 90, 173–174
    and Nevis, 52, 55–58
    offshore wealth, 11, 48, 65–71, 93, 177
    overseas property, 215–217, 219, 221, 223, 227
    sanctions, 133, 161
    Teva Pharmaceutical, 108–109
    and Ukraine, 13–14, 161
    and US 2016 presidential election, 14–15, 260
    watches, 230–231
    Yukos, 93–94
Rybolovlev, Dmitry, 212–213

Saez, Emmanuel, 225
St. Kitts, 55, 56, 135–160
and Nevis, 19, 22, 49, 86, 135–141, 269
    Economic Citizenship Program (ECP), 145–152
    See also Nevis
St. Lucia, 134, 150, 155–160
St. Vincent and the Grenadines, 3, 16, 19, 21

Sakvarelidze, David, 186–187, 189
Salinas, Raul, 96–97
Sanchez, Alex, 250
al-Sanea, Maan, 164
Sarao, Navinder, 53–54
Saviano, Roberto, 123
Savills, 216
Say Yes to the Dress (television program), 204–210
Schwebel, Gerry, 259
Scotland, 11, 63, 72, 141, 144, 261
Second World War, 27, 28, 31, 34, 38, 42, 69, 117, 118, 163
secrecy. *See* privacy
Securities and Exchange Commission (SEC, US), 108–109
Semivolos, Andrei, 103, 114
Serious Fraud Office (SFO, UK), 181–188
Seychelles, 11, 21, 75, 82, 86
Sharp, Howard, 179
Shchepotin, Igor, 101–103, 108–114
Shehada, Kamal, 149–150
shell companies, 12, 19, 21, 23, 53, 65, 67, 70, 71, 85–86, 90–96
Sheridan, Jim, 264
Sherpa, 87
Sherwin & Noble (S&N), 76–77
Shvets, Yuri, 200–201
Sidorenko, Konstantin, 102, 107–108
Sigma Tech Enterprises, 82
Silkenat, James, 87
Simmonds, Kennedy, 139, 143, 148
Singapore, 47, 118, 231, 253
Skripal, Sergei, 202
Skuratov, Yuri, 64–66, 70–71
Sloane Rangers, 214
Smith, Peter, 88
Smith, Vaughan, 166
Snyder, Shawn, 50–51
Soffer, Donald, 221–222
Soffer, Jackie, 222
Soffer, Jeffrey, 222
Soloman, Sam, 81
Somalia, 18, 89, 123
Sonangol, 207
Sooliman, Imtiaz, 133
South Dakota, 245, 248, 252–253, 255
South Sudan, 18
Soviet Union, 123, 139, 162, 179, 183, 195, 202, 213, 223
    and Angola, 206–207
    dissolution of, 6–7, 13, 67–68, 162

and eurodollars, 35
and *Goldfinger* (film), 30, 35, 65
healthcare, 101–104, 110, 259
See also Azerbaijan; Kazakhstan; Kyrgyzstan; Russia; Ukraine; Uzbekistan
SP Trading, 89–90
Spain, 95, 115, 116, 201
spending
    and Moneyland, 12–13, 15, 20–23, 26, 204–210, 211–232
    Say Yes to the Dress (television show), 204–210
    watches, 61, 113, 210, 218, 230–232, 234
    whisky, 231
    wine, 231–232, 236
    See also property
Spink, Mike, 216
Spira, Peter, 40, 41
Stephens, Mark, 156
Stolen Asset Recovery (StAR) initiative (World Bank), 87, 189
succession planning, 46, 60
sugar, 55–56, 140, 144–149
Sukholuchya shooting lodge, 6–7, 10–11, 15, 74
Sunny Isles Beach, Florida, 221, 222
Sutton, Heidi-Lynn, 57–59, 267
Sweden, 40, 177
Switzerland, 233–243
    asset recovery, 96–97, 177–178
    bank secrecy, 38–42, 69, 96, 233–243, 250–252
    sharing data, 242
    and United States, 26, 232–240
    watches, 230
Syria, 22, 271

Taiwan, 54, 58, 142, 148, 232
Takilant, 95
Tax Justice Network, 61, 87
TEAS (The European Azerbaijan Society), 263–265
Teliasonera, 95
Teva Pharmaceutical, 108–109
Thurlow, Edward, 88–89
Tintin, 38–39
Tobon, John, 85–87, 220, 266
Tonga, 139
Tornai, Pnina, 204–206, 208–210, 228
Transparency International (TI), 18–20, 87, 116, 123, 168–169

Trump, Donald, 133, 204, 271
  administration of, 268, 270
  election of, 4, 14–15, 68, 260
  and Manafort, 1, 3
  properties, 4, 213
  and Russian ties, 220
trust, 114, 223, 261
trusts, 59–60, 245–248, 251–255
Tunisia, 9–10, 164
Turover, Felipe, 71

UBS, 61, 235–239, 248, 251, 252, 265
Ukraine
  2014 revolution, 4–6, 9, 13, 74, 103–104,
    112–114, 180
  asset recovery, 180–189
  Aveiro, 265
  corruption, 1–2, 4–17, 19, 22, 55, 74,
    101–108, 112–114, 123–124, 164–165,
    181–182, 186–189, 250
  Crimea, 11, 13, 103, 133, 161, 199
  healthcare, 101–114, 165
  and Manafort, 1–4, 8, 15–16, 18–19, 21,
    68, 260
  Mezhyhyria palace, 4
  and Nevis, 55, 58
  sanctions, 161–163, 167, 188–189
  Sukholuchya shooting lodge, 6–7, 10–11,
    15, 74
ultra-high-net-worth people (UHNWs),
  98–99
UNITA, 206–208
United Kingdom (UK)
  anti-corruption agenda, 266
  asset recovery, 180–187
  and Azerbaijan, 263–265
  Brexit referendum, 133–134, 260–161,
    270–171
  Bribery Act, 87
  corruption, 18, 123
  currency crisis, 31, 35
  Financial Conduct Authority, 87
  inequality, 227
  inflows of money, 177
  libel laws, 164–169, 174–175
  and Nevis, 52
  pirate radio stations, 36–37
  and Russia, 173–174, 200–202, 215–217,
    226, 261
  and St. Lucia, 155–160
  sharing data, 248–250
  Skripal poisoning, 202

  and Ukraine, 181–189
  visas, 134
  Welfare State, 32
  See also City of London; London
United Nations, 89, 95, 123, 141, 155
United States
  2016 presidential election, 4, 14–15, 68,
    133, 260
  and Angola, 206, 207
  anti-bribery measures, 110
  asset recovery, 179–181, 186, 188–190
  bank secrecy, 251–253, 255
  banks, 32, 35, 44–46, 67, 240, 259–260
  Bretton Woods system, 28–35, 37, 43–45,
    69–70, 262–263, 267
  corruption, 18
  and Equatorial Guinea, 127, 178
  eurobonds, 43
  eurodollars, 35
  FATCA, 239–241, 243, 247–248, 251, 256
  Flash Crash, 53–54
  free speech, 169
  inequality, 16–17, 227–228, 232
  and Jersey, 60–61
  limited liability companies, 89
  Magnitsky laws, 173
  and Nevis, 49–59
  offshore wealth, 45
  and Russia, 67–69
  and St. Kitts, 148
  shell companies, 85–86, 90–96
  and Swiss banks, 26, 233–243
  trusts, 245–248, 251–255
  and Ukraine, 161, 180–181, 187–188
  visas, 22, 268–270
  See also individual states; Miami;
    New York
Uralkali, 212, 213
Uzbekistan, 95–96, 179, 253

Vanish (yacht), 147
Vedomosti (Russian newspaper), 230
Venezuela, 89, 132, 176, 220, 259
Ver, Roger, 149
VimpelCom, 95
Virchis, Andres, 195
Vlasic, Mark, 189
Vogliano, Ernest, 238

Wall Street Journal, 60–61, 187
Warburg, Siegmund, 37–39, 43, 45–46, 53,
  217, 252

Washington Post, 187–188
watches, 61, 113, 210, 218, 230–232, 234
Wealth-X, 98–99
weapons smuggling, 90, 116, 143
Wegelin, 239, 251
Weill, Sandy, 212
whisky, 231
White, Harry Dexter, 29, 262
Windward Trading Limited, 179
wine, 231–232, 236
Wisconsin, 245
World Bank, 37, 180
    Doing Business, 89–90
    and Equatorial Guinea, 127
    StAR initiative, 87, 189
Wyoming, 18, 50, 92, 248

Xiao Jianhua, 160

Yanukovich, Viktor, 1, 4–6, 8–11, 111–112,
    180–183, 188
    assets blocked, 181
    Cancer Institute visit, 101–103
    and Manafort, 4, 8, 15–16, 19
    Mezhyhirya palace, 4
    and Nevis, 55
    Sukholuchya shooting lodge, 6–7, 10–11,
        15, 74
Yeltsin, Boris, 64–66, 213
Young, Robert, 60–61
Yukos, 93–94

Zambia, 88, 229
Zhang, Lu, 89
Zlochevsky, Mykola, 165–166, 182–188,
    265
Zucman, Gabriel, 38, 46–48, 255